Data Visualization with Microsoft Power BI

How to Design Savvy Dashboards

Alex Kolokolov and Maxim Zelensky

Beijing · Boston · Farnham · Sebastopol · Tokyo

Data Visualization with Microsoft Power BI

by Alex Kolokolov and Maxim Zelensky

Published by O'Reilly Media, Inc., 1005 Gravenstein Highway North, Sebastopol, CA 95472.

O'Reilly books may be purchased for educational, business, or sales promotional use. Online editions are also available for most titles (*http://oreilly.com*). For more information, contact our corporate/institutional sales department: 800-998-9938 or *corporate@oreilly.com*.

Acquisitions Editor: Michelle Smith	**Indexer:** Potomac Indexing, LLC
Development Editor: Shira Evans	**Interior Designer:** David Futato
Production Editor: Clare Laylock	**Cover Designer:** Karen Montgomery
Copyeditor: nSight, Inc.	**Illustrator:** Kate Dullea
Proofreader: Piper Editorial Consulting, LLC	

September 2024:   First Edition

Revision History for the First Edition

2024-08-29:   First Release

See *http://oreilly.com/catalog/errata.csp?isbn=9781098152789* for release details.

978-1-098-15278-9

[LSI]

Table of Contents

Part II. Trusted Advanced Visuals

Part III.   Risky Advanced Visuals

Preface

Note from Alex Kolokolov

I have been involved in business intelligence projects since 2009, working with various BI platforms such as Power BI, Qlik, Tableau, and Cognos. I began my career as a data analyst, progressing to roles as a project lead and team lead. Eventually, I founded a company providing consulting and services in the field of data analytics.

My career progression was promoted by my ability to deal with customer requirements, especially when it came to reports. I could grasp what they wanted to see in a report and figure out how to present the data in a clear, understandable, and user-friendly manner. This skill was essential to me since university; I enjoyed designing presentations, drawing business process diagrams, and creating pixel-perfect charts.

Initially, I was puzzled by why it seemed so challenging for others. However, I later discovered that for experienced analysts and data engineers, visualization was entirely unnecessary. They comprehend the data structure, and the relationships are evident to them simply through tables. They genuinely don't understand the need for all these pie charts and graphs.

But on the other hand, visualization is crucial for business users. They initially need a visual representation of key indicators, and then they delve into the details. I trained my team in this skill: which types of data require specific charts and how to compose them into dashboards. I also educated our clients and developed guides to empower them to proficiently create reports in a self-service mode.

It's not enough to draw a visually appealing dashboard layout. It's crucial to understand the anatomy of diagrams and how they will be implemented in a specific BI tool.

My favorite tool is undoubtedly Power BI. It has undergone remarkable evolution, becoming part of the Microsoft Fabric ecosystem, where artificial intelligence provides incredible capabilities. Yet it remains user-friendly for a quick start, like its "parents"—PowerPoint and Excel pivot tables. You can read this book without a technical background and immediately apply the knowledge to create professional dashboards. Gradually, you can delve into advanced tools.

Certainly, AI will affect our analytical tasks, handling routine tasks and even suggesting insights. However, it's crucial not to forget the fundamental principles of data literacy. It's not just about following what your AI assistant suggests but making *conscious* choices. In this regard, books remain a reliable source of knowledge. I wish you an engaging reading experience!

Note from Maxim Zelensky

Throughout my professional experience, data analysis has been at the core. I have spent over 20 years in marketing and sales, where one of the most critical factors for success is the ability to work with data, analyze it proficiently, and present it effectively. Developing basic data visualization skills does not seem difficult—almost all of us can create simple charts in Microsoft Excel or design presentations in PowerPoint.

However, over time I have come to realize that effective data visualization and presentation should not rely solely on intuition but rather on a thorough understanding of the fundamental principles and techniques that take into account the peculiarities of our perception and cognition. To convey important information to a consumer, one must comprehend their needs, how they interpret information, and how it is assimilated. I began to delve into the science of data visualization, reading numerous books and articles on the subject, and I am still amazed at the breadth and complexity of this field of knowledge.

Ever since Microsoft Power BI emerged, I have been its avid fan and evangelist. Even within its core visuals, Power BI offers us extensive capabilities for interactive visualization, and when custom visual elements are used skillfully, these possibilities become practically limitless.

Since 2016, I have been professionally engaged in creating reports in Power BI: writing queries, building data models, performing complex Data Analysis Expressions (DAX) calculations, and, of course, visualization. I have actively participated in forums and online discussions, spoken at numerous conferences and meetups. For my professional expertise and contribution to the user community, I was awarded the Microsoft Most Valuable Professional (Microsoft MVP) status. Throughout the years, I have seen numerous examples of both brilliant and, conversely, terrible Power BI reports. However, merely seeing them is not enough; one must understand the capabilities of the tool being used. In simpler terms, it's not just about knowing how to create a user-friendly and visually appealing report, but also knowing how to achieve it.

Over the years, I have developed my own algorithm for setting up visual elements, which I share with my students and colleagues. When Alex asked me to participate in writing this book, I gladly agreed. I hope that my modest contribution to this work will help you avoid mistakes at the start and derive pleasure from the process of visualizing data in Power BI.

We wrote this book for everyone working with reports, financial and marketing data, information about employees, and projects. For those who want to communicate with data and develop data-driven culture within their companies. We define two target audiences for this book.

Who This Book Is For

This practical book shows data analysts as well as professionals in finance, sales, and marketing how to quickly create visualizations and build savvy dashboards.

Managers and Nontechnical Professionals

For those who are new to Power BI, this book serves as an excellent introduction. It provides a clear understanding of how Power BI works through the lens of the final visual output. Particularly if you are familiar with PowerPoint presentations or Excel pivot tables, many features will feel intuitive.

If your company already has Power BI Report Server with ready-made data models, the knowledge presented in this book will be ample. It enables you to craft professional dashboards based on clear data.

Data Analysts

If you are involved in data engineering, primarily working with Power Query and DAX, this book will be a valuable addition to your skill set. We understand that the design aspect can be tricky for a true analyst, making it challenging to anticipate what the client wants. Therefore, each chapter is supplemented with examples and explanations of why a particular visualization suits a specific case.

You don't have to memorize all the details; you can refer to the relevant chapter when necessary and cross-check the checklist to confirm whether all the configuration aspects for a particular chart have been addressed.

How This Book Is Organized

The book is organized from basic to advanced concepts. It begins with two introductory chapters. Chapter 1 delves into the Power BI interface, catering to those who are new to this tool. Chapter 2 serves as a refresher on the fundamental principles of visualization, providing a concise overview of the key rules you may have encountered in some capacity.

Part I is dedicated to classic visuals that you might have encountered in Excel and PowerPoint. In these chapters, we thoroughly explore all the nuances of setting up impeccable bar charts, line charts, and tables in Power BI. A single dataset is utilized for all the chapters in this part, allowing you to build the final dashboard. At the end of this section, there will be a quiz to reinforce the material.

Part II of the book will delve into advanced visualizations, aptly named "Trusted Advanced Visuals" due to the existence of best practices and specific use cases for them. Some chapters will also address necessary data transformation to create the desired charts. In this part, we will go beyond the basic set of Power BI visuals, downloading visuals from the AppSource gallery.

In certain chapters, we'll compare alternative options, highlight pros and cons, and explain how to avoid pitfalls. As before, a quiz will be provided at the end for material reinforcement.

Part III is titled "Risky Advanced Visuals" because these visualizations may appear unusual but can disappoint users. Sometimes analysts try to impress managers with innovative charts, but unusual shapes can make it challenging to find insights. Nevertheless, there are specific use cases for these diagrams. We will explain the data on which they should be built and how to avoid common pitfalls.

You can read the book sequentially or use it as a reference. When you need to understand a specific chart, simply go to the relevant chapter and follow the step-by-step guide on how to configure all the important details correctly.

We hope you enjoy exploring the realm of data visualization. These skills are anticipated to enhance your communication with colleagues and stakeholders, aiding them in making data-driven decisions. Your role as a dependable adviser will be highly appreciated, and your efforts will be duly rewarded.

How to Work with Practice Datasets

In this book, you will learn how to work with various datasets and create effective graphs based on them. At the beginning of each chapter or section, you will find a link to a dataset that can be used to build the graphs discussed in that chapter, housed in a GitHub repo for this book (*https://oreil.ly/DataViz-supp*).

To get started, you need to download the dataset and follow the instructions provided in the corresponding chapter. This practical approach will allow you not only to understand theoretically how different types of graphs work but also to apply your knowledge in practice by creating your own visualizations.

At the end of the chapter, you can download the final file. It contains an example of what you should have according to the instructions.

Conventions Used in This Book

The following typographical conventions are used in this book:

Italic
: Indicates new terms, UI elements, URLs, email addresses, filenames, and file extensions.

`Constant width`
: Used for program listings, as well as within paragraphs to refer to program elements such as variable or function names, databases, data types, environment variables, statements, and keywords.

`Constant width bold`
: Shows commands or other text that should be typed literally by the user.

 This element signifies a general note.

Using Datasets

Datasets are available for download at *https://oreil.ly/DataViz-supp*.

If you have a technical question or a problem using the datasets, please send an email to *support@oreilly.com*.

This book is here to help you get your job done. In general, if example code is offered with this book, you may use it in your programs and documentation. You do not need to contact us for permission unless you're reproducing a significant portion of the code. For example, writing a program that uses several chunks of code from this book does not require permission. Selling or distributing examples from O'Reilly books does require permission. Answering a question by citing this book and quoting example code does not require permission. Incorporating a significant amount of example code from this book into your product's documentation does require permission.

We appreciate, but generally do not require, attribution. An attribution usually includes the title, author, publisher, and ISBN. For example: "*Data Visualization with Microsoft Power BI* by Alex Kolokolov and Maxim Zelensky (O'Reilly). Copyright 2024 Data2Speak Inc., 978-1-098-15278-9."

If you feel your use falls outside fair use or the permission given above, feel free to contact us at *permissions@oreilly.com*.

O'Reilly Online Learning

 For more than 40 years, *O'Reilly Media* has provided technology and business training, knowledge, and insight to help companies succeed.

Our unique network of experts and innovators share their knowledge and expertise through books, articles, and our online learning platform. O'Reilly's online learning platform gives you on-demand access to live training courses, in-depth learning paths, interactive coding environments, and a vast collection of text and video from O'Reilly and 200+ other publishers. For more information, visit *https://oreilly.com*.

How to Contact Us

Please address comments and questions concerning this book to the publisher:

O'Reilly Media, Inc.
1005 Gravenstein Highway North
Sebastopol, CA 95472
800-889-8969 (in the United States or Canada)
707-827-7019 (international or local)
707-829-0104 (fax)
support@oreilly.com
https://www.oreilly.com/about/contact.html

We have a web page for this book, where we list errata, examples, and any additional information. You can access this page at *https://oreil.ly/DataViz_MicrosoftPowerBI*.

For news and information about our books and courses, visit *https://oreilly.com*.

Find us on LinkedIn: *https://linkedin.com/company/oreilly-media*.

Watch us on YouTube: *https://youtube.com/oreillymedia*.

Acknowledgments

First, I'd like to extend my thanks to my colleagues at Data2Speak Inc, who have supported me in working on this book for nearly two years, patiently rewriting and rethinking the material with me three times over. Thanks to Ksenia Koroleva for the technical writing and involvement in the project, Natalia Danilina for translating and adapting the final text, Yana Yakovleva for her effective project coordination, which helped bring it to completion. And, of course, thanks to my coauthor, Maxim Zelensky, for technical expertise and attention to detail. Also, thanks to the tech reviewers: Alan Murray, Ranjeeta Bhattacharya, and Nikesh Pahuja.

Second, thanks to all the clients I've worked with over the past 15 years. Thank you for presenting challenging tasks and being unwilling to compromise. We ventured into experiments with risky advanced visualizations, and it was through this real experience that the third part of the book was born. Once again, thanks to my colleagues—technical professionals from Data2Speak Inc who found unconventional solutions and explained complex matters to me in simple terms.

Third, thanks to all my students who completed assignments, provided feedback, and shared their success stories. During lectures and training sessions, I saw the spark in your eyes when you learned new useful features, found solutions to pressing problems, and understood how it would save you time and allow you to earn more. This gave me strength and inspiration to keep on with education activities and writing this book.

And a special thanks to my family and friends who believed I could bring something new to what seemed like a well-explored field, to create something valuable not just for a small circle of clients or students, but something that could truly enhance the quality of work for millions of professionals worldwide. Thank you, and I will do my best to justify your trust!

— *Alex Kolokolov*
CEO and Founder at Data2Speak Inc

PART I

Classic Visuals

In this part, we will introduce you to the most popular types of charts. You've likely seen and even used them before. According to our experience, around 90% of corporate reports consist of these visual elements:

- Column and bar charts
- Pie and donut charts
- Timeline charts
- Tables
- Key performance indicator (KPI) cards

Beginner Power BI users often try to build advanced charts right away and ignore the classics. As a result, they might fail, and the management might find it too complex, asking to revert to the "old ways" with presentation slides or spreadsheets.

However, complex shapes and forms are not always necessary. You can complete your tasks with well-configured familiar visual elements. In Power BI, many things work similarly to Excel pivot tables, but there are parameters that work entirely differently. This is why the very first chapter is called "Power BI Interface and Chart Anatomy."

We've designed this material to make it easy for you to learn on your own and explain to others why you chose a particular visualization. Use the step-by-step guides to convey the meaning of your data effectively through classic charts. If you're already well versed in the basics and are tired of explaining them to your colleagues, give them this book. It contains all the rules for creating informative reports with clear examples.

Beyond bar and pie charts, as well as graphs, the section about classic visualizations also includes chapters on configuring tables and KPI cards with summary values. Tables can be really helpful; you just need to make them visually appealing and comprehensible. KPI cards assist in highlighting critical business metrics, making them an integral part of an interactive report.

Each chapter goes from simple features similar to Microsoft Excel and continues to parameters unique for Power BI. Alternatively, you can read them in any order and use this book as a manual in the future. When a new task arises, take it and find the right chart and remember the right fine-tuning step.

OK, ready? Here we go.

CHAPTER 1

Power BI Interface and Chart Anatomy

This chapter is for those who are opening the Power BI Desktop application for the first time. You'll soon realize it's quite similar to other applications you know, like Microsoft Office Excel and PowerPoint. But there are some features that work a bit differently.

As of the time this book was written, the Power BI Desktop is available for Windows but not for macOS. If you're using macOS, you can use a virtual machine (VM) for Power BI Desktop on the Mac. The Power BI service is not really a like-for-like. The visualization side may be the same, but the queries, modeling, DAX, etc. are nothing like the same.

You can download the practice dataset (*https://oreil.ly/DataViz_dataset*) and make first steps in Power BI. This dataset is utilized for all the chapters in Part I, allowing you to build the final dashboard.

Power BI Key Elements

Let's go through the basic elements of the Power BI Desktop interface. When you launch the app, you'll see a screen that looks like Figure 1-1.

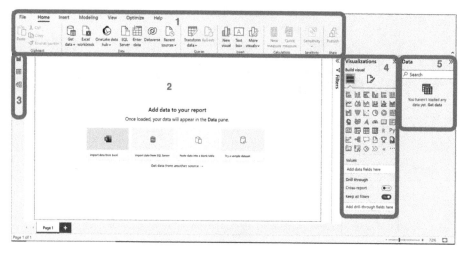

Figure 1-1. Key elements of the Power BI Desktop interface

The key elements of the Power BI interface are as follows:

1. The ribbon (top menu bar)
2. Workspace canvas
3. View mode selector
4. *Visualizations* pane for creating and editing visuals
5. *Data* pane, where loaded data is displayed

Top Menu Bar

The top part of the program looks like a ribbon, which is a common layout for Microsoft software. When you first open Power BI, you're on the *Home* tab (Figure 1-2), where you'll find the most commonly used buttons. These buttons are organized into groups based on what they do. For instance, in the group *Data*, you can import different types of data from various sources. The *Insert* group is where you add things like charts and text blocks.

Figure 1-2. The ribbon (top menu bar)

Most of these functions can also be accessed from context menus and other parts of the interface, so you won't need to use the ribbon very often.

Workspace Canvas

The main part of the screen is taken up by the blank page, which resembles a PowerPoint slide (Figure 1-3). This is where we'll place visualizations.

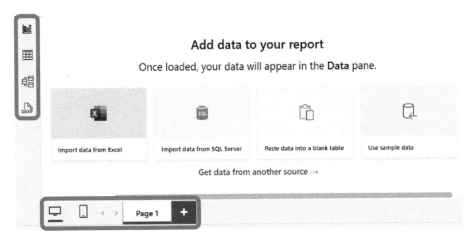

Figure 1-3. Page view mode and desktop/mobile view mode

In the bottom left corner, there are buttons to switch between desktop and mobile viewing modes. Right next to them is the page indicator. We can add pages similar to Excel sheets by clicking the plus button or remove them as needed.

View Mode Selector

In the top-left part of the screen, you'll find buttons for selecting the display mode. We are by default in the *Report view*. The next icon, resembling a table (*Table view*), switches our canvas to the original data view. The *Model view* shows all data tables and the relationships between them in the form of a schema. In the scope of this book, we will only work with the *Report view*. The other modes are equally important, but each of them would require a separate book to cover in detail.

Visualizations Pane

The *Visualizations* pane (Figure 1-4) is essential for creating and editing visualizations. To accomplish these tasks, there are two tabs at the top of the menu: *Build visual* and *Format visual*. After building the first visual, a third tab may appear: *Add further analysis to your visual*. Appearance of the third tab depends on the selected visual capabilities (not all visuals support this feature).

Below, there's a list of default visualizations in the form of icons. By default, there are six icons per row (if you change the width of the *Visualizations* pane, the number of icons per row could change).

The first row of icons consists of familiar bar charts in various combinations (vertical and horizontal, stacked, and clustered). The second row includes line and area charts and their combination with column charts. Once again, these will look quite similar to Microsoft Excel. We'll soon delve into their anatomy.

Next, you could find some charts we consider "advanced" and will discuss in the second part of this book: waterfall charts, funnels, and maps. Please don't search for an increasing order of complexity here. Following these is the scatterplot, which we've categorized as exotic visuals in Part III, and next to it is the classic pie chart.

The last button on the visualizations list, the "three dots" (or "ellipsis"), allows you to load new types of charts not included in the Power BI basic set.

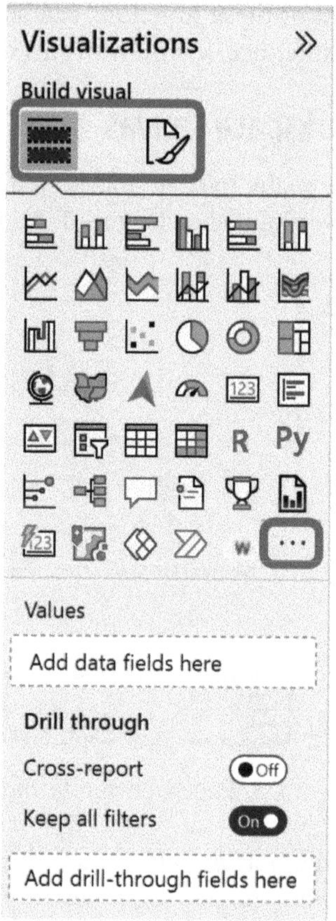

Beneath the visualization icons, you'll find a block with field placeholders where you input

Figure 1-4. Visualizations pane

the data to create a specific chart. Naturally, each visual requires its own set of fields, so when you select an icon, you'll see specific fields that need to be filled with data from the *Data* pane.

Data Pane

To demonstrate how the data panel works, we will load data from Excel. To do this, click on the green button on the empty canvas (*Import data from Excel*), specify the path to the file, and click *OK*. Next we describe the steps of loading to get the Cycles table.

We've loaded the data in Figure 1-5 from an Excel spreadsheet. In this example, you'll see planned and actual sales broken down by product categories and subcategories, by country, and by managers.

Date	Country	Product category	Quantity	Price per item	Sales fact	Sales plan
12.25.2021	USA	Accessories	2	303	606	398
05.17.2021	USA	Accessories	2	98	196	153
08.12.2021	USA	Accessories	2	138	276	210
01.15.2021	USA	Accessories	2	82	164	132
08.10.2021	USA	Accessories	2	24	48	43
10.02.2021	USA	Accessories	2	112,5	225	212
10.10.2021	USA	Accessories	2	3	6	6
12.29.2021	USA	Accessories	2	28	56	60
01.15.2021	USA	Accessories	2	18,5	37	32
01.02.2021	USA	Accessories	2	8	16	17

Figure 1-5. Source data

After loading the data to the model, in the *Data* pane you'll see a field list similar to Excel pivot tables (Figure 1-6). This is where you can select fields, and they will appear in the *Values* section on the neighboring *Visualizations* pane (Figure 1-7).

Figure 1-6. Uploaded data

Some fields have icons right away: a calendar icon for the *Date* field and a Σ icon for numeric fields like *Price per item, Quantity, Sales fact*, and so on.

Unlike the data source, the fields are sorted in ascending alphabetical order. If you didn't find a specific field right away, you can use the search function on top of the *Data* pane.

How Power BI Builds Charts

Let's start building our first visualization. On the *Data* pane, click on the square to the left of the *Sales fact* field to choose it. You'll see then a new chart has appeared on the report canvas, with a single column representing the sum of values in *Sales fact*. If the column you choose first is of a numeric type, Power BI will automatically create a clustered column chart. If we then add the *Product category* field in the same way, its values will appear on the chart as the x-axis and the new columns will appear per each product category (as shown in Figure 1-7).

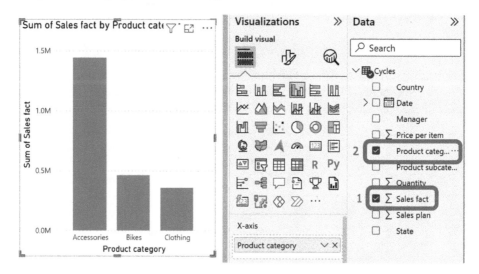

Figure 1-7. Default column chart drawn for numeric value

But you might get a different result. If you first select the *Product category* field and then *Sales fact*, you'll get a table (Figure 1-8). This is because Power BI displays textual data as a table by default. Afterward, you can change the table to a column chart or another visual.

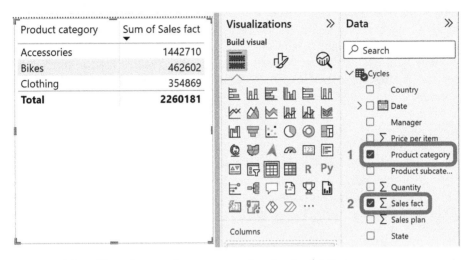

Figure 1-8. The table is drawn when text type data is selected first

To create a new picture or chart, first click anywhere on the empty area of the page to deselect the current one. Now, you can choose new data categories, and a new image will pop up for them. Let's take the *Country* category as an example, and you'll instantly see a map (Figure 1-9)! Even though this category doesn't have a specific symbol, Power BI recognizes that it's about places (like countries, states, cities, or addresses) and creates a bubble map for it. Next, choose the *Sales fact* field, which will determine the size of the bubbles on the map.

Figure 1-9. The default chart is drawn when geographic data is selected

If you think you don't need a map but would like a different way to display the data, you have options like bar charts, tables, or something else. This is the secret to success: choosing the right type of visualization that accurately represents the data's meaning. Throughout this book, we'll focus on this. You'll learn the fundamental rules for picking the right charts, and we'll explore specific cases when we make exceptions to those rules.

Format Visual

Let's go back to Figure 1-7, where we selected the fields *Sales fact* and *Product category*, which resulted in a column chart. In the *Visualizations* pane (Figure 1-10), click on the paintbrush icon (*Format visual*), and you'll see a list of parameters you can customize for the chart. This section is further divided into two parts:

Visual
> Here, you can adjust parameters that are specific to this particular chart.

General
> These parameters apply to all charts and include things like titles, background colors, borders, and more. In some versions this section may be called *Properties*.

Most of our work will be within the *Visual* tab. You'll notice that some options are active and enabled; however, the *Legend* section is inactive because we haven't selected data for it. The *Data labels* section is active but turned off. Click the *On/Off* switch (Figure 1-10) on the *Data labels* section, and you'll see them appear on the chart's columns.

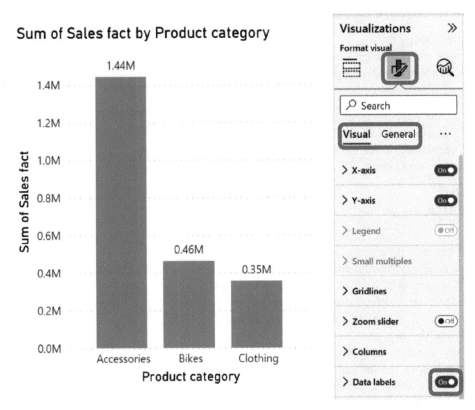

Figure 1-10. Enabling Data labels *in the* Format visual *pane*

You can fine-tune these items, and to do that, you need to open them up (see Figure 1-11). Since we turned on data labels, let's explore what's inside.

The structure of these parameters goes like this:

Apply settings to
In our case, there's only one set of data, so nothing changes here.

Options
This part includes things like orientation (horizontal/vertical) and positioning (top/center, etc.). For now, we don't need to alter anything here.

Values
This is a parameter that often needs some adjustments. Let's dive into it.

Within this parameter, we can tweak the font and its size, style, and color. Let's make the size a bit larger, say, 12 points. Pay attention to font color. It has a default color (dark gray), and it is adaptive. When the data label is positioned outside the bar, this default color will appear. When the data label will be inside the bar (or other shape), the font color will be switched to white to provide a contrast. But if you change the font color manually, your custom color will appear for both cases.

The next parameter is *Display units*. By default, it's set to "auto," meaning Power BI automatically decides whether to display values in thousands, millions, or billions based on the value range. We chose *millions* and *2* decimal places and the result is the same as settings by default. However, you can manually set the units and decimal places.

Figure 1-11. Data labels settings

There are quite a few parameters, and it can be challenging to remember where each one is initially located. That's why there's a search field at the top. If you can't recall where to set "decimal places," just type these keywords, and you'll find the corresponding menu item.

For numeric values, there is one more setting: the decimal separator. With its help, all values longer than three digits will be displayed with a space or comma between the digits (units, thousands, etc.). This makes it much easier to understand, especially in situations where you need to show the entire number without abbreviations (for example, in a drill-down table). But you cannot configure the division by digits in the visual settings panel; we can only do this in relation to a specific data field.

The first step is to select the required field in the data panel (we will work with *Sales fact*). Please note that we do not click on the field checkbox but rather select it by clicking on the text line. The top menu bar automatically switches to the *Column tools* tab. Here are all the settings related to the number format. We are interested in the *Formatting* tab, and on it there is a comma icon. After activation, the icon appears with a border and fill (Figure 1-12). Now the value of the *Sales fact* field on all visuals will be displayed with separated digits.

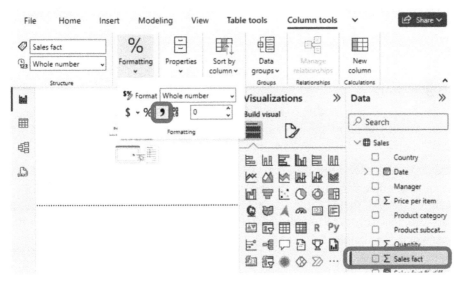

Figure 1-12. Value format settings on the top menu bar

Some parameters can be adjusted in a similar manner for all visuals, like data labels. However, others will differ; for instance, configuring the x-axis for a waterfall chart will be quite different from a Gantt chart. You'll also come across parameters that are specific to certain visuals, such as tables and cell formatting.

Chart Anatomy

There are best practices for designing charts that have stood the test of time. They are discussed in *Say It with Charts* by Gene Zelazny (McGraw-Hill), *Information Dashboard Design* by Stephen Few (O'Reilly), and other classic books. No matter what tool you use, you still follow these general rules. The elements of a chart may have different names in various tools and even within different Power BI visuals, but their purposes remain the same.

Value Axis

When we created the first column chart (Figure 1-7), you saw a y-axis on its left side. On this axis, you'll find data markers and an axis title. In the formatting pane, specifically for the column chart, this part is referred to as the *Y-axis*. If we were to create a horizontal bar chart, this part would be named the *X-axis*.

Once we turn on data labels on the actual columns (Figure 1-10), the value axis becomes less necessary because it essentially duplicates the data labels and takes up space. So, typically, we'll turn it off for most charts. However, there are exceptions to this rule: for instance, when the axis range is changed, and the axis doesn't start at zero.

Category Axis

The category axis displays the textual labels for categories. Depending on the chart's orientation, it will be positioned either at the bottom (in a column chart, this is the x-axis) or on the left (in a bar chart, this is the y-axis).

We always display the category axis. Challenges with it arise when there are many categories or when they have long names consisting of several words. The text can get cut off or rotated, making it harder to read. In such cases, we'll find a compromise by adjusting parameters like font size, text wrapping, and others. We will review these cases in detail in Chapter 3.

Legend

If your chart has different sets of data, like planned and actual numbers, these sets will have different colors. A legend explains which color represents which set. However, if your chart contains only one set of data, as in our column chart (Figure 1-7), you don't need a legend at all.

Here's an important rule: the legend should be positioned above the chart. The good news is that in Power BI, this is the default setup (unlike Excel, where the legend typically sits below the chart, and you have to move it up each time). You can change the legend's position in the settings, but it's usually fine as it is.

Shapes and Colors

The default color for visuals in Power BI is the classic blue. You can change it in the format options. For a column chart, this setting is called *Columns*, for a bar chart, it's *Bars*, for a line chart, it's *Line*, and so on.

The default settings for shapes in Power BI are quite neat and in line with minimalist business graphics. This is fortunate, because there's no way to make fancy 3D columns with highlights and shadows like in PowerPoint 2003.

Data Labels

By default, in most charts, this feature is turned off, but we've activated it. It's important to aim for showing data labels on your chart. This way, users won't have to make rough estimates by matching dots to the scale; they can directly see the precise values.

Yet, there are exceptions; for example, when there are too many data points on your graph, and data labels overlap. In such cases, we intentionally switch them off and instead display the value axis.

You've already learned that Power BI automatically adjusts units of measurement, which is quite handy. Labels with six to seven digits make reading cumbersome. The optimal number of digits is three to four in a label. For instance, compare the range of 12,720,000 to 8,340,000 with 12.72 million to 8.34 million.

If we were working with presentation slides, we'd suggest limiting labels to two to three digits. For example, 12.7 million and 8.3 million. However, in reports, we always have data filtering, and it's possible that after applying a couple of filters, your labels might display values around 0.1 or 0.4. We want to compare values starting from the first digit, not from zero.

Chart Title

By default, Power BI generates a title based on the selected fields' names, for example, "Sum of Sales Fact by Product Category." In our example, this is still a clear title. However, if we had chosen two or three more fields, the title would already span two lines. Besides, field names in the source data don't always precisely convey the business context.

The rule of thumb is that the title should fit within one line. We always find ourselves editing the title. In our example, we could make it shorter, like "Sales by Categories." You can adjust the *Chart title* parameter in the *General* section.

In each chapter, we'll be configuring these and other chart parameters following a step-by-step guide. Even if you have to work with other visualization tools, you'll consciously find the relevant chart element and make it clear. Just like in Power BI, new charts and options will keep emerging.

Responsive Mode

When reducing the chart size, there's another nuance to consider: the font size of labels and captions will automatically shrink to smaller size, even if you've set it to 12 pt. A warning icon next to the section title will notify you of this change (Figure 1-13).

Figure 1-13. Warning icon informing that the size of data labels has been changed

You can disable responsive mode in the *General* → *Properties* → *Advanced options* menu (Figure 1-14).

Figure 1-14. Enable/disable responsive mode

Tips and Notes

Power BI is easy to master on analogies with Microsoft Excel and PowerPoint. The main elements of the workspace:

- The ribbon (top menu bar)
- Workspace canvas
- View mode selector
- *Visualizations* pane
- *Data* pane

Power BI builds charts depending on the data type selected first:

- If it's a number, you get a column chart.
- If it's text, you get a table.
- If it's geographical data like countries, cities, or addresses, you get a map.

But you can create an empty visual container first and then fill it with the fields of your choice.

The main elements of a diagram might have different names in various tools, and even within different Power BI visuals, but their purposes remain the same:

- Value axis
- Category axis
- Legend
- Shapes and colors
- Data labels
- Title

CHAPTER 2

Visualization Compass: How to Choose Charts Correctly

Choosing charts for reporting remains a complex issue. Dozens of books have been written on this topic, catalogs of visualizations have been compiled, and schemes (so-called chart choosers) have been drawn up to suggest which chart to choose for your data. However, what seems right in theory may look unattractive, disproportionate, or simply displeasing to the report's client when applied to real data. In such cases, best practices yield to subjective opinion or familiar templates. Simply referring to the "right book" is not enough; you need to convince your users why a particular chart best conveys the meaning of the data.

And there's another issue. For true analysts, the most understandable way to present data is through tables. Analysts are deeply immersed in the meaning of the data and do not need charts. Perhaps you've also found yourself in a situation where you don't care about the format of the data—whether it's a bar chart, pie chart, or table—as long as the manager stops bothering you with their "pretty pictures." But we understand that visualization helps to perceive information more quickly, especially for those who don't look at reports every day or who are getting acquainted with a new report.

In any case, working with data visualization is primarily about working with people, and only then with Power BI (or another tool). We want to provide you with a methodology that will allow you to consciously choose charts and, importantly, persuade your colleagues, managers, and clients why such a visualization option will be optimal and most suitable.

Chart Choosers

One of the most well-known chart choosers is presented in Figure 2-1. It was developed by Andrew Abela. It is based on four basic types of analysis—comparison, distribution, structure, and relationships—and we move through one of them depending on what we want to show. The further choice of charts depends on the number of categories or time periods we have (many/few) and variables (1, 2, 3, or more).

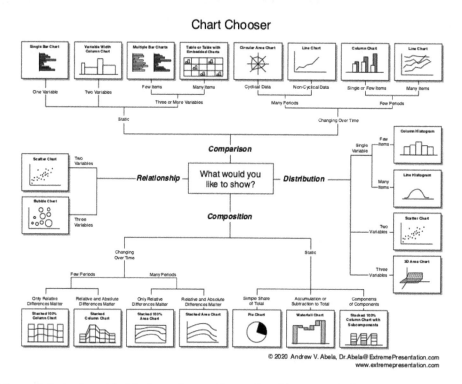

Figure 2-1. Andrew Abela's chart chooser (https://oreil.ly/epGJW): four basic types of data analysis

We find this to be a very useful tool for organizing charts and even used this and other chart choosers in our trainings. Unfortunately, we have found that our clients do not use them and find them too complex. Moreover, not all of these charts are used on dashboards, where we encounter dynamic visualization—data is updated and can change the range of values due to the application of filters. This is the difference between our genre of business analytics and creative infographics or data journalism.

We offer you a simplified methodology for choosing charts. In 90% of cases, dashboards contain data of three types:

Ranking

This is a quantitative comparison based on the "more-less" principle: who is in first place, who is in the top five and by what margin, and who is lagging behind and by how much; for example, employee rankings by sales volume, article expenditure rankings, or branch rankings by headcount. The basic figure for visualizing such data is a column (horizontal or vertical).

Dynamics

This is the change in indicators over time (year, month, day) or other ordered periods, such as project life-cycle stages. Here, it is important to show the overall trend: growth, decline, or seasonal fluctuations in the indicator. The basic figure. for dynamics is a line on a timeline axis (usually called a timeline). Also, a column chart is suitable for this purpose.

Structure

Analysis of the composition of the whole, where the emphasis is not on quantity, but on percentages. It helps to understand which segments and categories contribute the most to the overall result; for example, sales structure by markets, expenditure structure by projects. The basic figure is a circle divided into sectors. Hence the metaphor of "pie" and "donut."

After you have determined the data type, you need to understand how many categories you want to show: 5, 10, 15, or 50. Based on the project experience of the Business Analytics Institute, we divided the options into ranges and developed a metaphorical compass (Figure 2-2). Depending on how many categories you have, the arrow will indicate which chart is best suited for you. However, if you want to show 50 categories, then no chart will help you.

Figure 2-2. Visualization compass

Take this compass more as a metaphor, a simplified cheat sheet. The boundaries here are not strict: somewhere you may need to change the type of chart not at 10 categories but already at 8. Or conversely, a column chart with 11 categories may look appropriate. It also depends on the size of the chart: either you allocate half of the dashboard workspace for it, or one-sixth.

Let's examine each direction of the compass in detail.

Ranking

For visualizing quantitative comparisons on a scale, we use a column chart. It can have either vertical or horizontal orientation. In Power BI (as well as in Excel), these are two different types of charts—column chart and bar chart. The choice depends on:

- The number of categories on the chart
- The length of category labels
- The size of the chart

Number of Categories on the Chart

As you have already learned, by default, Power BI for numeric data formats generates one of these charts (depending on the program version). Let's consider the scenario where we automatically obtained a column chart. If there are a few categories (three to seven), the chart looks good and is easy to read. But if there are more categories, a problem arises: category labels are displayed at an angle or vertically, making it difficult to read. In most languages, we read horizontally from left to right, so we shouldn't disrupt this way of perceiving information. In Figure 2-3, you can see that a column chart with 3 product categories looks simple and clear, but when there are more than 15 subcategories, it becomes overloaded—labels are tilted, requiring careful scrutiny to understand which column the label belongs to, and data labels overlap each other or the columns.

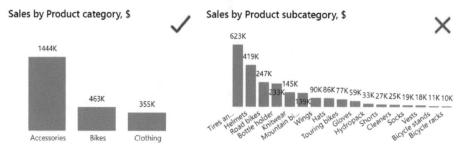

Figure 2-3. Correct column chart (left) and overloaded variant (right)

We can partially solve this problem by providing more space for the chart, but long subcategory names will still remain tilted, and some of them will not be fully displayed (Figure 2-4).

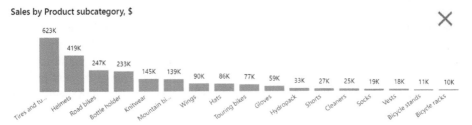

Figure 2-4. Stretched column chart: angled labels are difficult to read

This indicates that we need to use a different visualization—a bar chart. In this chart, we need to "flip" the proportions: the columns were stretched in width, and now, to accommodate all horizontal bars, we need more space vertically (Figure 2-5). In this variant, all labels are fully displayed horizontally and are large enough, which is the key advantage of a bar chart.

Figure 2-5. A correct alternative to the column chart with long category names—a bar chart

From a storytelling perspective, we could say that we need to focus attention on the most significant products. Against the backdrop of hundreds of thousands of values in the range of 10,000–30,000, they're not visible and could be grouped into a separate category, "Other." Then, with about 10 categories, we could place them on a column chart.

But the data on the dashboard is dynamic, and we cannot fix the top 10 with a value limitation because, with filtering, a difference of 10,000–20,000 could be significant.

The Length of Category Labels and the Chart Size

The category name can consist of one or several words. Power BI can wrap this text by words, but it will depend on the longest one. In Figure 2-6, this word is "hydropack." If there is not enough space for its horizontal display, then all labels on the x-axis will be angled (Figure 2-6 on the left). To neatly arrange the text into two lines as shown in Figure 2-6 (on the right), it is sufficient to increase the width of the chart area by 20%–30%.

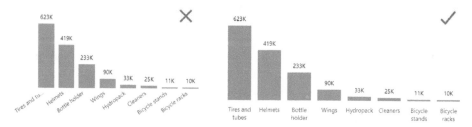

Figure 2-6. Options for displaying category labels: incorrect angled display (left) and correct horizontal display with word wrapping (right)

But what if we don't have additional space? Then, for seven to eight categories, we would use a bar chart. Another advantage of it is its compactness, and even if we reduce its size by almost half, data labels and category labels will still be clearly visible (Figure 2-7, right). At the same time, for small values in the range of 10,000–30,000, nothing significant has changed—they remain as thin bars, as they were.

Figure 2-7. Column chart with angled labels (left) and more compact bar chart (right)

In general, this boundary between horizontal and vertical placement of columns is around 10 categories. However, depending on the length of labels and the size of the chart, it can be shifted either downward or upward: for 7–8 categories with extended names, you will need to use a bar chart, while for 11–12 categories with short labels, you can stick with a column chart.

Dynamics

To show how one indicator has changed over time, a line chart is most commonly used. We're familiar with it from school. Its main idea is that we draw a horizontal axis of time (x-axis), which moves from left to right, from the past to the future, and plot the axis of values (y-axis) vertically. For each period on the x-axis, we plot a point and connect them with lines, which ultimately show us the trend: whether the indicator is increasing, decreasing, or has seasonal peaks and fluctuations.

With the same goal in mind, we can also use columns—they will also show us the time dynamics. The question arises: what to choose—a line chart or columns? The approach here is similar to ranking. If we have a few indicators, columns will look good—for example, data for several years or quarters (Figure 2-8 on the left). But if there are many intervals on the timeline (such as every day of the month or weeks of the year), then it's better to choose a line chart. It can be just a line (Figure 2-8 on the right) or an area chart.

Figure 2-8. Quarterly sales dynamics on a column chart (left) and daily sales dynamics on a line chart (right)

There exists a borderline interval—the 12 months of the year. Both columns and lines are suitable for it (Figure 2-9). Here, there is no issue with long category labels. Unlike rankings, the labels for time intervals are more concise: numerical date format, abbreviated month names, and days of the week.

Figure 2-9. Two possible ways to display sales dynamics for 12 months

Therefore, on our compass, there is a boundary at 12 periods. If there are more, for example, dynamics for two years, it is definitely worth building a line chart—it is easier to see the trend on it (Figure 2-10 on the right). However, a large number of columns looks overloaded (Figure 2-10 on the left).

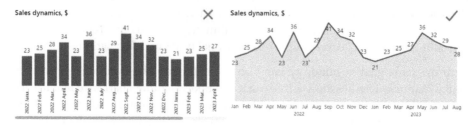

Figure 2-10. Dynamics with a large number of periods: incorrect column chart (left) and correct line chart (right)

If the data is grouped by quarters or years, on the contrary, a line composed of several points will look unclear. There won't be enough data for a convincing trend line (Figure 2-11 on the left), whereas columns clearly show the quarterly revenue changes (Figure 2-11 on the right).

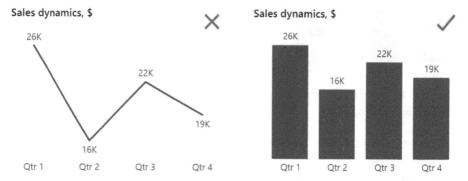

Figure 2-11. Dynamics with a small number of periods: incorrect line chart (left) and correct column chart (right)

Structure

Structure shows which segments and categories contribute the most to the overall result. For visualizing such data, a circle divided into sectors—a pie chart—is usually used. A donut chart has the same meaning, is built on the same parameters, and differs only in the space inside. In Figure 2-12, you see the sales structure by channels. Both charts look simple and clear.

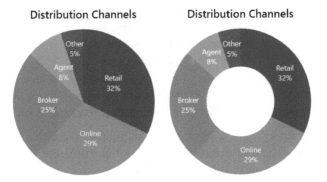

Figure 2-12. Sales structure by distribution channels: pie chart (left), donut chart (right)

What's the difference between them? Studies have shown that they are perceived almost equally. Our eyes gauge the size of the outer arc: a quarter, a third, half, and so on. We surveyed our students and clients to find out which option they prefer. Some say that the ring (donut) looks somehow fresher and more interesting because the pie chart has become boring. But for others, the circle seems clearer. You can choose according to your taste. However, we prefer classic pie charts because they utilize the entire area of the figure for visualization.

The charts in Figure 2-12 look good because there are only five sales channels represented, or more precisely, four main ones, while all the others are grouped into the "Other" category. Both types of charts vividly display data within the range of five to seven categories. However, if there are around 10 categories or even more, both charts will appear overloaded (see Figure 2-13).

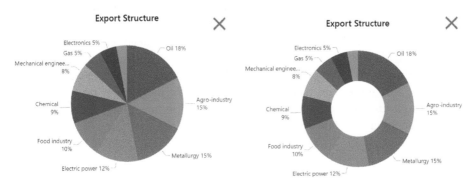

Figure 2-13. Overloaded pie and donut charts

In analytical projects, it's rare to be limited to only five to seven categories, yet the structure still needs to be displayed somehow. Because of this, pie charts have developed a bad reputation—they are often used for 10 or 15 categories, resulting in thin sectors that are difficult to distinguish from one another, with labels overlapping. Therefore, on our compass, we set the limit for pie charts at six categories. It's important to note that this is an average boundary; depending on the range of data and the size of the chart, it may effectively represent seven to eight categories as well.

What to do for seven or more categories? An alternative to pie charts is the relatively new treemap chart. The idea behind it is similar, but instead of cutting a circle into sectors, we divide a rectangle. Because we fill the entire rectangular area with data, it can accommodate 10–12 elements (see Figure 2-14).

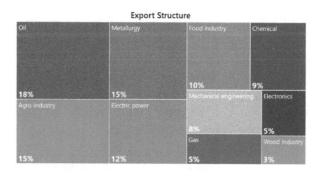

Figure 2-14. An alternative to pie charts—the treemap

The rectangular shape also gives us more flexibility than the circle. Depending on the available space on the dashboard, we can stretch it horizontally or vertically. Power BI automatically adjusts the optimal proportions of sectors. However, the treemap also has limitations. On our compass, we set the mark at 12 categories. As an exception, 13–14 may fit, but with 15–20 elements, it will definitely be difficult to discern anything beyond the largest 5–7 categories. Figure 2-15 depicts the sales structure by regions: you can see that more than half of it is accounted for by the first five regions, and beyond that, it turns into a multitude of small colored rectangles where category labels and even data labels don't fit.

Figure 2-15. Overloaded treemap with many categories

It turns out that there is no universal solution for representing structure. For a large number of categories, we can recommend the following options:

- If you can group everything that is not in the top 5 into an "Other" category, use a pie chart.
- If you can group everything that is not in the top 10 into an "Other" category, use a treemap.
- If grouping categories is not possible and it is important to show everything, then your option is a table with conditional formatting. We will examine this in detail in Chapter 7.

We have covered all the diagrams of the visualization compass. Now it will help you with initial "orientation on the terrain," and as you study the book, you will learn about the exceptions to the rules. But before moving on to the technical part, let's discuss common mistakes. They are not related to Power BI settings and can occur both on PowerPoint slides and in other applications.

Common Mistakes

Often, we become prisoners of our habits and no longer think about why we build a particular diagram. It's just "how it's done" in the company or "it's more convenient for me." Of course, there are exceptions to the rules, but we are talking about how most people perceive visual information. Let's consider examples of when a diagram can distort the meaning of data.

Line Chart for Ranking

Sometimes, a report consists entirely of bar charts, and you might want to diversify it somehow. For example, you might try to display sales by country on a linear chart, especially with a beautiful fill (Figure 2-16, left).

Figure 2-16. Ranking distortion on the line chart (left), and correct display on the bar chart (right)

From a visual perspective, everything looks fine here—you can see the data labels, and category labels are easy to read horizontally. However, from a logical point of view, the chart shows a linear relationship between categories and growth from the first to the last, as in the case of changes in indicators by quarters of the year. Only upon careful examination or clarification from the report's author will it become clear that this is a comparison of countries. The linear chart shows a continuous flow over time. In our example, there isn't—we rank individual categories by sales volume and sort them from largest to smallest. In this case, a bar chart should be used (Figure 2-16, right).

Bar Chart for Dynamics

Dynamics can be visualized using a line chart, as well as a bar chart. Sometimes there is a temptation to change its orientation to horizontal because the bar chart is more compact, accommodating more categories and longer labels (Figure 2-17 on the left). However, this would be a distortion: at first glance, such a chart will be perceived as a ranking, and then the question will arise why it is not ordered.

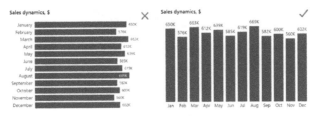

Figure 2-17. Vertical distortion of the time scale (left) and correct representation along the x-axis (right)

Remember: the time scale is placed on the x-axis and read from left to right.

Exceptions to this rule can occur in infographics when designers come up with unusual ways to display dynamics. But we have a different genre, and everything on the dashboard should be clear at first glance. Yes, to display the time scale, the chart will be more stretched horizontally, but we can always reduce the font size of the category labels or shorten the names of the months (Figure 2-17 on the right).

Pie Chart for Dynamics

Another mistake is to show the time axis as a circle. The only exception is for visualizations of the life cycle of iterative processes. However, for classical temporal dynamics, this is inappropriate. While a pie chart built on four quarters may look neat (Figure 2-18, left), it only shows roughly equal shares. In contrast, a bar chart (Figure 2-18, right) clearly demonstrates that there was uniform growth over three quarters followed by a decline in the fourth.

Figure 2-18. Distortion of the time scale on a donut (left) and correct representation of quarterly dynamics on a bar chart (right)

Tips and Notes

We offer you a simplified methodology for choosing charts. In 90% of cases, dashboards contain data of three types:

Ranking
> This is a quantitative comparison based on the "more-less" principle. The basic shape is a bar (horizontal or vertical):
>
> - Fewer than 10 categories: use a column chart (vertical).
> - Ten or more categories: use a bar chart (horizontal).

Dynamics
> This is a change over time (year, month, day) or other ordered periods. The basic shape is a line on an x-axis (timeline):
>
> - Twelve or fewer periods will fit on a bar chart.
> - For more than 12 periods, choose a line chart.

Structure
> This is a composition, part of a whole, where the emphasis is not on quantity but on percentages. The basic shape is a circle divided into sectors:
>
> - Within six categories, you can use a pie or donut chart.
> - With 7–12 categories, you can use a treemap (rectangle divided into sectors).

CHAPTER 3

Column and Bar Charts

Vertical columns or horizontal bars are the most popular data visualizations. These chart types are the first options you'll find in the list of visuals in any BI tool, including Power BI. In Chapter 1, you learned that as soon as it detects numeric data, Power BI automatically generates a column chart.

Technically, column and bar charts are quite similar, differing only in a few options. Often, people use the term "bar chart" to refer to both types, simply distinguishing them as horizontal or vertical. However, in Chapter 2, you discovered their distinct conceptual differences. The column chart is limited in the number of categories it can display clearly, while the bar chart is more suitable for longer lists.

In this chapter, we'll begin with a detailed setup of the column chart, providing a step-by-step guide. Then, we'll complement it with specific options for the horizontal bar chart. Finally, we'll address common mistakes associated with data filtration challenges.

You can download the practice dataset (*https://oreil.ly/DataViz_dataset*) and follow the step-by-step guide in this chapter. This dataset is utilized for all the chapters in this part, allowing you to build the final dashboard.

Column Chart

In terms of its purpose, this visual is suitable for two types of analysis (Figure 3-1):

Dynamics
> When we want to observe how a value has changed over time.

Ranking
> When we need to compare categories based on their magnitude, identifying leaders and laggards.

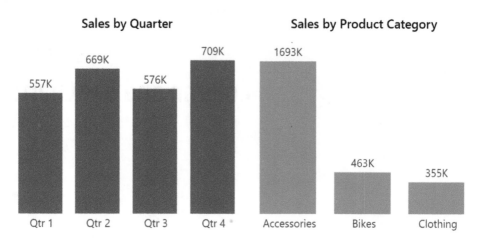

Figure 3-1. Column chart for dynamics (left) and ranking (right)

We'll delve into dynamics visualization and the intricacies of working with a time scale in Chapter 6. For now, let's focus on quantitative ranking. We have a sales volume of three product categories, and they will fit perfectly on the vertical columns (Figure 3-2).

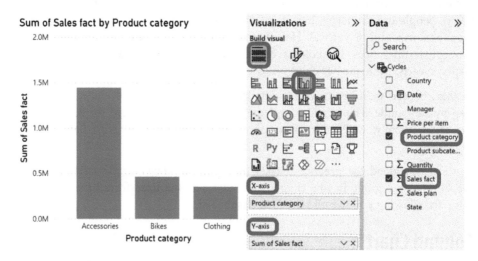

Figure 3-2. Default column chart displays ranking across product categories

However, the default appearance doesn't quite match the examples in Figure 3-1. We're missing data labels, and the axis labels on the left and bottom are repeating information from the title, making the chart look a bit rough. That's why, every time, we'll walk through the elements of chart anatomy and remember where to tweak them in the menu. In each chapter, we'll provide a detailed guide to make it easy for you to return to when you start creating visuals with your data.

Step-by-Step Guide for Column Chart

Here's what we have to do to create a column chart.

Step 1: Enable and Adjust Data Labels

This step is essential for almost any chart (with very rare exceptions). It's crucial to see the exact value right on the column instead of making an approximate estimation from the scale.

Turn on the *Data labels* option in the formatting panel and expand it (Figure 3-3). You'll see groups of options that can also be expanded:

Apply settings to

> If we had multiple data series, like a plan and actuals, we could choose to apply settings to all of them at once (which is the default option) or customize each one individually. In this case, we have only one data series, so nothing changes.

Options/Orientation

> You can change the default horizontal orientation to vertical, but it's strongly recommended not to do that. Just like category labels, users read data labels horizontally.

Options/Position

> By default, it's set to *Auto*, which is *Outside end* (Figure 3-3). However, if there's limited space on the chart, for the tallest column, the label will be placed *Inside end*. This parameter is optimal, and we won't change it.

Values (Figure 3-4)

> This parameter often needs customization. Typically, you should change the font style and color of the labels, and the default font size of 9 should be increased to 12 (or at least to 11 or 10 if you have limited space on your chart).

Figure 3-3. Customizing the Data labels *settings*

Display units (Figure 3-4)

By default, it's set to *Auto*, and Power BI automatically adjusts it based on the value range, converting numbers to thousands, millions, or billions as necessary. However, you can manually set the units and decimal places.

In Figure 1-11, we displayed labels in millions with two decimal places. However, data in your report can be further filtered, and you may get label values in the range of 0.01M, which isn't very informative. That's why in our sample case we'll display labels in thousands without any decimal places (Figure 3-4).

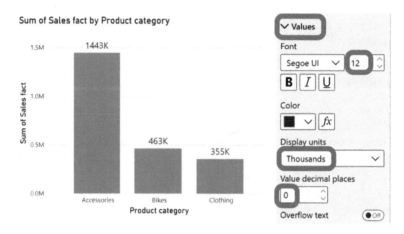

Figure 3-4. Customizing data labels

Step 2: Disable the Y-Axis

The values on the y-axis now duplicate the data labels and don't provide new information for analysis. It's a good practice to eliminate such "information noise," so simply uncheck the *Values* and *Title* options to turn it off (Figure 3-5). But as mentioned in "Chart Anatomy" on page 13, there are exceptions to this rule—for instance, when the axis scale is changed, and the chart doesn't start at zero.

When you turn off the *Y-axis*, the gridlines also disappear automatically. This is the right approach—without the y-axis the gridlines become unnecessary, and it's best to get rid of them.

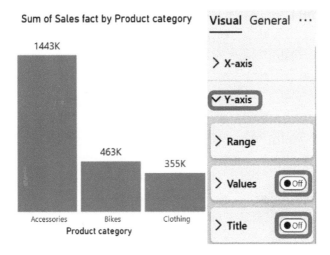

Figure 3-5. Disabling the Y-axis

Step 3: Customize Category Labels on the X-Axis

Category labels on the x-axis are necessary, so we keep the *X-axis* feature turned *On*. However, Power BI has this habit of automatically adding the name of the column with the data categories to the chart as an axis title. We'll deal with this the same way we did for the y-axis—we go into the menu under *X-axis* and uncheck the *Title* option (Figure 3-6).

In this context, we also want those category labels to be larger, with a font size of 12. However, increasing the font size too much might lead to a problem where the labels don't fit in neatly and appear at a slanted angle.

Max area height

> If these category labels are made up of multiple words, they might wrap onto more than one line. Sometimes this can balloon into three or four lines, eating up half of your chart's space. The software, by default, doesn't let them take more than 25% of the category area. You can change this ratio, but in our case, there's really no need to.

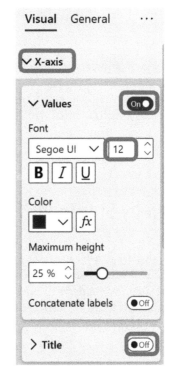

Figure 3-6. Adjusting the X-axis

Step 4: Edit the Chart Title

This part is common for any chart (we talked about it in "Chart Title" on page 15). Go to the *General* tab (Figure 3-7), choose *Title*, and type in your title in the *Text* parameter.

Figure 3-7. Title settings and final column chart after customization

The title should be larger than your data labels and category labels. The default 14-point font size works well for this. Keep the horizontal alignment to the left.

And that's it for setting up a column chart with a single data series. It took just four steps to turn the default option into a clear and informative visual element for easy data analysis (Figure 3-7).

Step-by-Step Guide for the Bar Chart

Bar charts are used to display quantitative comparisons, especially in cases where the data doesn't fit well in a column chart (we explored such examples in Figures 2-1 to 2-5). To create a bar chart, we will select the *Product subcategory* field, which contains more than 10 items with long names. The default chart view also doesn't meet our standards (Figure 3-8), so let's walk through a step-by-step guide again.

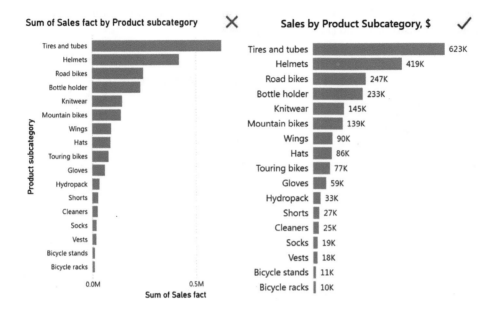

Figure 3-8. By default (left) and final view (right)

Step 1: Enable and Adjust Data Labels

This step is identical to the column chart. The *Data labels* section contains the same options as shown in Figure 3-3, so we won't repeat the description.

Notice that for the largest value the label could be positioned inside the end of the bar, while for the others, it's outside. This is the essence of the default *Position* parameter—*Auto* (Figure 3-3). Power BI automatically placed the label inside to provide more space for the bar and even inverted the label color on a dark background (Figure 3-9, right).

Step 2: Disable Value Axis (X-Axis)

In general, we talk about the "value axis": for a column chart, this is the y-axis, and for a bar chart, it's the x-axis. The rule is exactly the same: if we've turned on data labels, then the axis isn't needed, just like its title. You can adjust this in the same way as shown in Figure 3-5, but instead of the y-axis, you'll be working with the x-axis.

Here, we'd like to draw your attention to an exception to the rule. There are cases where the difference in data range is minimal, and the bars (whether vertical or horizontal) look quite similar (Figure 3-9, left). In our dataset, this happens when we compare sales by the manager field. In such cases, we can adjust the start of the value axis (either x or y). We display the scale to make it clear that the difference between first and last isn't threefold (Figure 3-9, right).

Figure 3-9. Left: X-axis is from zero; it's hard to see the difference. Right: X-axis is set from 35K; the scale has changed and the bar chart is clearer.

Step 3: Customize Category Labels on the Y-Axis

Technically, the category axis parameter works the same way, differing only in the name, *X* instead of *Y*. But there's a semantic difference for the *Max area width* parameter in the *Values* section. If we start reducing the width of the entire chart, the text will begin to get cut off. This isn't critical if we lose only the last few letters. However, as shown in Figure 3-10 on the left, we can see heavily truncated category names (Tires and…, Mountain…), and this is a small but perceptual barrier for the user.

Figure 3-10. How to customize Max area width *for categories—cropped titles on the left, enlarged area on the right, titles are fully visible*

By default, 25% of the category area is allocated, but we can increase it to 50% by entering a value or dragging the slider to the right. This doesn't guarantee that all labels will fit, but it's correct that you can't set it to more than 50%. After all, at least half of the chart area is needed for visualization. If you find that there's not enough space, just stretch the entire chart widthwise.

Step 4 (Optional): Adjust Bar Height

If we start reducing the height of the chart, at a certain point, a scroll bar will appear on the right. It's a good thing that Power BI prevents us from "flattening" the bars. But how do you control this parameter?

Let's move to the *Y-axis* section again. In the *Layout* section, *Minimum category height* determines how much the bars can "squeeze" (Figure 3-11). The default is 20 px, and that's also an optimal value. However, depending on the data range and the size of the chart area, we might need to adjust it.

Figure 3-11. Default 20 px for category height (left) and increased 30 px (right)

By increasing the thickness of the columns, we removed four smaller values beyond the scrolling area and emphasized the top categories. This step is not mandatory in our guide, but keep it in mind. In Power BI, of course, you can set a top-10 or another fixed value using filters or data transformations, but for now, we're focusing on the fundamentals of visualization and formatting options.

Step 5: Edit the Chart Title

This step is entirely identical to the column chart (Figure 3-7), as are other parameters in the *General* section. Expand the *Title* field and remove unnecessary words, shortening it to "Sales by Product Subcategory," as in the example in Figure 3-8, which is where our guide began.

Data Filtration Challenges

The Power BI report differs from presentation slides in that the data is updated, and the number of categories and the value range can change. Your beautiful chart may not look as good after applying a few filters. Let's discuss not only mistakes but also common challenges that we face with data refreshing and its impact. These challenges apply to both vertical and horizontal bar charts.

1. Too Small Values in the Data Labels

Let's say you fixed the display units to millions instead of using the *Auto* setting. Then, you applied filters by date and region. You'll end up with identical labels like "0.02M" for the first three bars with different values, making it unclear what the actual values are. In this case, it's better to switch to thousands or even leave the parameter as *Auto* (it will adjust the appropriate units of measurement), as you can see in Figure 3-12.

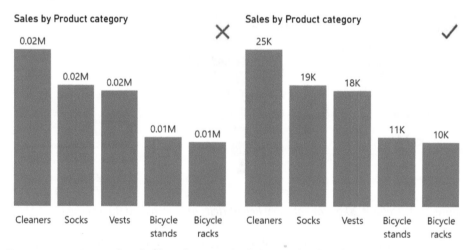

Figure 3-12. Meaningless (left) and correct (right) units for data labels

2. Category Labels Are Not Horizontal

It's not always possible to increase the chart size to make the text on the x-axis fit horizontally. Sometimes there's limited space on the dashboard. In these cases, it's worth deviating from the recommended font size of 12 pt and reducing it to 10 or even 9 pt to make everything fit without tilting (Figure 3-13).

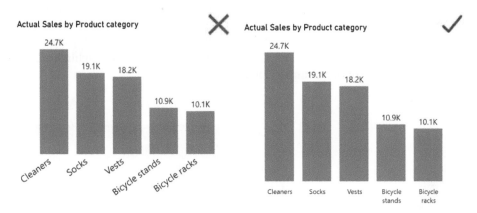

Figure 3-13. The x-axis labels should always be strictly horizontal

3. Charts Cross-Filtering and Highlighting

On a chart, you often want to show the inner details of categories, breaking them down into subcategories. While beginners sometimes try to squeeze all their data into a single column chart, experienced analysts avoid doing so. In Power BI, a powerful cross-filtering system connects all the charts in your dashboard. This means you can explore detailed data using filters applied to other visuals.

Imagine you want to display the latest sales for different subcategories in specific countries. If you create a stacked column chart, it can become cluttered and unattractive (Figure 3-14).

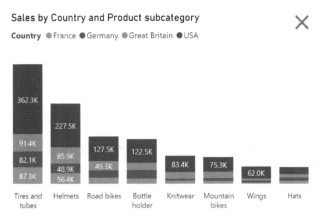

Figure 3-14. Stacked column chart on which it is difficult to read country details

We suggest placing two separate charts side by side: one for sales by country and another for sales by subcategory. By using cross-filtering capabilities, we can obtain all the sales data for each country within each subcategory. So, by clicking directly on the column for sales in the USA, on the adjacent chart, we can see highlighted sales for each subcategory in that country (Figure 3-15).

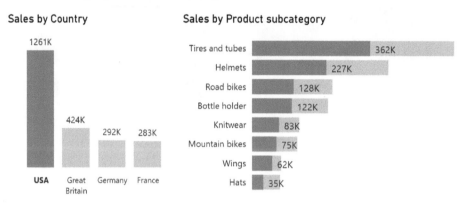

Figure 3-15. Cross-filtering of charts by USA

If we choose the *Helmets* column on the right bar chart, the left one will instantly display sales of this product category in all countries.

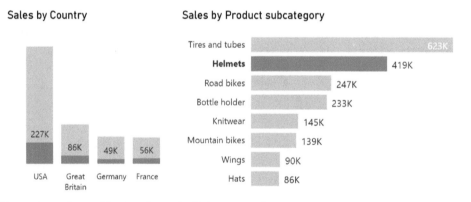

Figure 3-16. Cross-filtering charts by Helmets product category

Cross-filtering is a significant advantage of interactive Power BI reports, and we highly recommend making the most of this feature. We will clarify all the details of filtering and interactions in Chapter 9.

However, there are some nuances that you should consider in each specific case. For instance, if you set data labels in millions, during filtering, you might see zeros because, for example, one manager's sales could be in the tens of thousands. Therefore, when setting the data magnitude, you should consider how it will appear when filtered.

Tips and Notes

In terms of its purpose, a column chart is suitable for two types of analysis: dynamics and rating. Bar charts are used to display quantitative comparisons, especially in cases where the data doesn't fit well in a column chart.

Checklist for setting up a column/bar chart:

1. Enable and adjust data labels.
2. Disable value axis (Y for column and X for bar chart).
3. Customize category labels. For the bar chart, the category labels area usually needs to be enlarged from the default 25%.
4. Adjust bar width (optional).
5. Edit chart title.

Power BI reports differ from presentation slides in that the data is updated, and the number of categories and the value range can change. So double-check that your data and category labels are displayed correctly.

If you have difficulty setting up chart elements, or the menu item names in the current version of Power BI are different, you may download the *.pbix* file with customized visuals (*https://oreil.ly/up1GU*).

CHAPTER 4

Pie and Donut Charts

A great visual metaphor for representing structure is the pie chart. We divide it into slices and examine who got the largest piece, or, for example, how market players split half of the market between them. The emphasis is not on quantitative comparison (bigger or smaller), as with bar charts, but on the part of the whole (percentages).

A donut chart serves the same purpose as a pie chart, built with the same parameters, with the only difference being the hole (or properly termed, the "donut hole") in the center (Figure 4-1, right). In this chapter, we will provide you with a guide for a pie chart, but you can configure a donut chart in the same way.

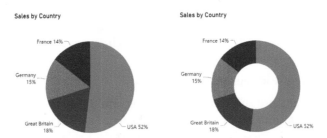

Figure 4-1. Pie chart (left) and donut chart (right)

What purpose does the hole serve? Nothing special. We can put the total value there, but there is no such standard option. We can get this result combining two visuals: donut chart and card with total value (Figure 4-2). But let's not complicate things for now and instead understand the basic setting.

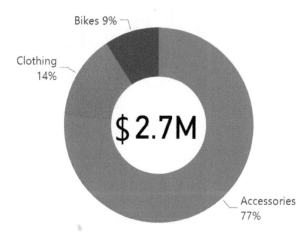

Sales by Category

Bikes 9%

Clothing
14%

$2.7M

Accessories
77%

Figure 4-2. Donut chart with total sales in the center

We remind you that the practice dataset (*https://oreil.ly/DataViz_dataset*) is utilized for all the chapters in this part, allowing you to build the final dashboard. You can continue practicing with your file from the previous chapter. If you face any technical problems, you will find a *.pbix* file with all the settings at the end of this chapter.

A pie chart is quite simple to create. You just have to put categories in the *Legend* field and the quantitative measure in the *Values* field. It doesn't look so bad by default (Figure 4-3):

- The chart is sorted in descending order, which is correct (we need to see first which country has the largest share of sales).

- Data labels are already enabled on the slices.

- The slices' colors are sufficiently contrasting and do not blend with each other (although this also depends on the color theme of your report, and you must be aware of color-blindness issues when selecting sector colors).

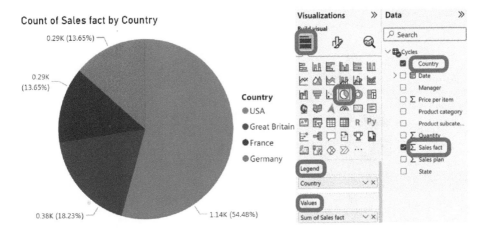

Figure 4-3. Default pie chart and fields selection for it

Let's go step-by-step and make the necessary changes to improve the pie chart's capacity to visualize the structure. This guide will be short because pie and donut charts don't have the concept of x- and y-axes.

Step-by-Step Guide for Pie and Donut Charts

Here's what we have to do to create a pie or donut chart.

Step 1: Adjust Data Labels

Unlike bar charts, here the data labels appear right away, and you don't need to enable them. However, in Figure 4-3, you can see absolute and percentage values. We understand that it can be important to see both. However, in terms of visualization, you should prioritize. If we try to display "everything at once," nothing will be seen at a glance.

Don't be startled if you don't see the data labels item in the visual formatting options; it's called *Detail labels* in pie charts (Figure 4-4).

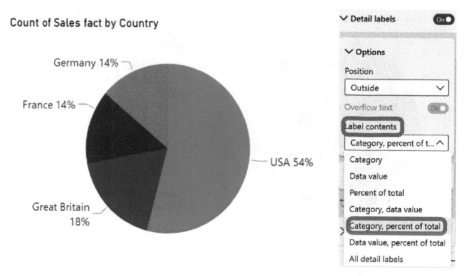

Figure 4-4. Options for detail labels

Let's take a closer look at the *Label contents* parameter; it offers several options to choose from:

- *Category* will display only the category name.
- *Data value* will show only the numerical value, in our case, the sales sum.
- *Percent of total* is usually the most important aspect of a pie chart, showing the segment's share of the whole.

Following these are various combinations of these elements, and you can even choose *All detail labels*. As we are primarily concerned with structure, we advise choosing *Category, percent of total*.

Now let's move on to the *Values* section (Figure 4-5) and configure it following the same algorithm as the bar chart in Chapter 3:

- It's better to increase the font size to 12 points, but ensure that the category names on the chart are fully visible (they could be automatically cut if they are too big). If they don't fit, reduce the size to 11, 10, or even the default 9 points.
- Leave the *Display units* on *Auto* (or you can set it to *None*). There's no need to transform our data into thousands or millions since it's in percentages (it would add unnecessary zeros).

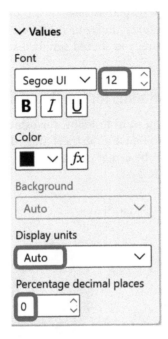

Figure 4-5. Values for detail labels

For *Percentage decimal places*, it's best to set it to 0. We assume that we have only a few sectors and a range of values like 10%, 20%, etc. Decimal places, in this case, would be redundant.

Step 2: Remove the Legend

This is important to display the value alongside the category label rather than attempting to correlate the pie slice with a small colored dot at the legend. In Figure 4-6 (left) you see the default view.

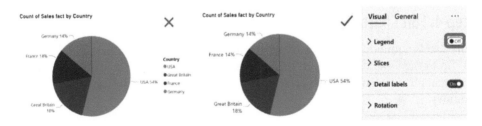

Figure 4-6. Remove the legend if you have displayed category labels

The category names are now displayed next to the data labels. Consequently, the legend contains redundant information, much like the y-axis in bar charts. There's no need for the legend anymore; you should simply disable this element (Figure 4-6, right).

Step 3: Adjust the Inner Radius for the Donut Chart

To format the donut chart, you need to follow the same first two steps as setting up the pie chart. Here, though, you have an extra setting: the inner radius, which affects the size of the empty space in the center of the chart. You can find this setting in the *Slices → Spacing* section (Figure 4-7).

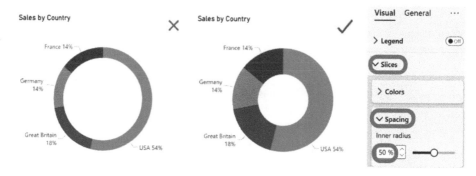

Figure 4-7. The inner radius of 80% makes the chart too tiny (left); at 50%, it looks balanced (right)

By default, the inner circle's radius is set at 60%. You can leave it as is, but we don't recommend increasing it, as shown on the left in Figure 4-7. The radius is set at 80%, and as a result, it dominates the empty space, making the visualization too subtle, with no clear focus. Based on our experience, we recommend reducing this radius to 50%, as shown on the right in Figure 4-7, for a balanced appearance. If you reduce the radius to 0, the donut will turn into a pie.

Step 4: Edit Chart Title

This step is common for any chart type, and we discussed it in "Chart Title" on page 15. Go to the *General* tab, select *Title*, and enter a concise title in the *Text* parameter. For example, instead of "Sum of Sales fact by Country," you can use "Sales Fact by Country."

Common Mistakes

A pie chart is quite simple to create, and sometimes you may want to add a unique feature or "cherry on the pie." However, experiments with such traditional visualizations often lead to unsuccessful results. For classic visualizations, it's best to follow the principle of "one thought, one chart." In the second part of the book, we'll introduce you to advanced visualizations for handling complex data.

Rotation

Rotation is the final parameter in the visualization panel, and it applies to both pie and donut charts. By default, the chart is sorted from largest to smallest, and the first sector starts at 0 degrees (imagine a clock face, starting from 12 o'clock). This is the conventional way to present such data.

You can certainly be creative and change the starting point, for example, to 90 degrees, as shown on the left in Figure 4-8. In this case, you will see Germany first, then France, and finally the USA with the largest share. However, this may raise questions about the sorting principle used in the chart. It's not an epic failure, but we recommend keeping the default rotation angle of 0 degrees.

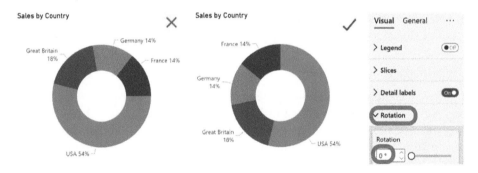

Figure 4-8. Incorrect rotation at 90 degrees (left) and correct default rotation at 0 degrees (right)

Details (Hierarchical View)

We put in the *Legend* and *Values* sections when we created the default pie chart (Figure 4-3) at the start of this chapter. However, there's one more field to consider, which is *Details*. This field allows us to create a hierarchical representation. In Figure 4-9, we see the structure of sales by categories, distinguished by color. Each large colorful sector is divided into smaller segments, representing the sales share of subcategories.

Figure 4-9. Messy hierarchical view with details

We understand that a regular pie chart may seem too simple, and you might want to add more information to it. However, when you add details, it can become overloaded: the sectors become too narrow, and for some, the category labels and values may not even be displayed, as is the case in Figure 4-9.

This representation can be effective only if each category contains two to three subcategories, no more. We could create such a teaching example, but in practice, we have never encountered such a scenario. The second level of hierarchy usually contains more than 10 elements, and they do not fit on a pie or donut. For this purpose, we have a treemap and other types of charts, which we will explore in the following chapters.

Timeline at the Pie or Donut

And here's another warning—displaying the timeline at the pie or donut (Figure 4-10). It may seem like a good idea to show quarterly sales shares, and the chart will look neat. But this will distort the meaning: the timeline should be directed horizontally from left to right, from past to future. The same works for any time period: days, months, years. This is a common pattern of perception, and we do not recommend breaking it. We'll tell you more about working with the timeline in Chapter 6.

Figure 4-10. Incorrect timeline on pie (left) and donut (center) charts; correct bar chart (right)

Tips and Notes

Pie and donut charts have the same purpose—visualizing the structure for a small number of categories (usually no more than six). These charts are built using the same parameters, with the only difference being that the donut chart has an inner space. They don't have x- and y-axes, and for customization, you need to follow simple steps.

Checklist for setting up a pie/donut chart:

1. Set up detail labels: category and percentage of the total.
2. Remove the legend, which duplicates the information in the labels.
3. Adjust the inner radius (for donut chart).
4. Edit the chart title.

In addition, you should handle these parameters with care:

Rotation

> Do not change the rotation angle (leave it at the default 0 degrees, i.e., at 12 o'clock on the clock face).

Details

> Do not add subcategories within the sectors; it makes the chart overloaded.

If you have difficulty setting up chart elements, or the menu item names in the current version of Power BI are different, you may download the *.pbix* file with customized visuals (*https://oreil.ly/pEUHD*).

CHAPTER 5

Treemap

Treemap is a visualization type used to display hierarchical data in a more structured way than pie or donut charts. In a treemap, rectangles are used instead of sectors. A treemap utilizes space more efficiently and accommodates a larger number of elements. The treemap in Figure 5-1 illustrates the sales structure by subcategories.

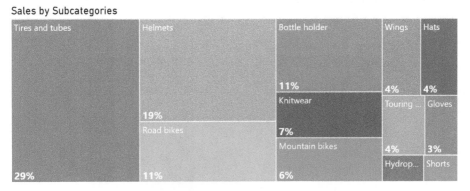

Figure 5-1. Treemap for one level of category

But what does this have to do with trees? Originally, this visualization method was applied to hierarchical, tree-structured data. Each branch of this "logic tree" is represented by a rectangle, which is then divided into smaller rectangles to represent subbranches. At the end of the previous chapter, we recommended not filling in the *Details* field for a pie chart because it overloaded the chart with information, as shown in Figure 4-9. However, a treemap is better suited for such data. In Figure 5-2, you can see that approximately two-thirds of the sales are related to accessories, and it provides insights into the share of each subcategory.

Sales by Product Categories/Subcategories

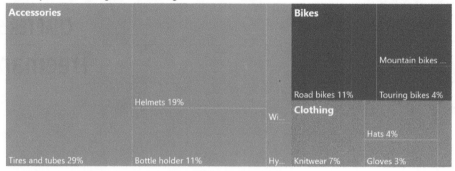

Figure 5-2. Treemap for hierarchy

The proportions of the rectangles (height and width) are automatically determined based on the size of the chart area. Some elements may end up as squares, while others may be stretched horizontally or vertically.

This is the weak point of the treemap. The data label will not fit in a narrow horizontal sector, and even the category label will show only a few of its beginning characters. In Figure 5-3, we've reduced the chart area by half compared with Figure 5-2, and data labels for categories are hidden almost everywhere.

Figure 5-3. The issue with "hidden" data labels

But this is not a treemap-specific issue; the same problem would occur with any visualization when there's limited space and you try to display a lot of data.

We hope that you have downloaded the practice dataset (*https://oreil.ly/DataViz_data set*). It is utilized for all the chapters in this part, allowing you to build the final dashboard. You may continue practicing with your file from the previous chapter. If you face any technical problems, you will find a *.pbix* file with all the settings at the end of this chapter.

Building a treemap is as simple as creating a pie chart. Let's start with a single-level example: place the *Sales fact* field in the *Values* section, which defines the rectangle's size, and put *Product subcategory* in the *Category* section. You may also put it in the *Details* section in this one-level example. In either case, as shown in Figure 5-4, you'll get a colorful "carpet."

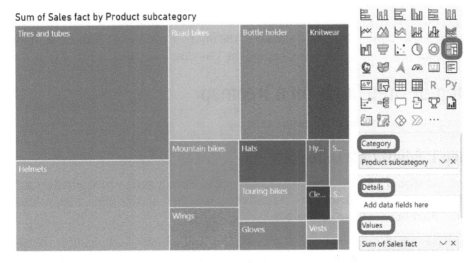

Figure 5-4. Default treemap

If you want to create a treemap with grouping like in Figure 5-2, you should place the *Product category* field in the *Category* section. This will give you three colorful "bricks" for these categories. To further divide them into subcategories, you'll place *Product subcategory* in the *Details* field (Figure 5-5).

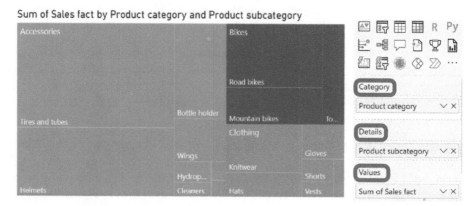

Figure 5-5. Default treemap with subdivision

What do we want to improve on the default treemap (Figures 5-4 and 5-5)? There will be just a few steps in this guide, similar to the ones for pie/donut charts. In addition, we'll show you some new features beyond the *Visualizations* panel.

Step-by-Step Guide for a Treemap

Here's what we have to do to create a treemap.

Step 1: Adjust Data Labels Size

First, we should add data labels. It's challenging to visually assess the share of even the largest items without them. Do tires and tubes take 20% or 30% of the sales volume? Is the share of road bikes 10% or 20%?

We have to turn on *Format visual → Data labels* and adjust it such that it is readable and visually appealing. In our case, we increased the font size, made it bold, and kept it white; set *Display units;* and put 0 value decimal places. In your case, the settings may be different, but the key is to ensure that the numbers are as visible as possible. Unfortunately, the labels in the lower right corner are not visible, as you can see in the treemap shown in Figure 5-6.

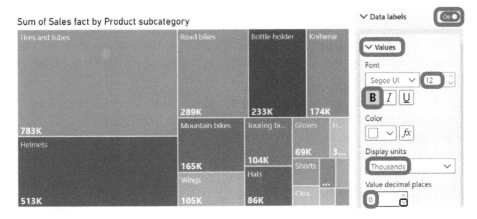

Figure 5-6. Data labels for the one-level treemap

The situation is much more complicated in the case of hierarchies. In this scenario, the data label of the inner section occupies more space because by default it represents the category and its value combined (Figure 5-7). Once more, we have to find the ideal ratio between readability and size.

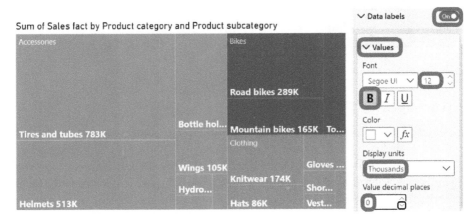

Figure 5-7. Data labels on the two-level treemap

Step 2: Display Percent of Total

The structure, shown as percentages, is what we require, not the absolute values that the data labels now indicate. The data label display options available for a pie chart (where we could choose any combination of category, value, and percentage) are not present in the treemap.

However, we will show you how to solve this issue. In the *Build visual* pane, click the small chevron on the right of the field name in the *Values* section (Figure 5-8). In the pop-up window, select *Show value as*, and then *Percent of grand total*. Now the values (and their data labels) will be shown as percentages of the total. Remember this option; you'll find it useful in the future! Data labels in percentages are now available (Figure 5-8).

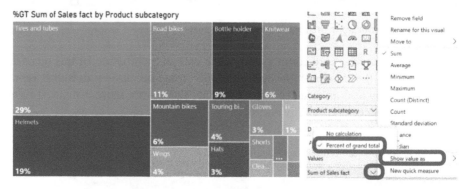

Figure 5-8. Adjust value display mode

Step 3: Adjust Category Labels

We modify category names while adhering to the same guidelines and standards in an effort to make them all readable and noticeable (Figure 5-9). Unfortunately, as we've mentioned before, even with the smallest font size, the last category labels will remain invisible if there are too many. However, it will be challenging to read the key categories in small font size. Decide on the best font color and size for your particular circumstance.

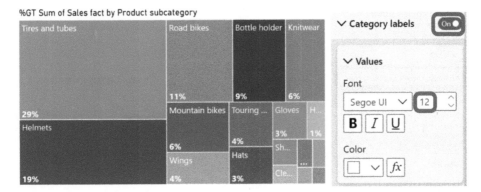

%GT Sum of Sales fact by Product subcategory

Figure 5-9. Category labels *settings*

Step 4: Adjust Colors

A treemap containing many categories almost always looks like a colorful parrot. The easiest solution to this, if a little labor-intensive, is to manually change the colors. The *Colors* section in the *Visual* format menu is where you can do this (Figure 5-10).

The *Advanced controls* option (with the *fx* symbol) in this section (Figure 5-10) allows us to create a monochromatic solution with a gradient. When you press the *Advanced controls* button, a pop-up menu appears (Figure 5-11), with the following default parameters (these are the ones we need):

- *Format style*: Gradient
- *What field should we base this on?* Sum of Sales fact
- *Minimum*: the lightest color
- *Maximum*: the darkest color

Figure 5-10. Color options

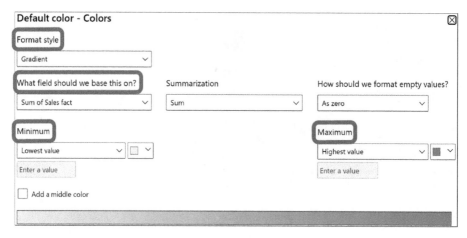

Figure 5-11. A pop-up menu window for customizing the gradient

But this solution is too light (Figure 5-12), and the entire right portion appears boring and unsightly as it merges into one. To make the treemap brighter, we will adjust the gradient range.

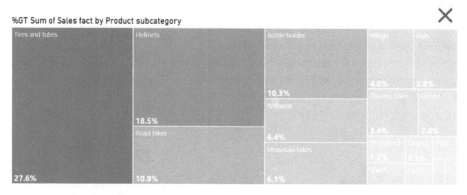

Figure 5-12. The default gradient of the treemap

Instead of starting with such a light hue, we will make the maximum slightly darker (Figure 5-13). Although these changes don't require a sharp contrast between neighboring sectors, the differences are still discernible. We will combine a portion of the formatting window and a portion of the treemap into a single picture because the top parameters (the formatting and summary fields) stay the same.

Figure 5-13. Gradient treemap with brighter colors for highest and lowest values

Note that the *Add a middle color* option (Figure 5-14) is also available for selection.

Figure 5-14. Gradient treemap solution with a middle color

Let's incorporate some variety. We'll select hues that are close together in intensity in the purple spectrum, and at the very least, we'll use a neutral gray that is nevertheless highly saturated. As a result, we'll have more contrast for sectors with small shares.

Step 5: Edit Chart Title

This part is common for any chart. We talked about it in "Chart Title" on page 15. Go to the *General* tab, choose *Title*, and type your short title in the *Text* parameter.

Strengths and Weaknesses of the Treemap

Let's summarize. The treemap is a good alternative to pie and donut charts. Compared with them, it has several advantages:

- In a treemap, you can visually represent 10–15 categories (while in a pie chart only up to 6). Of course, this depends on the dashboard's area size.
- The treemap is flexible and adaptable to proportions. You can fit it into a square area of the dashboard or stretch it horizontally or vertically.
- The treemap is suitable for displaying two levels of hierarchy (category and subcategory).

Despite these advantages, we expected the treemap to be a more mature, refined visualization. In terms of data labels, we hoped to see more options for fine-tuning:

- There is no native option for displaying percentages, which is essential for a structural visualization. We are accustomed to percentages from the old days of pie charts in Excel. It seems strange that you need to make additional transformations in the *Values* field parameters on the treemap (Figure 5-7).
- There is no subtotal for the top level (*Legend* field). It's difficult to tell at a glance how much is in accessories in the example in Figure 5-2—is it 60% or perhaps 75%? While you can mentally add up the subcategory proportions, it would be more helpful if the visualization assisted with this.
- Data labels often don't fit within the sector. This issue is relevant to the second level of hierarchy (the *Details* field, Figure 5-5). If a category has a long name, it pushes the numerical value to the right. In a narrow sector, this name may not be displayed. Even in Excel's treemap, this problem is addressed by an option to show data labels on a new line, and we would like to see this in Power BI as well.

These weaknesses aren't crucial, and newcomers might not even notice them. We're just warning you in advance so you won't think there's something you don't know. These are simply the limitations of this visualization.

Tips and Notes

Treemap is a visualization type used to display hierarchical data in a more structured way than pie charts. It utilizes space more efficiently and accommodates a larger number of elements.

Checklist for setting up a treemap:

1. Adjust the size of data labels.
2. Display percent of total.
3. Adjust category labels.
4. Adjust colors manually or set up a rule for gradient color.
5. Edit chart title.

But there are some options that we expected to have "ready-made":

- "Display percent of total" as an option for data labels (without transformations in the value field parameters).
- Subtotals for the top level (*Legend* field). There is no way to display it.
- Wrap text for category labels and display value on a new line.

These weaknesses aren't crucial, so feel free to build a treemap if you have about 10 categories.

Download the *.pbix* file with customized visuals (*https://oreil.ly/DkQdk*).

CHAPTER 6

Timeline Charts

In Chapters 3, 4, and 5, we have already acquainted ourselves with classic visualizations for rating and structure. Now let's move on to dynamics: analyzing changes in a metric over time. For this purpose we are accustomed to using line charts. They are made up of points with coordinates (x, y) that are connected by a line. In Figure 6-1, you can see a chart with two measures—actual and planned sales by month.

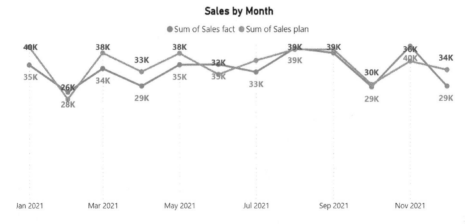

Figure 6-1. Line chart for two measures

It may happen that we don't have planned values, and we are displaying only the actual values, evaluating their dynamics. In this case, a semitransparent fill under the line will look good (Figure 6-2). Technically, this is another Power BI visual—the area chart—but it functions similarly to the line chart.

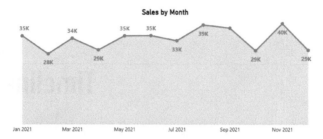

Figure 6-2. Area chart for a single measure

In this chapter, we will guide you on how to fine-tune these visuals to achieve a pixel-perfect view and introduce you to features unique to line charts.

Furthermore, when we say "line chart," we mean the full family of visuals that can be used with a time axis:

- Line chart
- Area chart, stacked area chart
- Combined chart: line + stacked column, line + clustered column
- Ribbon chart

Column chart also joins this family when we add the date to the x-axis. We will cover all of them throughout this extensive chapter. But first, let's pay attention to understanding how Power BI works with the date format. At first glance, this may not be obvious. Although there are many commonalities with Excel pivot tables, the behavior of some elements will be drastically different.

Date Hierarchy: How It Works

When Power BI recognizes the *Date* data type, it provides a calendar icon to that column and creates a *Date Hierarchy* automatically. This means it breaks the date down by years, quarters, months, and days. Let's create the line chart visual with the *Sales fact* field on the y-axis. On the x-axis we'll add the *Date* field to see selected measure dynamics over time. The result, however, may surprise you: instead of a graph, you will observe a single point, as illustrated in Figure 6-3.

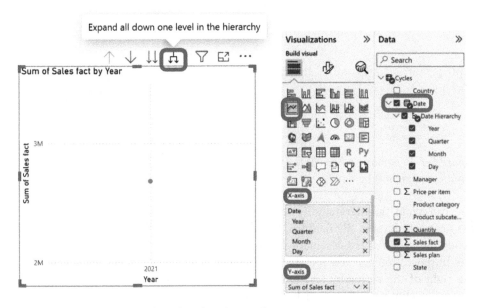

Figure 6-3. Building a graph with a date hierarchy

Let's expand the *Date* field on the *Data* pane. There is a *Date Hierarchy* group within it, and within that are *Year*, *Quarter*, *Month*, and *Day*. Power BI presents this hierarchy by default, beginning with the top level, which is the year. Again, by default, this hierarchy doesn't expand; that's why we received only one point on the chart (our dataset contains data for only one year). However, by drilling down, we can advance to the next level. There are icons with arrows above the chart to help you with this. In Figure 6-3, the "splitting" arrow, *Expand all down one level in the hierarchy*, is highlighted. It correctly takes us to the quarter, month, or day.

By sequentially expanding the hierarchy, we get sales charts by quarters, by month, and by day (Figure 6-4). If you need to go back up or down one level, press the *Drill up* or *Drill down* arrow.

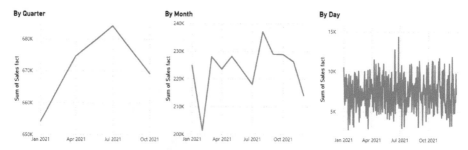

Figure 6-4. Expanding a line chart by date hierarchy (left is by quarter, center is by month, and right is by day)

You can avoid the hierarchy by selecting only the necessary level in the field list, which eliminates the requirement for arrows above. For this purpose, you can use the small crosses to the right of the hierarchy levels in the *X-axis* section to eliminate unwanted levels from the visual (Figure 6-5).

Figure 6-5. Date *hierarchy levels*

Using reports, we typically look at data by month, compare plans to actuals, or observe specific trendlines. A chart by day looks like a cardiogram, making it difficult to discern trends. On the other hand, quarterly charts often smooth out trends too much, and you might want to see more details. As the most common choice, we will construct a line chart by month step-by-step.

Step-by-Step Guide for Line Chart

Here's what we have to do to create a line chart.

Step 1: Customize Timeline on the X-Axis

Let's continue the discussion on date hierarchy. If you select only the month in the hierarchy field list, you may get x-axis labels at an angle (Figure 6-6, top). The reason for this is that "September," the longest name, doesn't fit horizontally. Of course, you can decrease the x-axis text size or widen the chart. But typically, there isn't much room on the sheet.

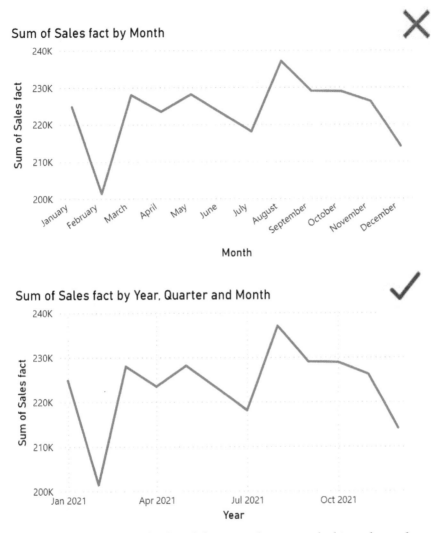

Figure 6-6. Full month name (top) and short month name at the hierarchy mode (bottom)

To address this issue, you can use abbreviated month names: Jan, Feb, etc. It's good if your data source has them prepared. Creating such an additional category can be done with DAX formulas, but that's at an advanced level. We are here to introduce you to standard Power BI features accessible to users at any level.

You can get an abbreviated date format using hierarchy. Select the chart where the full *Date Hierarchy* is used on the *X-axis*, and then click the split arrow on the chart until you reach the month level. In Figure 6-6 (bottom), you can see that x-axis labels are displayed with a two-month interval: Jan 2021, Apr 2021, and so on.

Category labels fit horizontally as a result of this. In Figures 6-1 and 6-2, the x-axis of our benchmark line charts is built in the same way. Only there the chart is wider, and months are displayed with a one-month interval: Jan 2021, Mar 2021, and so on.

Furthermore, observe that in Figure 6-6, the x-axis is labeled "Month" on the top and "Year" on the bottom (since the hierarchy began with the year). In both cases, don't forget to turn off the axis title since the period is already indicated in the chart title.

Step 2: Adjust the Y-Axis Scale

By default, Power BI constructs a line chart starting the y-axis from the smallest value among the data (Figure 6-7, left). The y-axis in our case begins at this value, which is the February value of about 200K.

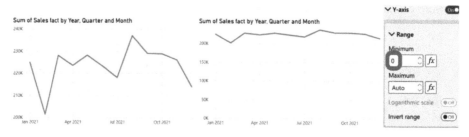

Figure 6-7. The y-axis on the left is plotted from 200K by default, on the right manually set from zero

The chart will appear differently (Figure 6-7, right) if we go into the axis parameters and adjust the y-axis to start from zero. The drop in sales from August to December won't seem as dramatic. We can say that sales were more or less stable throughout the year, with a slight dip in February and a peak in August.

In *Y-axis Range* options, we don't label one as correct and the other as wrong. Both are logically correct (unless, of course, on the left chart, we claim a dramatic drop in sales, which could be misleading). The choice depends on what you want to emphasize: the overall trend (on the right) or zooming in to observe fluctuations (on the left).

Step 3: Add Data Labels

Data labels are optional for line charts, even if they were required for pie charts and bar charts. After all, we are comparing not specific values with each other but evaluating the trendline. This is especially true if there is limited space for the chart on the report page. However, if there's enough space, correctly configured data labels will always be a useful addition.

Position is recommended to be left on *Auto*, as Power BI will automatically choose the optimal position for labels—either above or below the line.

The line chart has an interesting parameter—*Label density* (Figure 6-8). By default, it is set to 50%, meaning only half of the labels (every other one and peaks) will be displayed. This helps avoid overload and overlapping of labels. If you absolutely need to display all data labels, increase the density to 100% or choose another density value suitable for your data range.

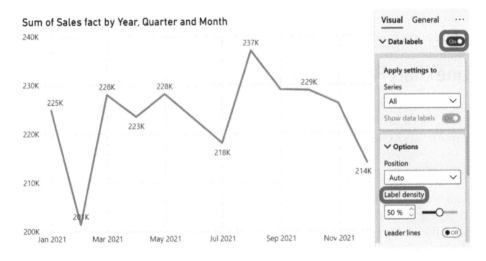

Figure 6-8. Data labels density

Note: Figure 6-8 shows a case where we display both data labels and the y-axis. We are doing it to remind the user once again: this is not the actual data scale but fluctuations within the range of 200K to 240K.

As usual, you can adjust display units and font size under the *Values* section.

You can also adjust the font size in the *Values* area, but make sure the chart maintains its coherence. In our case, we recommend changing the color of the labels to match the line color and choosing a bold font (Figure 6-9).

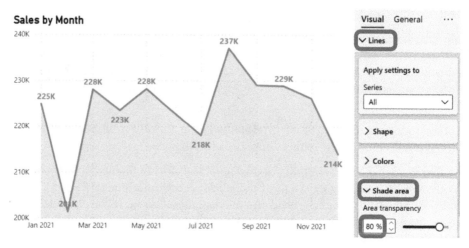

Figure 6-9. Area chart with increased transparency

And as always, don't forget to add an overall title to the chart.

"Line Chart Family" Features

Before we mentioned the full family of visuals that can be used with a time axis, such as area chart, as well as combined charts (line + stacked column, line + clustered column). Let's explore its features.

Area Filling

When we have only one indicator on a line chart, it can sometimes look empty or incomplete. This emptiness between the line and the x-axis can be filled nicely with a light fill. To do this, all you have to do is select the already created line chart on the page, and on the *Visualizations* pane click on another visual icon, the *Area chart*. The previous customization steps will be retained, so you will immediately get a beautiful area chart (Figure 6-9). The only thing we recommend doing is to increase the transparency of the fill so that it doesn't look too bright. This setting is located here: *Lines → Shade area → Area transparency*. We set it to 80% of the main line color.

To maintain a consistent style for the chart, we've also used blue for the data label font, and we made the labels bold. As always, you can customize this in *Data labels → Values*.

Markers

If desired, you can activate data point highlighters for both line and area charts. The form and color of the markers can be customized under the *Markers* section in the *Visual* formatting pane (Figure 6-10).

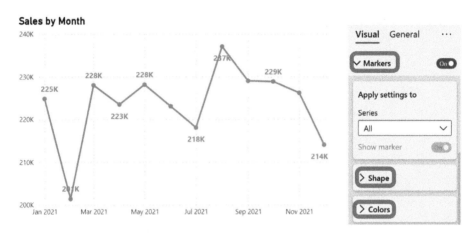

Figure 6-10. Enabling and setting up markers

You can change marker shape and color, but there is no need to do so without a special purpose. Default round markers look neat, while triangles or squares may look outdated. By default, the marker color matches the line color, and this is also an optimal combination.

Apply Settings to Specific Series

A chart may show two or more lines rather than just one. Power BI does not limit the number of lines displayed on the chart, but the general recommendation is to have no more than three to four lines. Usually we compare actual values versus some baseline: target, previous year, forecast, etc.

Sometimes, the lines in your color theme are adjacent colors that are difficult to distinguish. We can format each series individually. In the *Data labels* settings section, choose *Apply settings to* and then select the element you want to change—it's the *Sum of Sales plan* in this case (Figure 6-11).

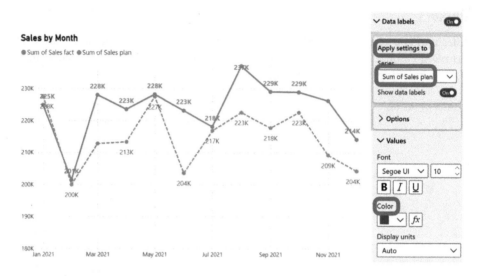

Figure 6-11. Customizing one of the chart elements

Afterward, you can change all the usual data label settings, but these changes will affect only the *Sales plan* element. In our example, we changed the color of the data labels. Using the same principle, go to the *Lines* settings section, choose *Apply settings to/Sum of Sales plan*, and change the color and line type. We've applied gray color and dashed type to the *Sum of Sales plan* there to highlight the main line on the chart—*Sum of Sales fact*.

Secondary Y-Axis

As we've mentioned, you can add multiple data series to a line chart. It may happen that the values are of different orders of magnitude. In Figure 6-12, we try to compare the dynamics of sales in dollars and in units. However, the range for dollars is in the hundreds of thousands, while for units, it's in the thousands, making them compressed against the x-axis and appearing as a straight line, although, in reality, that's not the case.

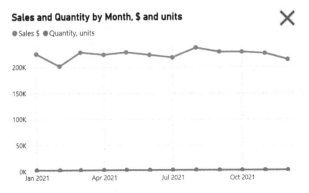

Figure 6-12. Incorrect combo of two measures with one y-axis

By default, the *Quantity, units* field was in the *Y-axis* section, and now we'll move it to the next section—the *Secondary y-axis*. Now we can discern correlations in Figure 6-13: there was a drop in sales in both units and dollars in February and a rise in March. In the second half of the year, unit sales remained relatively stable, while revenue fluctuated. We can see it thanks to separate axis ranges: on the left from 200K to 240K for sales in dollars, on the right from 1,800 to 2,100 for units.

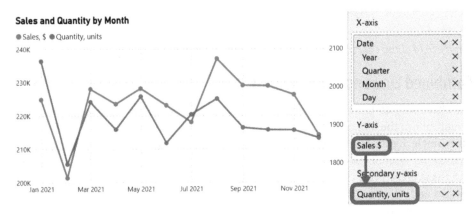

Figure 6-13. Line chart with secondary y-axis to compare indicators with different units

Enabling the secondary y-axis caused both scales to be displayed not from zero but in the default mode for Power BI: in the range from the minimum to the maximum. It's important to set the axis start to zero for both the primary and secondary axes if you want to compare in real proportions.

Along with this, in Figure 6-14, we'll show you another trick. As you already know (we're advocating for it), we make sure that text is read from left to right horizontally. However, axis labels have to be read from bottom to top vertically, and there are no other options. To address this issue, we'll disable the axis labels, and as for the values (intervals on the scale), we'll color them based on the series color, corresponding to the legend. We'll place the legend in the center so that it's equidistant from both scales.

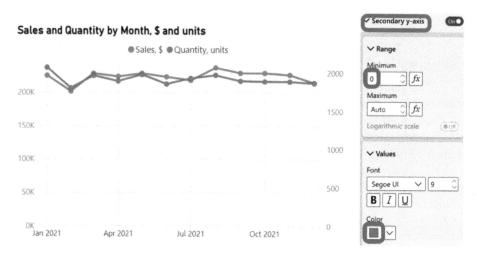

Figure 6-14. Line chart with color coding for primary and secondary axes

Combined Line and Column Chart

An alternative to the solution shown in Figure 6-14 could be using another type of visualization: the line and stacked column chart. We can display various kinds of data on a single figure by using this widget, which combines two chart types that we've already explored. Let's create a chart with comparison of actual sales and target sales and the average price (Figure 6-15). Place *Target Sales, $* and *Sales, $* in the *Line y-axis* section and *Average Price* in the *Column y-axis* (we removed the prefix *Sum of* from the field names).

Figure 6-15. Line and stacked column chart

We obtained a chart with three metrics, where the average price is displayed as columns, and the planned and actual sales are represented as a line chart.

Ribbon Chart

The last type of visualization in the series of line and area charts is the ribbon chart (Figure 6-16).

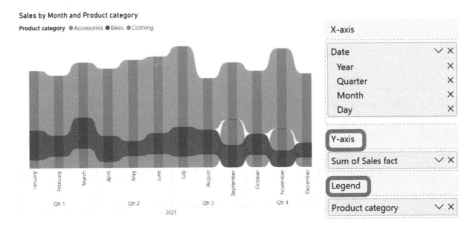

Figure 6-16. Ribbon chart

For this example, we took a single-line chart (the same as in Figure 6-10) and changed its type to *Ribbon chart* on the *Visualizations* pane. We also added a *Product category* to the *Legend* section in addition to the date and measure. As a result, we've got several intertwining ribbons (Figure 6-16): the top one is the widest and blue

(*Accessories*), with the largest number of sales. *Bikes* are mostly in second place, but they were ranked third in September and November, while *Clothing* rose higher in the rating. This is the feature of the ribbon chart—to show both the proportions between categories and changes in their positions in the ranking.

But the ribbon chart has a significant limitation. Data labels are in fact enabled, but there is not enough space to display them: the columns themselves are narrow (and there's no option to change columns width), and more space is allocated for the beautiful connecting lines that form the ribbon pattern. Thus, in favor of aesthetics, we lose functionality. An example of this delicate balance is shown in Figure 6-17. We show the quarterly sales dynamics by country. Data labels with two digits fit on the columns, but where it's already over 100K, there's no space for a third digit, and the labels are not displayed at all. If we build a stacked column chart, there will be enough space on the wide columns for both three and four digits.

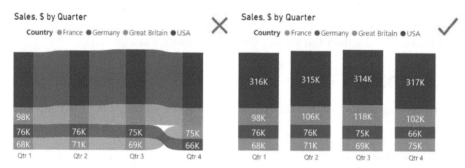

Figure 6-17. Data labels over 100K are not labeled on the ribbon (left), but fit on the column (right)

Of course, we can reduce the font size, but is it worth it? We only see the change in positions of the two smallest categories in one quarter on the ribbon chart. Overall, the image is fairly static, and a classic column chart would be more appropriate. Everything is evident on it, and there is no need to explain why ribbon charts begin to cross in the last period.

According to our book outline, this chart could be classified as exotic. For some cases with significant changes in rankings, it might be useful. But there won't be enough material for a whole chapter, and the principle of building a ribbon chart is the same as for line charts. So reconsider whether you really need "flashy" ribbons on your dashboard.

That's it; we have learned the basic principles of working with a time axis, date hierarchy, and features of the line chart family. The most essential thing to remember from now on is to avoid attempting to display 10 rows on a single chart. When we compare two indicators, we can compare up to three (the third is usually already established on the secondary axis).

Tips and Notes

We use line charts for analyzing changes over time. When Power BI recognizes the *Date* data type, it automatically creates a *Date Hierarchy*, breaking it down by years, quarters, months, and days.

In addition to the column chart, there are several charts designed for the time axis, which we have called the "line chart family":

- Line chart, stacked line chart
- Area chart, stacked area chart
- Combined chart: line + stacked column, line + clustered column
- Ribbon chart (make sure you really need it)

Checklist for the line charts:

1. Customize the x-axis. You can expand date hierarchy to the required level, and the system will correctly display the names. If you choose only one level, make sure that the period names are displayed horizontally and legibly.

2. Adjust the y-axis scale range. By default, Power BI starts the y-axis not from zero but from the smallest value, which may distort the real trendline. The choice depends on what you want to emphasize: the overall trend or zooming in to observe fluctuations.

3. Add data labels. They are optional for line charts, particularly if you have limited space on the report page. However, if there's enough space, correctly configured data labels are always a useful addition.

Features:

- Use the secondary y-axis if you want to compare values of different ranges. This axis should be configured the same way as the primary one to maintain proportions.
- In any chart of this type (line, area, stacked area, ribbon), do not display too many series—no more than five. Otherwise, it will become visually cluttered.

Download the *.pbix* file with customized visuals (*https://oreil.ly/b6KMC*).

CHAPTER 7

Tables and Matrices

While dashboards are often associated only with colorful charts and graphs, it's important not to forget about tables—a highly effective tool for presenting data. When you have dozens of categories and multiple indicators with varying ranges, tables come to the rescue.

Technically, we are talking about two elements in Power BI—tables and matrices. They are externally similar and sometimes may look the same, but they differ in the settings of the data fields.

And if we skillfully work out all the details, it won't just look like a table; it will resemble a combo visual! In Figure 7-1, you can see sales by managers for various metrics (quantity, average price, and actual sales).

Manager	Avg Price, $	Quantity, ps.	Sales fact, $		% plan
Carlos J. Pampliega	203	315	45K	●	7%
George Pitagorsky	185	307	41K	●	-3%
Eileen Roden	198	299	41K	●	-0%
Nicole Reilly	207	286	39K	●	-1%
Jurgen Appelo	209	289	38K	●	-12%
Jim Highsmith	217	267	38K	●	-8%
Cornelius Fichtner	190	280	38K	●	5%
Drew Davison	184	291	38K	●	5%
Glen Alleman	189	282	38K	●	2%
Total	**184**	**17392**	**2261K**		**-3%**

Figure 7-1. Table with visualization inside columns

Note that in the *Sales Fact* column header, there is a downward arrow. This indicates that the rows are sorted in descending order based on this field. Users can choose their sorting field in the table, but we recommend defaulting to sorting not by the alphabetical order of categories but by the ranking of one of the metrics.

If you've used pivot tables in Microsoft Excel, you're familiar with a hierarchical way of presenting data. It's like when you click on the plus sign in rows to see more details. In Power BI, this is a separate visual called a matrix, but it operates similarly to a table.

The matrix enables a more compact tabular presentation of data by grouping it (Figure 7-2). However, to view all elements, you need to expand the relevant position by clicking the plus sign next to it. In Figure 7-2, you can observe a matrix displaying sales by categories and subcategories, with the *Accessories* category expanded.

Product category	Quantity, ps.	Avg Price, $	Sales fact, $
⊟ **Accessories**	13247	147	1443K
Tires and tubes	6731	118	623K
Helmets	2045	314	419K
Bottle holder	3481	81	233K
Wings	424	268	90K
Hydropack	153	335	33K
Cleaners	327	95	25K
Bicycle stands	52	374	11K
Bicycle racks	34	354	10K
⊞ **Bikes**	1651	434	463K
⊞ **Clothing**	2494	217	355K
Total	17392	184	2261K

Figure 7-2. Matrix rows with drill-down

Figure 7-3 is an example of data visualization within a matrix—a heat map. The color of each cell depends on the sales plan performance. The higher the positive deviation, the brighter the shade of green; the lower the negative value, the more intense the red color. In Figure 7-3, we can immediately identify the most prominent points from the entire dataset—those products and months where sales deviated significantly from the plan.

Product subcategory	January	February	March	April	May	June	July	August	September	October	November	December
Bicycle racks	-5%	19%	4%	28%	42%	6%	26%			7%	3%	
Bicycle stands	3%	-18%	-41%	-56%			16%	-1%	-13%	-8%	19%	-58%
Bottle holder	-1%	-8%	-8%	1%	1%	-2%	-9%	-5%	-7%	-8%	-10%	-5%
Cleaners	12%	-16%	-11%	-4%	-11%	-10%	-8%	-26%	13%	-13%	-21%	0%
Gloves	-9%	6%	2%	12%	2%	10%	7%	11%	5%	-12%	10%	-17%
Hats	-18%	-14%	-11%	-10%	-16%	6%	-4%	-9%	-7%	-13%	-9%	-10%
Helmets	-24%	-18%	-15%	-2%	-26%	-20%	-20%	-11%	-19%	-14%	-16%	-4%
Hydropack	-18%	-4%	9%	11%	-25%	15%	-7%	17%	15%	-47%	-71%	-37%
Knitwear	-17%	-18%	-23%	-41%	-23%	-18%	-20%	-23%	-32%	-24%	-4%	-36%
Mountain bikes	15%	5%	8%	10%	1%	15%	-10%	-2%	13%	7%	4%	-5%
Road bikes	-21%	-18%	-23%	-14%	-30%	-27%	-12%	-18%	-19%	-19%	-2%	-18%
Shorts	-35%	-22%	-21%	-14%	-1%	13%	-35%	-41%	3%	22%	-66%	-40%

Figure 7-3. Matrix with conditional formatting in the style of a heat map

Creating a table is quite simple. We have a single *Columns* field where we put all the necessary data, and each item is represented in a separate column. In Figure 7-4, you can observe that the default table looks significantly different from our more polished examples. At this point, it resembles a draft or raw data.

Manager	Average of Price per item	Sum of Quantity	Sum of Sales fact
Adrian Turner	181.42	278	35543
Alfonso Enrique Nunez Nieto	176.83	207	24815
Anne Gabrillagues	159.76	233	29277
Bart Vermijlen	177.59	241	28949
Ben Aston	184.96	261	30338
Bernardo Tirado	163.68	264	34728
Bert Heymans	190.43	248	32636
Bill Dow	165.53	265	31953
Bill Mabry	203.75	235	32518
Bob Galen	192.41	201	25445
Bob Sutton	157.63	254	30418
Brad Egeland	215.50	216	34695
Bruce McGraw	184.15	270	28927
Carlos J. Pampliega	196.58	310	44755
Cliff Gilley	188.09	232	31670
Total	**182.80**	**17372**	**2260181**

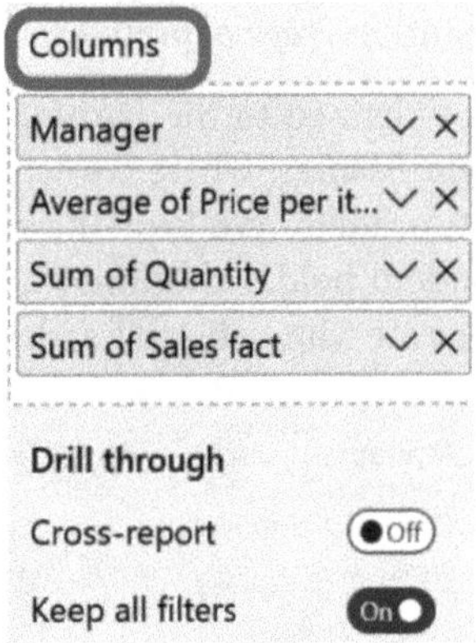

Columns

Manager ∨ ×

Average of Price per it... ∨ ×

Sum of Quantity ∨ ×

Sum of Sales fact ∨ ×

Drill through

Cross-report ● Off

Keep all filters On ●

Figure 7-4. Table by default

Many people stop at this stage, not even realizing that everything can be customized. Indeed, formatting tables in Power BI differs from Excel. Together, we will go step-by-step and discover all these intricacies.

Step-by-Step Guide for a Table

Here's what we have to do to create a table.

Step 1: Edit Column Headers

The column width is determined by the longest value in the row or header. In the *Manager* column (Figure 7-4), it is based on the longest name, and in the value columns, it's the longest text in the headers, which display field names with the prefixes *Sum of* or *Average of*. As a result, the columns have different widths and a lot of empty space between them.

You can arbitrarily compress a column by dragging the edges of the header, but it's better to choose short names for them. You can edit them directly in the *Build visual* section in the *Columns* field where we placed them. To do this, double-click on the name and write what is needed (Figure 7-5). We will remove the *Sum of* and *Average of* prefixes.

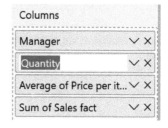

Figure 7-5. Column headers editing

Now let's go to the *Format visual* menu → *Column headers*, where we will change the font of the headers. We kept the size at 10 points but made it bold. Additionally, we set the background color to gray to visually highlight the row with column headers (Figure 7-6).

Manager	Avg Price, $	Quantity, ps.	Sales fact, $
Carlos J. Pampliega	202.51	315	45427
George Pitagorsky	185.25	307	41065
Eileen Roden	198.35	299	40600
Kurt Schmidt	182.76	298	37766
Drew Davison	184.46	291	37917
Jurgen Appelo	208.93	289	38365
Laura Fraser	187.23	287	36338
Nicole Reilly	207.41	286	39350
Soma Bhattacharya	165.36	285	31926
Hala Saleh	168.69	283	31918
Falk Schmidt	181.82	282	34935
Glen Alleman	189.36	282	37899
Robyn Reynolds	158.53	282	31460
Total	**183.86**	**17392**	**2260853**

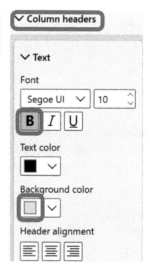

Figure 7-6. Column headers *setup*

Unfortunately, we don't have an option to align column widths as we are accustomed to doing in Microsoft Excel. Therefore, we manually adjust the width based on visual estimation. However, this is not critical; the intervals between them do not have to be strictly equal.

Step 2: Adjust Values

Similar to data labels on charts, we need to improve how values are presented. Remember that the optimal range is two to three digits. While *Avg Price* is in the hundreds of dollars, displaying unnecessary cents in the column results in five digits. As for *Sales Fact*, which is measured in tens of thousands, we don't need to show every dollar either.

To configure the settings for values in the table, start by going to the *Format visual* menu → *Values*—this section pertains to all values in all columns. Here, you can adjust the font size and color, as well as the background color. However, if the default values suit your preferences for now, there's no need to make any changes here.

To change the number of decimal places or display data in a different format, we need the *Format visual* menu → *Specific column* section. Under *Apply settings to*, select the desired column, and below, in the *Values* section, adjust the parameters as needed (Figure 7-7).

Manager	Avg Price, $	Quantity, ps.	Sales fact, $
Carlos J. Pampliega	203	315	45427
George Pitagorsky	185	307	41065
Eileen Roden	198	299	40600
Kurt Schmidt	183	298	37766
Drew Davison	184	291	37917
Jurgen Appelo	209	289	38365
Laura Fraser	187	287	36338
Nicole Reilly	207	286	39350
Soma Bhattacharya	165	285	31926
Hala Saleh	169	283	31918
Falk Schmidt	182	282	34935
Glen Alleman	189	282	37899
Robyn Reynolds	159	282	31460
Total	**184**	**17392**	**2260853**

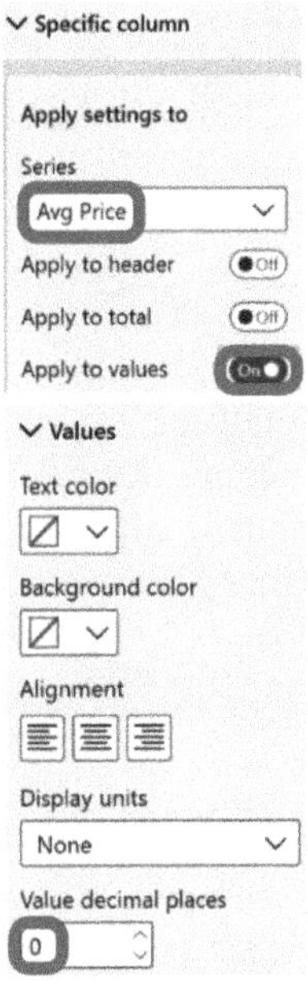

Specific column

Apply settings to

Series
Avg Price

Apply to header — Off
Apply to total — Off
Apply to values — On

Values

Text color

Background color

Alignment

Display units
None

Value decimal places
0

Figure 7-7. Adjusting values for a specific column

So, in the *Avg Price* column, we removed unnecessary decimal places, and for the *Sales fact* column, we displayed the values in thousands of dollars. The table now appears slightly neater, and each small improvement in the details adds to the creation of a professional dashboard.

Step 3: Set Up Style and Grid

Power BI provides several table styles that you can choose in the *Style presets* section. Unfortunately, most of the options provided are quite old-fashioned and overloaded with unnecessary details, and we strongly advise against using them (Figure 7-8, left). Among all the available choices, we prefer the *Minimal* style (Figure 7-8, center) and recommend sticking with it.

Figure 7-8. Style options for table formatting; Contrast alternating rows (left) versus Minimal (center)

After selecting a style, you can customize it in the *Grid* section. There are many options for fine-tuning: change line thickness and line color, enable vertical lines, and configure them. In our case, we will only change the *Border → Color* to match the manually added gray background of the top header row. We'll also add some spacing by increasing *Row padding* to 4 (Figure 7-9).

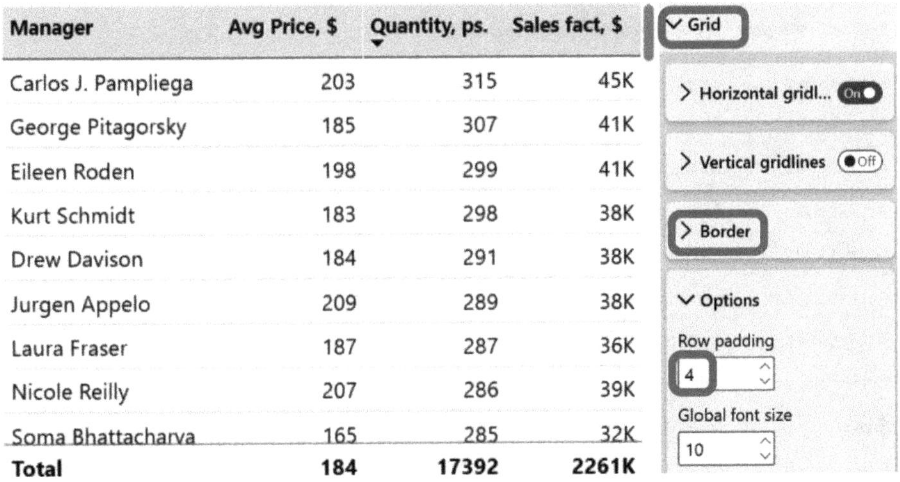

Manager	Avg Price, $	Quantity, ps.	Sales fact, $
Carlos J. Pampliega	203	315	45K
George Pitagorsky	185	307	41K
Eileen Roden	198	299	41K
Kurt Schmidt	183	298	38K
Drew Davison	184	291	38K
Jurgen Appelo	209	289	38K
Laura Fraser	187	287	36K
Nicole Reilly	207	286	39K
Soma Bhattacharva	165	285	32K
Total	**184**	**17392**	**2261K**

Grid settings panel:
- ∨ Grid
- ＞ Horizontal gridl... On
- ＞ Vertical gridlines Off
- ＞ Border
- ∨ Options
- Row padding: 4
- Global font size: 10

Figure 7-9. Grid settings

As a result, you'll have a clean, neat table without visual noise or unnecessary elements. You'll be able to read the data without distractions. Let's stick with these adjustments for now and move on to getting familiar with the matrix. We'll come back later to incorporating visual highlights using conditional formatting.

Matrix—Drill-Down Table

Similarly to Microsoft Excel, we are accustomed to using hierarchical tables where we can expand rows and navigate to lower levels. We demonstrated such an example at the beginning of the chapter in Figure 7-2. Let's explore how to transform a table into a matrix and consider the nuances involved.

A matrix becomes meaningful when there are elements that can be grouped or nested within each other. Let's create a new matrix on the worksheet. If we select fields like category, subcategory, and then quantity, Power BI will automatically generate a "flat" table where each subcategory is listed in every row along with its parent element (Figure 7-10).

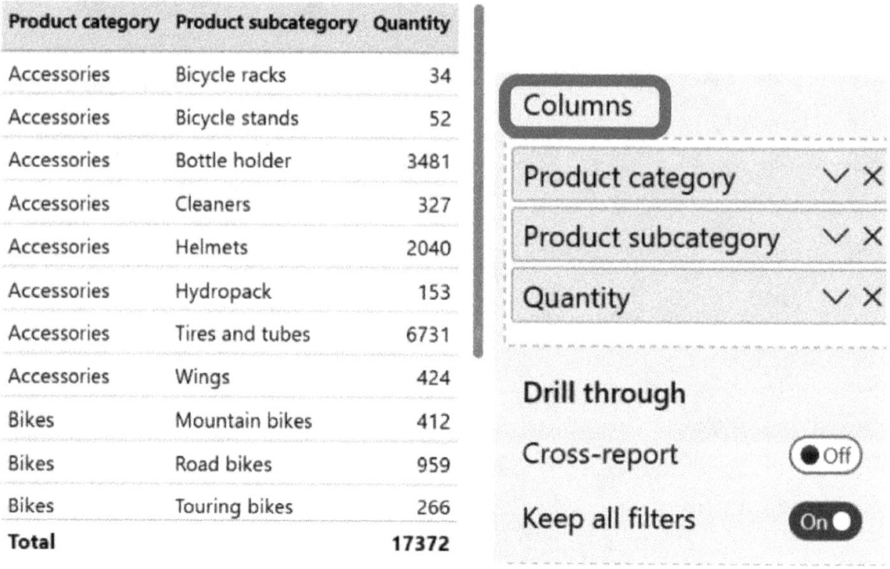

Product category	Product subcategory	Quantity
Accessories	Bicycle racks	34
Accessories	Bicycle stands	52
Accessories	Bottle holder	3481
Accessories	Cleaners	327
Accessories	Helmets	2040
Accessories	Hydropack	153
Accessories	Tires and tubes	6731
Accessories	Wings	424
Bikes	Mountain bikes	412
Bikes	Road bikes	959
Bikes	Touring bikes	266
Total		**17372**

Columns

Product category ∨ ✕

Product subcategory ∨ ✕

Quantity ∨ ✕

Drill through

Cross-report ● Off

Keep all filters On ●

Figure 7-10. Original table for further matrix construction

The *Matrix* icon is located to the right of the table in the visualizations list. If we click this icon when the created table is selected, we may get a strange view that does not resemble our sample (Figure 7-11).

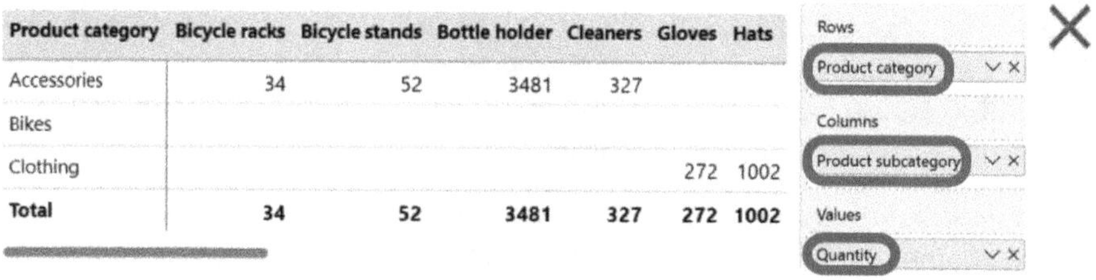

Product category	Bicycle racks	Bicycle stands	Bottle holder	Cleaners	Gloves	Hats
Accessories	34	52	3481	327		
Bikes						
Clothing					272	1002
Total	34	52	3481	327	272	1002

Rows

Product category ∨ ✕

Columns

Product subcategory ∨ ✕

Values

Quantity ∨ ✕

✕

Figure 7-11. Matrix draft with incorrect field positions

The reason is that the table had only one type of field, columns, whereas the matrix has three different types: rows, columns, and values. The system keeps the first element in *Rows* (*Product category*), moves the next one to *Columns* (*Product subcategory*), and fills the *Values* with the data at the intersection of these two elements (*Quantity*).

To make the matrix more user-friendly, we take *Product subcategory* and move it from *Columns* to the *Rows* field, right under *Product category*. We achieve a neat and compact matrix in Figure 7-12, where we can expand the desired categories as needed.

Product category	Quantity
⊞ Accessories	13242
⊟ Bikes	1637
Mountain bikes	412
Road bikes	959
Touring bikes	266
⊞ Clothing	2493
Total	17372

Rows
Product category ∨ ×
Product subcategory ∨ ×

Columns
Add data fields here

Values
Quantity ∨ ×

Figure 7-12. Correct matrix with hierarchical rows

It is possible to leave the *Columns* field empty, or you can add new data to it, such as *Country*. In Figure 7-13, we have a classic matrix view where we can compare data at the intersection of rows and columns, as well as expand the rows.

Product category	France	Germany	Great Britain	USA	Total
⊞ Accessories	1818	1751	2324	7349	13242
⊟ Bikes	197	199	402	839	1637
Mountain bikes	44	44	93	231	412
Road bikes	127	121	222	489	959
Touring bikes	26	34	87	119	266
⊞ Clothing	335	271	510	1377	2493
Total	2350	2221	3236	9565	17372

Rows
Product category ∨ ×
Product subcategory ∨ ×

Columns
Country ∨ ×

Values
Quantity ∨ ×

Figure 7-13. Total matrix by category and subcategory, organized by country

We can take it a step further and add several elements to the *Columns* field, allowing us to expand both rows and columns. For example, if we place a date hierarchy in *Columns*, we will see the option to *Drill on Rows or Columns* above the matrix (Figure 7-14). When we choose to drill on columns, we can expand the matrix by quarters and months.

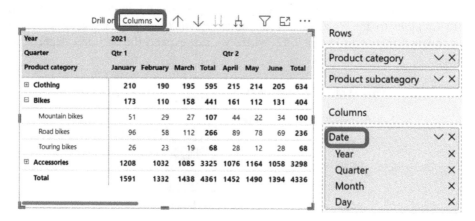

Figure 7-14. Matrix drilled on rows and columns looks overloaded

However, this representation already looks overloaded and resembles a spreadsheet. Our aim is to create clear visuals for dashboards. Therefore, be cautious and avoid delving too deeply into data hierarchy in both rows and, especially, columns.

We don't have a special guide for matrices; the same three simple steps apply: setting up column headers, adjusting values, and customizing grid settings. Next, we'll show you how to add striking visual accents to this foundation of columns and rows using conditional formatting.

Conditional Formatting

This feature is loved by many Microsoft Excel users. We can add fills, icons, and even mini bar charts to cells in a few clicks. This function works in Power BI on the same basis. There are four possible ways in the *Cell elements* section:

- Background color
- Font color
- Data bars
- Icons

This formatting works equally well for tables and matrices; we'll consider examples for both visuals. Let's start with the most popular and impactful one—data bars.

Data Bars

We can directly add a small bar chart to a cell by applying conditional formatting to columns. To do this, in the menu *Format visual → Cell elements → Apply settings to*, select the desired column (in our case, *Sales fact*), and enable *Data bars* for it. In Figure 7-15, you can see that bars appear in this column, visually highlighting sales leaders.

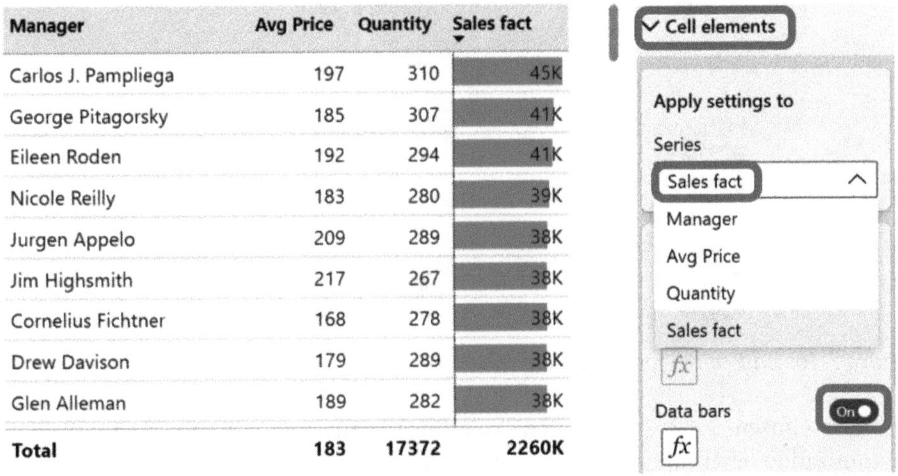
Manager
Avg Price
Quantity
Sales fact
Carlos J. Pampliega 197 310 45K
George Pitagorsky 185 307 41K
Eileen Roden 192 294 41K
Nicole Reilly 183 280 39K
Jurgen Appelo 209 289 38K
Jim Highsmith 217 267 38K
Cornelius Fichtner 168 278 38K
Drew Davison 179 289 38K
Glen Alleman 189 282 38K
Total 183 17372 2260K
Cell elements
Apply settings to
Series
Sales fact
Manager
Avg Price
Quantity
Sales fact
Data bars
On
fx

Figure 7-15. Switch on conditional formatting of the Sales fact column

There is a small issue—the data value is not easily visible against the blue background of the bar. We cannot make it white because part of the value will end up on a white background. The solution is to change the bar color to a lighter shade. To fine-tune this, click the *Conditional formatting (fx)* button and, in the pop-up menu, choose lighter colors for *Positive and Negative bars* (Figure 7-16).

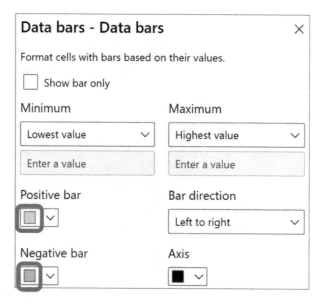

Figure 7-16. Edit colors for data bars

We have chosen not to display the table once again; you will see the result of the customization after the next step: adding icons (see Figure 7-18). We don't have negative sales amounts here, but if there were any, the bar would be red.

Icons and Quick Measure Calculation

Now, we want to see the deviation from the sales plan for managers, indicating who is falling short and who has exceeded the plan. But such data is not available in the source data table. Here we'll introduce you to the *Quick measure* calculation feature.

There are buttons with a calculator icon on the *Home* ribbon closer to the right edge. Click on the one with a lightning bolt icon: *Quick measure*. A panel will appear where you first need to select the type of calculation. It includes several groups with the most popular operations:

- Aggregation per category
- Filters
- Time intelligence
- Totals
- Mathematical operations
- Text

In the Mathematical operations list, select *Percentage difference* (Figure 7-17).

Then, choose two parameters that we will compare:

Base value
This is our plan, the deviation from which we are interested in.

Value to compare
These are the actual sales.

Select *Sales plan* and *Sales fact* from the field list and drag them to the corresponding sections.

Click *Add*, and a new field appears in the *Data* list: *Sales fact % difference from Sales plan*. This name was automatically generated; let's rename it for convenience to *% plan*. We'd like to tell you about all the useful features of quick measures, but that would require a new chapter. In general, you can study the huge possibilities of Power BI endlessly. But let's first establish a solid foundation for basic visualization.

Next, add this field to the table, and it will be displayed in the column header with this concise name. Now let's add conditional formatting with color icons: in the *Cell elements* menu →

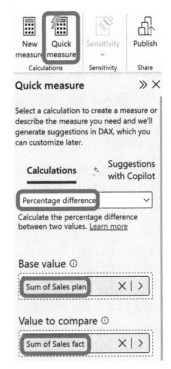

Figure 7-17. Quick measure parameters

Apply settings to, choose *% plan*; this is the column we will work with. Enable *Icons* for it (Figure 7-18).

Manager	Avg Price	Quantity	Sales fact		% plan
Carlos J. Pampliega	203	315		45K	7%
George Pitagorsky	185	307		41K	-3%
Eileen Roden	198	299		41K	-0%
Nicole Reilly	207	286		39K	-1%
Jurgen Appelo	209	289		38K	-12%
Jim Highsmith	217	267		38K	-8%
Cornelius Fichtner	190	280		38K	5%
Drew Davison	184	291		38K	5%
Glen Alleman	189	282		38K	2%
Total	**184**	**17392**		**2261K**	**-3%**

Figure 7-18. Default formatting icons for the % plan field

Default formatting works according to the following principles:

- The lowest 33.3% of values receive an icon with a red diamond.
- The next 33.3% receive a yellow triangle.
- The highest 33.3% of values receive an icon with a green circle.

However, such boundaries usually make little sense because from the sales point of view 50% or even 65% realization of the plan is not a yellow zone, it should be red. We want to establish a clearer rule so that all positive deviations are green. Deviations within –5% are yellow, and all deviations below –5% are red.

For a more specific and meaningful rule for conditional formatting, where positive variances are green, variances between –5% and 0 are yellow, and variances below –5% are red, define new rules. Click on the *fx* icon (*Conditional formatting*), then in the pop-up window, select the *% plan* field under *What field should we base this on?*

- If the value is greater than or equal to *Min* in the *Number* dimension and less than –*0.05* in the *Number* dimension, mark it with a red circle.
- If the value is greater than or equal to –*0.05* in the *Number* dimension and less than *0* in the *Number* dimension, mark it with a yellow circle.
- If the value is greater than or equal to *0* in the *Number* dimension and less than *Max* in the *Number* dimension, mark it with a green circle.

These rules will ensure that positive variances are green, variances between –5% and 0 are yellow, and variances below –5% are red for the *% plan* field (Figure 7-19).

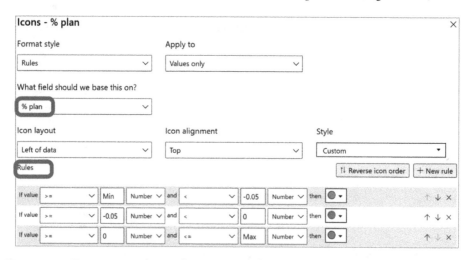

Figure 7-19. Formatting rules configuration window

As a result, in Figure 7-20, we get a sample similar to the one at the beginning of the chapter. Note that we used the same shape—a circle for all three colors—because the shape of the icon (triangle, rhombus) did not convey additional meaning. The only difference is in the color depending on the *% plan*.

Manager	Avg Price, $	Quantity, ps.	Sales fact, $	% plan
Carlos J. Pampliega	203	315	45K ●	7%
George Pitagorsky	185	307	41K ●	-3%
Eileen Roden	198	299	41K ●	-0%
Nicole Reilly	207	286	39K ●	-1%
Jurgen Appelo	209	289	38K ●	-12%

Figure 7-20. Final view for icon conditional formatting

Font Color

Another formatting option is changing the font color based on a given rule. Let's analyze the average price and highlight the most expensive product subcategories (over $300) in green font and the cheapest ones (less than $100) in red (Figure 7-21).

Product category	Quantity, ps.	Avg Price, $	Sales fact, $
⊟ **Accessories**	13247	147	1443K
Tires and tubes	6731	118	623K
Helmets	2045	314	419K
Bottle holder	3481	81	233K
Wings	424	268	90K
Hydropack	153	335	33K

Figure 7-21. Font color formatting for the average price

Now let's set up a rule for font color coding. Last time, we accessed the formatting rules setup window through *Format visual → Cell elements → Data bars → Conditional formatting* (Figure 7-15).

But there's a quicker way (Figure 7-22). Right in the *Build visual* menu to the right of the field for which we're creating a rule (in our case, *Avg Price*), click the down arrow. In the pop-up menu, choose *Conditional formatting* and then select the type of formatting you need. We'll choose *Font color*.

Figure 7-22. Alternative way to enable conditional formatting

In the menu, set up the rule (Figure 7-23). Choose *Rules* in the *Format style* field. Make sure that *Summarization* is set to *Average* since we are working with the average prices, and you can't sum them up. In the *Rules* field, set two rules:

- *If value >= 300 (Number) and <= Max (Number)*, then the font will be green.
- *If value >= 0 (Number) and < 100 (Number)*, then the font will be red.

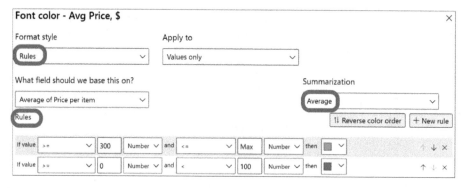

Figure 7-23. Color-coding of the average price

In the end, we get the matrix shown in Figure 7-2. So, font color conditional formatting works the same way as icons. It also works with gradient rule, but this approach fits better for cell color rule.

Cell Color / Heat Map

Similar to text color, you can set rules for cell background. If the default gradient style for text wasn't quite effective—making the numbers too pale—it might be more suitable for cell background. This technique works well, especially for a matrix, where one value is distributed across columns and rows. In Figure 7-24, sales by product subcategory and months are visualized this way.

Product subcategory	January	February	March	April	May	June	July	August	September	October	November	December
Tires and tubes	52K	53K	53K	49K	57K	52K	55K	49K	53K	51K	45K	55K
Helmets	32K	34K	29K	36K	35K	28K	32K	43K	32K	47K	38K	33K
Road bikes	25K	17K	27K	25K	20K	18K	23K	13K	23K	20K	14K	20K
Bottle holder	20K	15K	19K	19K	21K	19K	21K	20K	18K	20K	21K	19K
Knitwear	17K	10K	13K	8K	14K	10K	10K	14K	10K	10K	15K	13K
Mountain bikes	16K	9K	9K	16K	7K	12K	11K	19K	11K	8K	13K	8K
Wings	6K	7K	5K	10K	9K	7K	7K	7K	6K	9K	8K	8K
Hats	6K	6K	8K	8K	7K	9K	8K	7K	7K	7K	8K	6K
Touring bikes	7K	6K	7K	8K	3K	9K	3K	4K	9K	7K	8K	5K
Gloves	6K	2K	5K	5K	4K	5K	4K	5K	9K	3K	7K	3K
Hydropack	1K	6K	2K	3K	3K	3K	2K	6K	3K	2K	1K	1K

Figure 7-24. Matrix with conditional formatting in the style of a heat map

You can see the most prominent clusters of cells for *Tires and tubes* throughout the year. However, for *Road bikes*, the pale cells in August and November are noticeable. Thus, against the backdrop of general trends, we can immediately observe peaks and declines. Sometimes, the heat map effectively illustrates seasonal trends and anomalies. Moreover, it can be used to identify "hot" and "cool" segments based on age groups, employees, average check amounts, and other interval categories.

The settings for cell color are exactly the same as for font color, so we won't repeat them step-by-step. Instead, let's take the example of the heat map in Figure 7-3. For formatting icons, we created the *% plan* measure. In the matrix, we replaced *Sales fact* with *% plan* and added a middle color rule in the settings (Figure 7-25).

We don't set strict boundaries with rules as we did for icons and font color. For the central value, we specified *0* and a white color. This means we don't pay attention to data where the plan is met; instead, we use color to show deviations. The greater the deviation, the brighter the cell: for negative deviations, red; for positive deviations, green.

Conditional formatting helps highlight specific data in the table or indicate trends. However, it's essential not to overdo it.

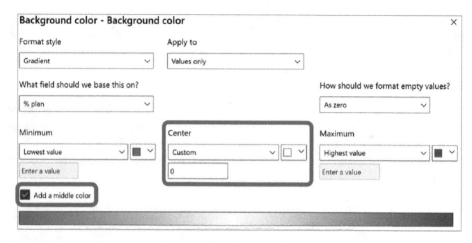

Figure 7-25. Gradient rule with a middle color for cells

Tips for Conditional Formatting

Here's how to properly apply conditional formatting and avoid common mistakes.

Apply one rule per column

That is, for one column, it's not advisable to use more than one rule. If you've shown bars, there's no need to highlight columns additionally or add icons (Figure 7-26).

Figure 7-26. Excessive (left), where two rules are applied to one column, and correct (right) conditional formatting

Don't try to color the entire table and format all columns

One or two columns in the table are quite enough (Figure 7-27).

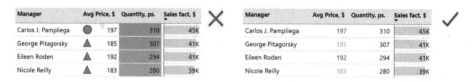

Figure 7-27. Excessive (left), where rules are applied to each column, and correct (right) conditional formatting

Contrast bar charts with the data labels

The number remains the main element in the table, so any additional elements should not obscure or overshadow it. Therefore, use subtle colors and small elements (Figure 7-28).

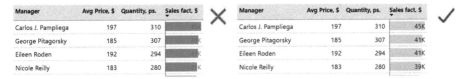

Figure 7-28. Excessive (left), where the color bars obscure the numbers, and correct (right) conditional formatting

---

Tips and Notes

Tables are excellent tools for visualizing data when dealing with dozens of categories and multiple indicators with varying ranges.

Checklist for setting up a table:

1. Edit column headers
2. Adjust values
3. Set up style and grid

If we want to show hierarchy on the rows and/or columns, we can create a matrix.

For matrices and tables, we can also set up conditional formatting in four ways:

- Background color
- Font color
- Data bars
- Icons

And don't forget a few tips for conditional formatting:

- Apply one rule at a time.
- Don't try to color the entire table and format all columns.
- Keep a clear contrast with the number.

Download the *.pbix* file with customized visuals (*https://oreil.ly/Ozrot*).

CHAPTER 8

KPI Cards

Toward the top of nearly every dashboard, you'll find cards displaying summary values. These are the first elements that catch the user's attention, so we position key performance indicators (KPIs) on top of the report page. The term "KPI" can have various contexts. From a business perspective, it is the target against which we compare the current indicator value. From a simpler technical standpoint, it is any total value that we deem important and place on the cards. In Figure 8-1, you can see an example of the most straightforward cards providing us with a summary: we have earned $2.26M, selling with an average price of $270 about 17K units of the product.

Figure 8-1. Several basic cards with a single value

Usually, a KPI card contains not only a single value but also an additional indicator by which we can assess whether it's good or bad (sometimes called a reference value). Let's take an example of selling a digital product with three subscription plans: basic, advanced, and premium. In Figure 8-2, you see a series of three cards that provide a more detailed picture of the financial results:

- Sales for the advanced plan amount to $232K, falling short by 19% of the target, which is considered poor—indicated in red.

- On the other hand, advertising expenses were $38K, staying within the budget limit, resulting in a favorable negative deviation of –13%, indicated in green.

- Profitability is measured by the return on investment (ROI; in this simplified example, calculated as sales divided by expenses). If this ratio is above the threshold (in our case, the threshold is 4 and the value is 6.1), then it's in the green zone.

Figure 8-2. Several basic cards with additional indicators, filtered by the advanced subscription plan

For the premium subscription plan, we observe a different situation, shown in Figure 8-3:

- Sales fall short of the target by 13%, indicated in the red zone.

- Expenses exceed the limit by 28%, also in the red zone.

- Profit amounts to $134K, falling into the yellow zone of the ROI indicator—3.0. If the ROI were below 3, it would be in the red zone.

Figure 8-3. Several basic cards with additional indicators, filtered by the premium subscription plan

Sometimes cards can be quite sophisticated, containing multiple deviation indicators (versus target, previous year) and even sparklines or bullet charts. In Figure 8-4, such a set of cards looks like a small dashboard on its own.

The subject of cards is highly significant, and we believe that half of a dashboard's success depends on them. In this chapter, we'll start with the basics, explaining essential principles through simple examples and helping you avoid common mistakes. In Part II, we'll explore building sophisticated cards similar to those in Figure 8-4. Finally, in Part III, we'll review visually cool but not always appropriate cards.

Figure 8-4. Advanced KPI cards

For now, let's focus on the concept of a card. Its primary purpose is to prominently display a key figure, making it the center of attention.

Suppose we want to show a single value of actual sales. We can choose a single numeric field or measure in the data pane, standing on a clean canvas, and by default Power BI will generate a column chart with a single column. However, the significance of the column lies in its comparison with others. If it stands alone, its meaning is lost. Moreover, the total value will be displayed with a subtle data label. Therefore, for KPIs, the card visualization is more suitable, as you can see in Figure 8-5.

Figure 8-5. Default column chart generated when selecting Sales Actual data (left) and a simple card for the same data (right)

Here's what we'll get if we select the *Sales fact* measure and replace the default column chart with the *Card* visual (Figure 8-6).

Figure 8-6. Default card

It's clear that we can resize the card, but there are other things to be improved:

- The data label should be rounded to one decimal place in millions. The value "2M" looks quite strange, and for once, we want to add more decimal places for greater accuracy, not remove them.
- The category label looks somewhat pale and disproportionately small compared with the giant data label. And, as always, the auto-text needs editing.
- We'd like to add a background to make the card stand out as a separate element rather than a number written on a blank canvas.

We fixed this manually for many years, until the new card was released. It configured these items correctly by default. But we decided to explain to you the evolution of the card anatomy. If you are already familiar with the new card, you can skip to "New Card" on page 118, or even to Chapter 18. Or let's go through a step-by-step guide for the old card. It will consist of three simple steps, after which we'll move on to additional features.

Step-by-Step Guide for a Card

Here's what we have to do to create a KPI card.

Step 1: Adjust Data Label (Callout Value)

Following the analogy with other visuals, we refer to this element as the data label and begin with its customization. However, following one of the Power BI interface updates, it is now called the *Callout value*. In essence, this is the most crucial element of the card, and displaying it as "2M" looks too rounded. After all, there's a significant difference between 1.6M and 2.4M.

Let's remind ourselves of the principles we follow when choosing units and decimal places. The optimal choice according to our experience is typically two to three digits. For example:

- 3,871,520—a large value; let's convert it to millions and keep two decimal places: 3.87M.

- 13.83M—here we are dealing with tens of millions, and one decimal place is sufficient: 13.8M.

- If the order of values is closer to a hundred, for instance, 78.7M, then rounding to 79M is acceptable (similar for thousands).

Indeed, on dashboards, we usually allow for a margin of one digit for data filtering. We could keep units in millions with two decimal places—2.26M. However, when selecting categories or countries on the dashboard, this value might end up around 0.3M or even less, and that would be insufficiently accurate again. Therefore, in Figure 8-7, we opted for thousands with zero decimal places. Yes, initially, we see four digits, but with any filtering, there will be three, and sometimes even two.

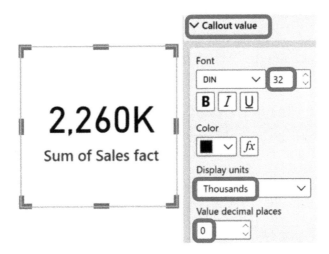

Figure 8-7. Configuring Callout value

Additionally, we reduced the font size because the default 45 pt appeared disproportionately large. A value within the range of 25–35 pt will be sufficient; we'll set it to 32.

Step 2: Adjust Category Label

Let's continue discussing proportions and move on to the second formatting point: *Category label*. The default font size is only 12 pt, although conceptually, it serves as the title of the visual, similar to other charts on the dashboard. We recommend maintaining a consistent font size for all visual titles, ranging from 14 to 20 pt. On the other hand, a harmonious relationship between the size of the category and callout is 1:2. Therefore, with a callout size of 32 pt, we'll set the category size to 16 pt.

We also want to make the font itself more vibrant. As an alternative to the *Bold* option, you can choose the semibold style from the font list; it will look both vivid and neat (Figure 8-8).

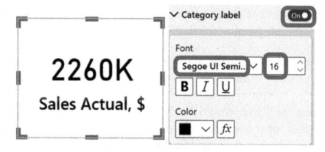

Figure 8-8. Configuring Category label

And don't forget to correct the title. In *Build visual* mode, double-click on the field in the *Fields* pane and edit the text. We replaced *Sum of Sales fact* with *Sales Actual, $* (for details, see "Chart Title" on page 15).

Step 3: Add Contrasting Background

Data value and category label, although written in large font, still might not be prominent enough against the background of other visuals on the dashboard. Therefore, a good practice is to add a background. Like with other visuals, we can customize it in the *General* section: expand the *Effects* item, and there you will find *Background* (Figure 8-9). Technically, it's already enabled, just in white.

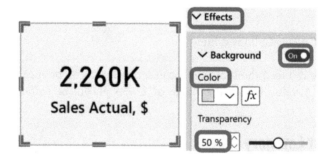

Figure 8-9. Adding a semitransparent background to the card

Let's change it to the most neutral light gray (the one called *White, 10% darker*). Even such a shade looks a bit dark, and we recommend making the background for cards even lighter. To avoid manually selecting the color, you can use the transparency parameter. Now the background looks light and neat and helps highlight the card but doesn't conflict with the text.

Sometimes, the dashboard style requires a dark-colored background for the card. However, this can disrupt the contrast, making it difficult to read dark text on a dark background. If you choose to use a dark background color, make the font for the title and indicator on the card white (Figure 8-10).

Figure 8-10. The text should be white on a dark background

There's another issue with Figure 8-11 on the left. The blue text would be suitable for a white background but not for a gray. In this form, they blend together, lacking contrast. It's crucial to draw the user's attention to the key indicator, not the background color of the card. Therefore, let's make the text dark blue and the background light gray.

Figure 8-11. Increasing the contrast between the background and text

In the *Effects* section, we got acquainted with the *Background* option, and there are also options for *Visual border* and *Shadow*. By default, they are disabled, and we strongly recommend leaving them that way. At first, it might seem original to add shadows and bold borders, but it would be excessive. The background and border on the card serve the same purpose—to unite data value and category label into one object and separate it from other dashboard elements.

If you decide to add a border, then the background is no longer necessary. Follow the "one effect at a time" rule (Figure 8-12). Shadows, rounded corners, and other embellishments on the card are unnecessary; otherwise, it will look more like a text bubble from a comic than a corporate report. You can round the corners, but do so carefully, in the range of 5–10 px.

Figure 8-12. One effect at a time: if you enable the border, disable the background

We have completed the three basic mandatory steps and obtained a properly configured card. However, usually there is not just one card on the dashboard but a whole series. You don't have to repeat all these steps; instead, you can use an example that you've done, copy it, and then modify it further. This approach will save time, and all your cards will immediately be in a consistent style.

How to Create Multiple Cards

We've obtained one card for the field *Sales fact*. Now let's copy it and paste it on the same report sheet. If we click on the arrow at the right of the field name, in the list of options after *Remove field* and *Rename for this visual*, there is a list of aggregation methods. By default, it's set to *Sum*, and we will change it to *Average* (Figure 8-13). Now the card will have a different business meaning—average price. This is how we will rename the field instead of the automatic *Average of Sales*....

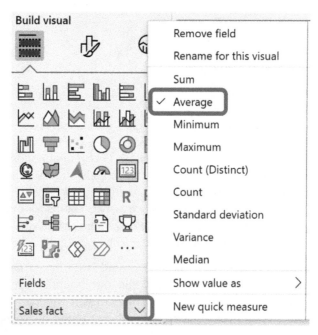

Figure 8-13. Changing the aggregation type

Now, let's once again copy our "reference" card and paste it on the sheet. However, this time, we will remove *Sales fact* from the *Build visual → Fields* and replace it with *Quantity* (don't forget to remove the auto-text *Sum of...*). As a result, we get a series of cards in a unified format (Figure 8-14).

Figure 8-14. Several KPI cards

The standard card does not provide the option to add another measure if, for example, we want to show the deviation of sales from the plan. The solution in this case is simple: place two cards side by side, visually combining them. Here's another useful property of the background—it visually merges two elements into one logical block!

We add a card to the canvas with the deviation from the plan, which we calculated using the *Quick measure* in Figure 7-17. We will do this using the copy/paste method from the first card, remove *Sales fact* from the *Build visual → Fields*, and replace it with *% plan*. You can see the result in Figure 8-15.

Figure 8-15. Two KPI cards that will be further combined into single

You may find that the deviation is displayed in the format of *0K*. This is because we configured display units for the *Sales* measure in thousands. In this case, change the display units back to *Auto* or *None*.

Place both cards side by side without a space between them and compress them slightly horizontally. In Figure 8-16, we have a logically unified card that technically consists of two elements.

Figure 8-16. Two cards combined into one

Step 4: Add Conditional Formatting

We've gone through the first three steps of setting up the main card parameters: callout value, category label, and background. We then copied the created card and made changes to the measures and data aggregation methods. The next step, while not mandatory, is typically performed for one or more dashboard cards: *conditional formatting*.

We learned about conditional formatting in Chapter 7, when we set up rules for the color of icons in a cell, as well as the color of the font. We can do the same in a card, but using a slightly different approach. The idea is to have the color of the deviation from the plan change in our "grouped" card, specifically the callout value for the *% plan* field. If the deviation is positive, indicating the plan is exceeded, the color should be green. If the deviation is negative, the color should be red.

As you've already noticed, a card has only two simple parameters to configure, and there's no separate option for conditional formatting, as we managed for tables. However, we can invoke this function in the font color setting for the callout value. In Figure 8-17, next to the color selection, you see the familiar button *fx*, which will open the formatting rule configuration window.

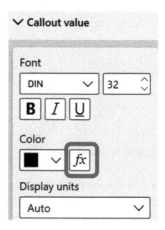

Figure 8-17. Conditional formatting button

Let's set simple rules for Figure 8-18: if the deviation (*% plan* field) is < 0, the font color will be red, if >= 0, the font color will be green.

Color - Callout value ✕

Format style

| Rules | ⌄ |

What field should we base this on?

| % plan | ⌄ |

| Rules | | ⇅ Reverse color order | + New rule |

| If value | >= ⌄ | Min | Number ⌄ | and | < ⌄ | 0 | Number ⌄ | then | ■ ⌄ | ↑ ↓ ✕ |
| If value | >= ⌄ | 0 | Number ⌄ | and | < ⌄ | Max | Number ⌄ | then | ■ ⌄ | ↑ ↓ ✕ |

Figure 8-18. Conditional formatting rules for Callout value

In Figure 8-19, you can see how the card will look in cases when the plan is not met (a red deviation indicator, left) and when the plan is exceeded (a green one, right).

Figure 8-19. Card states for negative and positive deviations

Actually, we can apply such formatting rules to the color of any element. Let's consider this using our exemplary single card for the *Sales fact* field, which we obtained after the three steps in the guide. As usual, we go to *General → Effects → Background* and see that there is also a button to press: *f(x)*. Pay attention to the parameter *What field should we base this on?* By default, the field on which the card is built is selected, but we can change it to any other. In our example, in Figure 8-20, we will choose the *% plan* field. The rule conditions will be the same, but the shades of red and green will be paler. After all, we need to adhere to the contrast rule: with dark text, the background should be pale.

Color - Effects - Background   ✕

Format style

| Rules   ∨ |

What field should we base this on?

| % plan   ∨ |

Rules   ↑↓ Reverse color order   + New rule

| If value | >= ∨ | Min | Number ∨ | and | < ∨ | 0 | Number ∨ | then | ■ ∨ | ↑ ↓ ✕ |

| If value | >= ∨ | 0 | Number ∨ | and | < ∨ | Max | Number ∨ | then | ■ ∨ | ↑ ↓ ✕ |

Figure 8-20. Conditional formatting rules for the card background

And here's what we get: depending on different filters, our entire card can be high-lighted in either green or red (we could have added a rule for yellow or another state as well). The reader sees red cards to show the values that are under the plan and green ones to show the values exceeding the plan (Figure 8-21).

Figure 8-21. Card conditions for positive and negative deviations, indicated by background color

Our experience shows that it is sufficient to change the font color, especially if each card has some deviation indicator. If you change the background for each card, it may look too colorful on the dashboard. However, there are cases when there is a single important card, and for its critical deviations, you can use the entire background.

Step 5: For Perfectionists: Put Category Label on Top

We have the title of visuals at the top, which seems logical. But for the card, it's at the bottom. Of course, with a large title, we will still see it, but it's a small dissonance: reading top to bottom, I first see the large number 2,260K—what does it mean? And so, I can read it sequentially: Sales, 2,260K. It is considered good practice to place all elements in a unified logic. If the titles are at the top for visuals, then that should be the case for cards as well.

We would like to have an option in the category label settings for positioning, similar to how it is available for legends (top left, center, bottom, etc.). Unfortunately, this option is not available for the classic card. While this can be configured in other more complex cards, which we will get acquainted with in Parts II and III of the book, for now, let's solve this issue with the minimal tools available to us.

- Turn off the *Category label*.
- On the *General* tab, enable the *Title*.
- In the *Text* field, write the title of the card.

In the same settings section, you may change font style and size (Figure 8-22). Use *Horizontal alignment* to align it to the center.

Figure 8-22. Card title styling

It is important to remember that now, when we copy/paste this card, the title will be preserved and will not be automatically changed, as was the case with the category label. Therefore, keep in mind that for each new card created by copying, the title text needs to be adjusted.

This option has a drawback: the card title is positioned very close to the top border, leaving empty space between it and the value. In Power BI, you cannot adjust the padding for such a title. Therefore, while this approach solves the problem logically, it may not be entirely successful from a design perspective. There are two alternatives: use a text box or add an additional rectangle for a background:

Text box

Turn off the card title and category label, then simply insert a text box (Figure 8-23, left). Remember, you can do this through the top menu tab *Insert* → *Text box*. Don't forget that the background of the title should be either 100% transparent or the same as the card background.

Background

This option is more flexible in terms of setting the card size. When inserting a text box, we need to fit it into the space between the data label and the top edge of the card. At the same time, a fairly large and useless space remains under the data label to the bottom edge (where something could also be entered). If we set the shape of the KPI card as a separate element, then there will be no such problem (Figure 8-23, right).

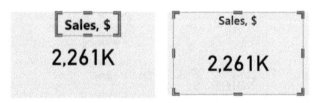

Figure 8-23. Adding a text box as the title of the card (left) and shape for a background (right)

To add a background shape, go to the top menu tab *Insert* → *Shape* → *Rectangle*. Resize it to your card and then disable the background (and border if you have one) for the card. Put the rectangle under the card; to keep layer order, go to *Format* and select *Send to back*.

Yes, this step is required for perfectionists. Usually, it would be enough to follow the first three steps:

1. Adjust callout value within the range of 25–35 px.
2. Adjust category label within the range of 14–20 pt (or consistent font size for all visual titles).
3. Add a background and keep the color contrast between it and the text.

But if you want your dashboard to be flawless, don't forget to put a title on top. This means turning off the category label and displaying it with a title or a text box.

New Card

Most of the issues we described above are addressed by the new Power BI visual: *Card* (*New*). This visual appeared in 2023, and it accounts for and fixes most of the shortcomings of the basic card. Some options may change in the future; we are not covering them here.

If we switch to the *Card (New)* visual after step 2 of our guide, we get quite acceptable results (Figure 8-24). Here, the *Category* label is instantly formatted as the title on top, everything is aligned to the left, and there's even a border.

Figure 8-24. Card (New) *default alignment*

Here we can add not just one but several values in the *Data* field, and then we will get an equivalent of a card row without multiplication and copy/paste steps (Figure 8-25). In the card settings, there is a magical option called *Apply settings to*, so we can work with individual elements of the card—we can change the position, size, and color of fonts, backgrounds, and borders.

Figure 8-25. Card (New) *with several values*

We will not go through all the steps again; the approach for *Card (New)* remains the same. Why didn't we start with this new card right away, instead of explaining the tricks with text boxes and combining cards with a common background? Because you first need to understand the anatomy of visuals and be able to correctly configure cards using simple tools (even with PowerPoint and Excel). We will return to the topic of advanced options for KPI cards in Part II of the book, but for now we will move on to mastering other classic visuals.

Tips and Notes

From a technical standpoint, KPI is any total value that we deem important and place on top of the dashboard. This element is called a card. There are three simple steps to follow:

Checklist for a card:

1. Adjust the callout value within the range of 25–35 px.
2. Adjust the category label within the range of 14–20 pt (or similar font size for all visual titles).
3. Add a background and keep the color contrast between it and the text.

Optional steps:

1. Add conditional formatting rules, if you have a value to compare (plan, previous year, etc.)
2. If you want your dashboard to be flawless, don't forget to put a title on top. It means you must turn off the category label and display it with a title or a text box.

Usually we display from three to six cards on the top of the dashboard. To save time, copy your first designed card, then paste it and modify further. Or you can use the new card for this purpose.

Download the *.pbix* file with customized visuals (*https://oreil.ly/lfjeR*).

CHAPTER 9

Slicers and Filters

In this chapter, we will discuss an important tool that is part of the basic visualizations in Power BI: the slicer. It is a utility element, meaning it does not visualize data itself but allows filtering of the charts on the dashboard based on a selected field. In practice, no Power BI report is complete without slicers.

The conversation about slicers becomes relevant when we have at least one chart that we want to filter. By default, any slicer filters all visual elements that have related data, including other slicers. We will demonstrate how to influence this option later on, but for now, let's understand how to build slicers and the different types they can be.

In Figure 9-1, a fragment of a dashboard with a slicer for countries is presented. After selecting *Great Britain* in the slicer, the charts on the right show sales by categories and monthly sales dynamics in that country.

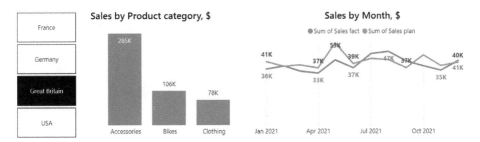

Figure 9-1. The slicer filters both charts based on the selected country (Great Britain)

In most tasks, slicers are built based on categorical data (such as countries, products, managers, etc.) or dates, and less frequently on quantitative values. In the case of dates and numerical values, the slicer can take the form of a slider—we drag its edges to adjust the range. In Figure 9-2, the first slicer selects the period from March 11 to August 12, while the second slicer filters the price range from $300 to $1,000. The table on the right is filtered to display data that satisfies both conditions.

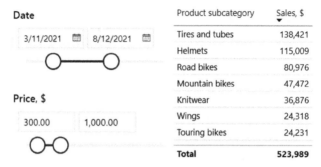

Product subcategory	Sales, $
Tires and tubes	138,421
Helmets	115,009
Road bikes	80,976
Mountain bikes	47,472
Knitwear	36,876
Wings	24,318
Touring bikes	24,231
Total	**523,989**

Figure 9-2. Slicers/sliders (left) set filter conditions for the table (right)

Creating a slicer is straightforward. When you select a field with categorical data on the data panel, Power BI will present it on the dashboard as a table. To change it to a slicer, choose the corresponding type of visualization: *Slicer* (on the *Visualizations* pane, its icon is located immediately to the left of the table). By default, you get a list of categories (in our example, countries) with checkboxes to the left of the labels (Figure 9-3).

Figure 9-3. Default slicer by countries

Currently, these checkboxes do not look as modern as those in Figures 9-1 and 9-2. Let's explore the options available for fine-tuning their appearance.

Step-by-Step Guide for a Slicer by Category

Here's what we have to do to create a slicer.

Step 1: Define Slicer Style

The first section, *Slicer settings*, for categorical data allows you to choose one of three display options (Figure 9-4):

- Vertical list (set by default)
- Tiles (as shown in the examples in Figures 9-1 and 9-2)
- Drop-down list (the third slicer from the left in Figure 9-4)

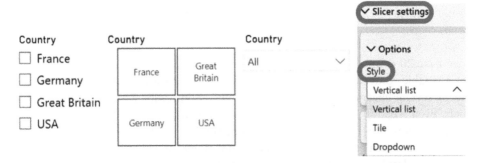

Figure 9-4. Three slicer styles: Vertical list *(left),* Tile *(center), and Dropdown (right)*

The tile style looks the most stylish and is well suited for tablets—large buttons are easy to tap. In our example, with only four categories, they are immediately visible as tiles, whereas a drop-down list may not be as ergonomic for such data: an extra click is needed to expand the list and see the same names.

In the case of an increase in the number of categories, stylish tiles may not be the most optimal option. If the space allocated for the slicer is not sufficient, a horizontal scroll bar will appear, indicated by a small arrow on the right (Figure 9-5, left). Many users may not notice it or may not think to click on it to see the remaining categories. You can make the slicer area wider and arrange the names in two columns or stretch it vertically to fit all the tiles, of course, if you have enough space on the dashboard for this. Typically, for categories numbering more than 10–12, the default vertical list proves to be the most compact option.

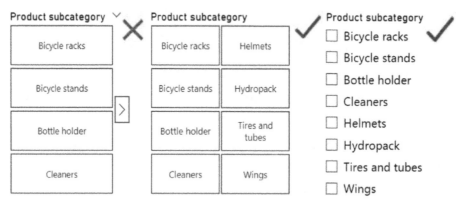

Figure 9-5. Choosing the slicer style for a moderate number of items: tiles with scrolling are not suitable (left); tiles in two columns are acceptable (center); a vertical list is optimal (right)

If we have 20 or more categories, scrolling is unavoidable even in a vertical list. It's not advisable to occupy half of the dashboard workspace to display all elements of one or several slicers and complicate user perception with a large number of text labels. Even a list of 15 items, especially if they are long, will be difficult to read and navigate. Therefore, in such cases, we recommend using a drop-down list. It allows for compact placement of the slicer block in a single row at the top (Figure 9-6) or side of the dashboard. Additionally, a drop-down list can include a search option, significantly simplifying users' interaction with large lists.

Country	Product category	Product subcategory	Manager
All ⌄	All ⌄	All ⌄	All ⌄

Figure 9-6. Block of four Dropdown-*style slicers*

If you are wondering how to set a specific number of columns and rows for the slicer, the answer is: you can't. Power BI determines the number of columns proportionally to the slicer's proportions. If you stretch the slicer downward, it will have one column, and if you stretch it sideways, it will have one row (Figure 9-7). Without scrolling, around 10 items fit into a row, depending on the length of the category names.

Product subcategory

Bicycle racks	Bicycle stands	Bottle holder	Cleaners	Gloves	Hats	Helmets	Hydropack	Knitwear

Figure 9-7. Horizontal Tile-*style slicer arrangement*

In 2023, a new *Slicer* visual was added to the list of default visuals. It comes with more customization options, including the ability to set the number of rows and columns. However, for now, let's focus on understanding the logical principles of slicer functionality rather than delving into design intricacies.

Step 2: Define Selection Type

The next section in the *Slicer settings* is the *Selection* section. Here, we configure how the slicer behaves when interacting with it. *Single select* (Figure 9-8) locks the selection to one item and doesn't allow filtering by multiple items or resetting the filter to see the data for all categories. In practice, it's not used frequently but can be useful in situations where you cannot aggregate metrics across different categories, and the dashboard always needs to show information for one country or one manager, for example. Another example is switching between different currencies.

When single selection is enabled, other options in the settings disappear because they are logically impossible in this context.

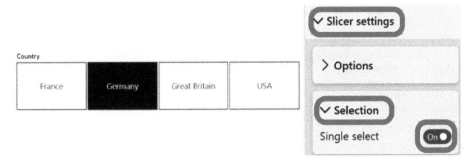

Figure 9-8. Single selection for the slicer: only one country can be chosen

Multi-select with CTRL is set by default (Figure 9-9). It allows you to choose several elements on the slicer by clicking on the desired ones while holding down the Ctrl key (this is especially convenient when working with tiles). If you disable this mode, you can simply click the buttons sequentially for multiple selection. The downside of this option is that if you want to reselect a single category, you will need to deselect each category that was previously selected. This is not very convenient and not obvious for all users.

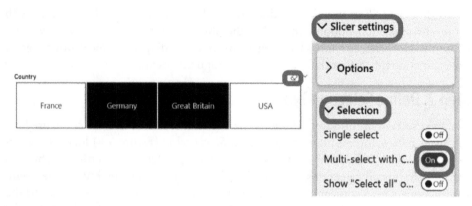

Figure 9-9. Slicer with multiple selection using CTRL allows you to select any number of items, while the Deselect *button clears the selection*

To help with this, there is the *Clear selections* button (eraser icon in the top right corner of the tiles, Figure 9-9). It resets the selected categories, but it is not always easy to see.

In the case of *Multi-select with CTRL*, to deselect all categories, you simply need to double-click on the same category twice. Therefore, for convenience, we recommend leaving this option enabled.

The last option is *Show "Select all"* (Figure 9-10). There is no special need for it, so it is disabled by default. It provides the same result as the *Clear selections* button or double-clicking on the same category when using *Multi-select with CTRL*, but it adds one more button (or row in the vertical list). In the case of working with drop-down lists, this option can be activated.

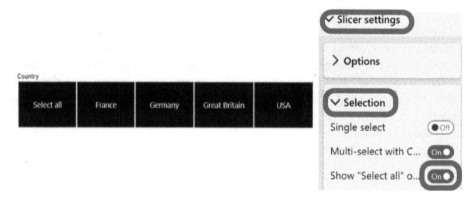

Figure 9-10. Show "Select all" option *adds a button that selects all items at once.*

Step 3: Slicer Formatting

After configuring the slicer parameters, you can proceed with its formatting. Often, this is not necessary because the slicer is primarily a functional tool, and the main requirement for it is functionality. However, if you want to customize this element and unify its style with the entire dashboard, you can do this in the *Value* settings. Available formatting options include:

Values
> Font size and color of category labels in the slicer, as well as the size of spacing between them in pixels.

Borders
> Their position, color, and line thickness. It's worth mentioning that while borders can be used for tiled slicers, they should not be added to lists (both vertical and drop-down), as additional lines can complicate reading the text.

Background
> Similar to borders, backgrounds can be set for tiled slicers but not for vertical lists. For drop-down lists, a faint or semitransparent background is acceptable.

Additionally, besides the slicer's elements, you can format its title. First, you need to enable it and change its text if necessary (it is automatically generated based on the field on which the slicer is built). Then, you have the same settings as for values: font, border, and background. Here are some recommendations applicable to all slicer styles:

- The title color should match the color of category labels in the slicer or the color of titles of all visualizations on the dashboard.

- Use only bottom borders to "underline" the title. All other lines will visually weigh it down.

- Do not give the title a background that differs from the slicer's background (if there is no background for the slicer, it is not necessary for the title).

There is no separate parameter for setting the background for the entire slicer; it is located, like all visual elements, in the *General → Effects* section. Examples of slicer formatting are shown in Figure 9-11.

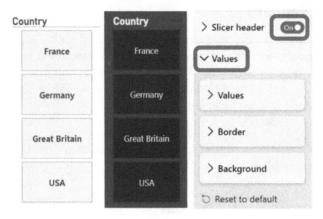

Figure 9-11. Examples of slicer designs and configurations

With the basic setup of slicers covered, let's now move to exploring other scenarios of working with slicers and the peculiarities of their formatting.

Slicer for a Range of Values and Dates

Often in practice, examples of filtering data by categories or dates are more common, but slicers can also include numerical values. In this case, if we are building a slicer from scratch (rather than modifying a previously formatted slicer), by default it will appear not as a list but as a slider. Figure 9-12 presents such a slicer based on product price, with only products priced between $500 and $2,000 selected. You can adjust the selection either by moving the start and end of the slider along the axis or manually entering the desired values in the boxes provided.

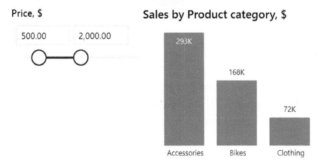

Figure 9-12. A slicer with a price range for products in the form of a slider

It's important to note that if you modify a slicer previously configured for categories, it will retain the same style you manually set (list or tiles). To change it to a slider, you need to choose the *Between* option (or *Before/After* if you want to limit the slider from one side) from the style options. We'll discuss the new styles in more detail later on.

If we use a date as the source field, Power BI will also build a slicer in the form of a slider (Figure 9-13). The start and end of the slider axis will determine the date range in the source data. As with working with a slicer with numerical values, you can adjust the range boundaries by typing dates into the boxes provided, or click the calendar icon to pick a date from a calendar pop-up.

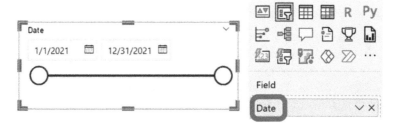

Figure 9-13. Default date slicer

For a slicer with dates, there are even more styles available than for values (Figure 9-14). Let's consider all possible options:

Vertical list
> The default style for categorical data (typically not used for dates and values).

Tile
> A stylish option for a small amount of data. Not used for values, but for dates it's applied for hierarchy levels like years, months, or weekdays.

Between
> The default style for numerical values and dates, which we saw in Figure 9-13.

Before
> A slider limited from the left. In this style, the start date (or minimum value) is fixed, and we can change only the end date (or maximum value). This allows us to see the range from the start to the selected value.

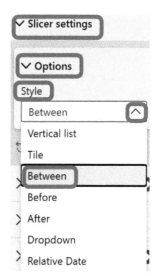

Figure 9-14. Styles for date slicers

After

The reverse of *Before*. In this style, the end date (or maximum value) is fixed, and we can move only the start date (or minimum value) to see the range from the end to the selected value.

Dropdown

An alternative option to the slider.

Relative Date (only for date format)

Allows you to set rules for selecting dates for the entire slicer.

Relative Time (only for date format)

Similar to the previous option, but the rules will apply to selecting time.

The default *Between* option is optimal when working with numerical values, but it's not always convenient when dealing with dates. Tasks requiring filtering by an entire month or quarter are much more common than those requiring the option of selecting arbitrary dates. For users, it's more convenient to click on a single button (tile) rather than adjusting dates on a slider.

In this case, it may not be obvious how to create a slicer for months in tile format. If you simply switch to this style from the default, you will get a button for each date, as shown in Figure 9-15. Scrolling through them to reach the end of the period while holding Ctrl would be impractical.

Date

Friday, January 01, 2021	Tuesday, January 05, 2021	Tuesday, January 12, 2021	Monday, January 18, 2021	Friday, January 22, 2021
Saturday, January 02, 2021	Thursday, January 07, 2021	Wednesday, January 13, 2021	Tuesday, January 19, 2021	Sunday, January 24, 2021
Sunday, January 03, 2021	Friday, January 08, 2021	Thursday, January 14, 2021	Wednesday, January 20, 2021	Monday, January 25, 2021
Monday, January 04, 2021	Saturday, January 09, 2021	Sunday, January 17, 2021	Thursday, January 21, 2021	Wednesday, January 27, 2021

Figure 9-15. Date slicer with hierarchy in Tile *style: not practical*

In Chapter 6, we explained how Power BI works with date format: it automatically creates fields for year, quarter, month, and date, and it organizes them into a hierarchy. The slicer by default displays data from the lowest level of the hierarchy: days. To correct this, expand the *Date Hierarchy* in the *Data* pane and place the level you want to use for the slicer in the *Field*—in our case, *Month* (Figure 9-16).

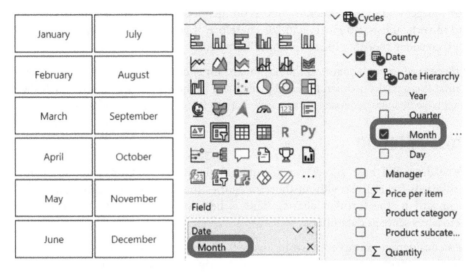

Figure 9-16. Creating a slicer for date by month

You can configure such a slicer as tiles or a vertical list, following steps 1–3 from our guide.

Keep in mind that if your data spans multiple years, you need a separate slicer for years; otherwise, data for all months with the same name will be summed up. You can create such a slicer, as well as separate slicers for quarters or days, in a similar way.

Technically, it's possible to show all levels in one hierarchical vertical list (see Figure 9-17 on the left), but we don't recommend doing so. It's better to create separate slicers for each hierarchy level and arrange them vertically side by side (as shown in Figure 9-17 on the right). This approach is not only visually more appealing, but it is also more user-friendly since all selection options will be visible at once.

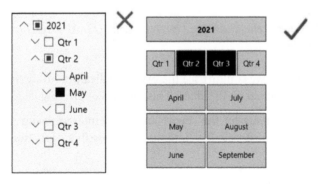

Figure 9-17. Hierarchical slicer by date versus three separate slicers in Tile *style*

Don't forget that in tile slicers, it's not recommended to show more than 10–12 items, and in vertical lists, no more than 20. Therefore, if you're adding a separate slicer for days, consider choosing the drop-down list style.

If there's not enough space on the dashboard for slicers in tile form, it's acceptable to format them as drop-down lists and place them in the report header row. Such slicers must have headers because we can't see what's in the slicer until we expand it.

Cross-Filtering

We've discussed how slicers work, but sometimes you can do without them on dashboards (or at least without those categories that are already represented on the dashboard in the form of charts). This is because, in Power BI, visual elements themselves serve as data filters.

Let's consider an example shown in Figure 9-18: a column chart (on the left) displays sales by category, while a pie chart (on the right) shows sales by country. If we highlight a country on the pie chart, for example, the USA, the values for it on the column chart will remain brightly colored, while the overall indicators will become semitransparent. This method of interaction is called *highlighting*.

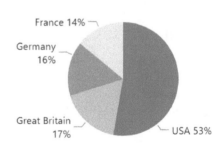

Figure 9-18. The column chart is filtered by sales in the USA through highlighting this segment on the pie chart

When we used a slicer, we couldn't see the overall indicators—only the values for the selected category remained on the chart. This method of filtering is called a *filter*.

By default, visual elements on the report are set to interact using the highlighting principle (except for those visuals where this is impossible—for example, KPI cards or line charts).

But this approach has its drawbacks. If we choose a category on the column chart, then inside the segments on the pie chart, only the sales shares of the selected category in each country will remain (Figure 9-19, center). The figure will be original, but incomprehensible: against the background of the total values, it is difficult to compare these small sectors, especially when they are of different heights.

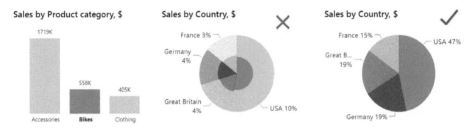

Figure 9-19. The filter by category on the column chart (left) ambiguously filters the pie chart using the highlight principle (center) and correctly filters using the filter principle (right)

For analytics, it is important to show the distribution of the selected category by country in a logical sequence (from largest to smallest) and with correct values. Therefore, it is necessary to change the type of cross-filtering from highlighting to filtering here (Figure 9-19, right).

To configure the types of cross-filtering between visualizations on the dashboard, you need to select the visualization that will be used for filtering. In the ribbon, go to the *Format* tab and click the first button on the left of the ribbon, which says *Edit interactions*. After you do this, all visual elements on the sheet will display icons representing interaction options (see Figure 9-20):

- The column chart icon with the slicer symbol (left) represents filtering using the filter principle. Data is filtered based on the selected element on another chart, similar to a slicer.

- The column chart icon without the slicer symbol (center) represents filtering using the highlight principle. Data related to the selected element on another chart is highlighted against the background of the overall data. This option may be absent for some visualizations.

- The ⊘ icon (right) represents *disabling* or enabling interaction. If this is disabled, the chart will not respond to filtering.

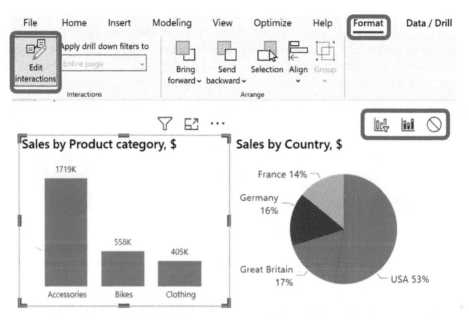

Figure 9-20. Configuring interactions between elements on the dashboard. The icon of the active interaction type has a dark gray fill.

Interaction is changed by clicking on the icon with the desired type. It is important to click specifically on the icon buttons, not on the visual element itself; otherwise, we will change the selection and end up modifying not the desired visual's filtering but its interaction with other elements.

Interaction settings between elements need to be done individually for each visual element. This means that if we change the interaction of a bar chart to a pie chart, it doesn't mean that the pie chart will also change its influence on the bar chart. To achieve this, we need to select the pie chart first, and then click on the icon of the desired interaction type above the bar chart.

When there are many elements on the dashboard, you may need to edit dozens of interactions. It's not difficult, but it requires attention. In Figure 9-21, you can see the directions of interactions from the selected line chart: toward all the cards, the bar chart, the pie chart, the graph, and the table. Once again, note that cards, line graphs, and slicers do not have interaction filtering types, as there is nothing to highlight within them.

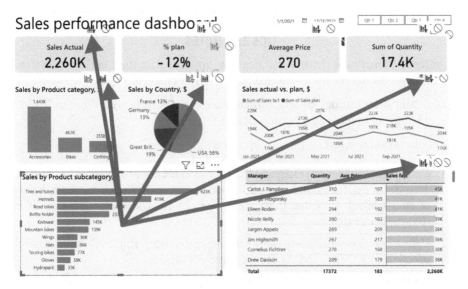

Figure 9-21. Dashboard with Edit interactions *mode enabled. Arrows indicate active interaction types from the line chart to other visual elements.*

By the way, it's important to configure interactions not only between visual elements but also from slicers to them. Although slicers can only filter (there won't be an option for highlighting when selecting a slicer), it's important to disable slicers' influence on certain visualizations. For example, to prevent a trend chart from collapsing into a single point when selecting a single month, we need to disable its interaction with the slicer for months (select the corresponding slicer and click the ⊘ icon above the chart).

Charts do not interact with slicers, so there's no need to configure reverse cross-filtering. However, slicers interact with each other. To avoid unexpected filtering, it's almost always necessary to disable the influence of lower-level slicers on higher-level ones: quarters don't affect years; months don't affect quarters and years; days don't affect months, quarters, and years. All other situations should be considered case by case. When designing a dashboard, always keep in mind the cross-filtering capabilities and discuss with the report's users which elements should influence others and which should not. This can affect not only the visual aspect but also the data model.

Tips and Notes

A slicer is a functional element that does not visualize data itself but allows filtering all charts on the dashboard by selected category, date range, or values.

The default slicer settings are well chosen. Here, a checklist is needed not to "fix" the visual but to consciously adapt it to your data.

Checklist for slicer setup:

1. Choose slicer style: for categorical data, you can choose a vertical list, tiles, or drop-down list; for value range, additional options exist such as between, before, or after (slider); for dates, there are all the options above plus you can set up relative date or time.

2. Define selection parameters (only for categorical data): single selection, multiple selection with CTRL, and display the "select all" option.

3. Format the slicer: fonts, borders, and background for values and headers in the standard slicer plus shapes and layout in the new slicer (indicated by a lightning bolt symbol).

In the interaction settings of slicers with other elements, there are two modes:

Highlight (default for all visual elements except cards and line charts)
   Highlights the filtered value against the total.

Filter
   Shows only the values of the selected category.

Additionally, you can always disable the influence of elements on each other. It is important to do this if logic requires it.

Download the *.pbix* file with customized visuals (*https://oreil.ly/q-fEu*).

Download layout image: dark (*https://oreil.ly/KaUGk*) or light (*https://oreil.ly/njEYI*).

CHAPTER 10

Putting It All Together: Dashboard Design Tips

So, we are approaching the end of the first part of the book. And in your toolkit, you now have classic visuals:

- For displaying rankings: bar and column charts
- For depicting structure: pie and donut charts, as well as treemaps
- For showcasing dynamics (timelines): a family of line charts
- For an overview: tables and matrices
- For key metrics: KPI cards
- For data filtering: slicers, as well as cross-filtering options

With these tools, you'll be able to address 80% of tasks in the corporate reporting sphere. Through regular practice, the step-by-step guide for each visual will become second nature, allowing you to create neat and proficient charts within a matter of minutes.

However, a chart by itself is not the final product; our task is to learn how to create interactive dashboards. This is a broad topic that encompasses data storytelling and information design, and it has dedicated books. In one chapter, we've aimed to distill key points. Even if you are an experienced analyst eager to move on to Part II's discussion of advanced visuals, we recommend reading this chapter to ensure that you are doing everything correctly.

In this chapter, we'll cover the basics of dashboard design. We won't be talking about creatively choosing colors and fonts, but rather about the composition of the dashboard as a whole—how to assemble individual visual elements into a unified information product. There won't be any exclusive content here—our task is to briefly systematize best practices. Even experienced managers and analysts sometimes make typical mistakes and overlook important details, especially if their supervisor demands "another pie chart on top." We've compiled a guide that will help you avoid such mistakes and set up your dashboard professionally—as if a designer had also worked on it.

Beginner dashboard developers often find that their dashboards look something like Figure 10-1.

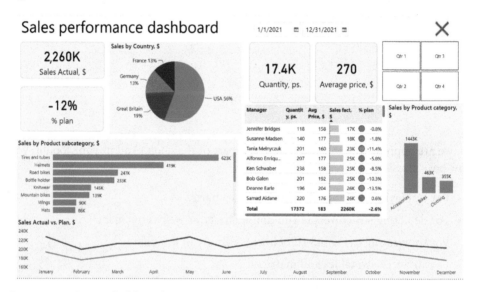

Figure 10-1. Messy dashboard

Charts are configured according to checklists, but still, there's a desire to call in a designer to "make it look better." Let's figure out what's wrong with this dashboard:

- At the top, KPI cards, a pie chart, and slicers in tile form are scattered around. It seems that elements with different purposes are visually grouped together on the same level, and we perceive them together, which can be confusing.

- In the center of the dashboard, there's a table. It seems like it was placed there at the last moment, roughly compressing the column chart (its labels becoming rotated) and disproportionately compressing the line chart showing sales dynamics.

- Overall, the visuals have different proportions, backgrounds, and borders, with uneven spacing between them, creating a sense of chaos.

The issue lies not in the colors and fonts but in the lack of organization, a failure to separate elements into logical blocks. If we fix this, we'll get a version where the same visualizations are arranged in a logical structure from general to specific (see Figure 10-2). This is quite sufficient for corporate reporting.

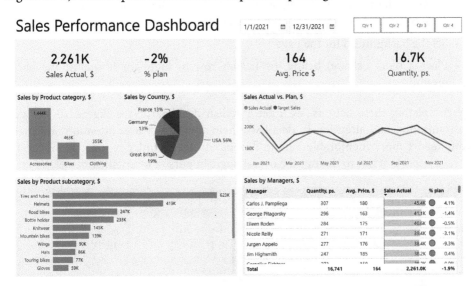

Figure 10-2. Organized dashboard of classic visuals

Let's take a closer look at what can be improved to make the dashboard even more attractive:

- Change the standard cards to new ones with category labels at the top and align all elements to the left edge.
- Add the planned value to the first card.
- Apply conditional formatting to the deviation indicator in the card.
- Apply the same font style to all charts and the table.
- Work with the table:
  - We've already added a header in the previous version (the table header is not the same as the title).
  - Rearrange the column sequence logically for storytelling purposes: sales actual, deviation, quantity, average price.
  - Apply conditional formatting to the cell background for the average price indicator to highlight the highest prices; format minimum values with a different background color.

- — Turn off the background of the main part or set it to the background color of the block.
- — Add a separator line for the header row and totals.
- — Align the totals in all columns exactly below the values (performed in the *Specific column* setting for each indicator separately).
- Set the background for the page.
- Place a block (shape) below the header row to highlight it against the background.

By completing these actions, we'll get a stylish dashboard (see Figure 10-3). Such customization and attention to detail will help you attract user attention and make your report more memorable among dozens of other similar reports. However, it's always important not to disrupt the overall logic in pursuit of artistic finesse.

Figure 10-3. Dashboard with "more stylish" blue background

In Figures 10-2 and 10-3, we adhered to a simple rule of dashboard composition. The page is divided into several zones, each designated for specific purposes and charts. These zones are arranged from top to bottom, descending from the general to the specific, from global context to details:

Header (level zero)
> This includes the title, navigation buttons, and individual slicers (or a button to invoke the slicer panel). It can also contain the company logo, report generation date, and other common elements related to the entire dashboard.

The first level—KPIs

Here, cards are placed. The rule is that we always start the dashboard with cards at the top, and only cards, period. We defined that rule this way because we want users to pay attention to the most important information (main KPIs) first, and only then provide them additional information that adds details to the KPIs.

The second level—visualized subtotals, trends

Below the cards, in the upper half of the working area, we place high-level visualizations, categorized by items such as regions and timelines. These visuals also serve as filters—clicking on a column reveals details about it on the next level.

The third level—details

Here, we present more granular data, usually in tables with conditional formatting. However, belonging to the third level is determined not by the form (chart or table) but by the content. In Figures 10-2 and 10-3, at the bottom left, there's a bar chart, "Sales by Product subcategory," which belongs to the third level, while the categories belong to the second.

Now, we realize that in Figure 10-1, a fundamental rule of levels was breached:

- Slicers and a pie chart were present on the first level. We moved the slicer to the header and shifted the pie chart to the second level.
- The central table belonged to the third level, as did the bar chart "Sales by Product subcategory." We relocated them downward and elevated the line chart to the second level.

The priorities of arranging visual elements can be determined by the rule of information levels. It is schematically presented in Figure 10-4.

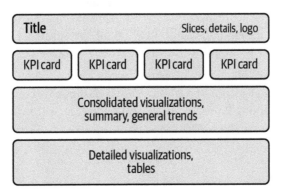

Figure 10-4. Dashboard information level scheme

Now we understand that in the initial version of the dashboard (Figure 10-1), a fundamental rule of information levels was violated:

- Slicers and the pie chart ended up in the KPI card level. We moved the slicer to the header level, and the pie chart to the second level.
- The table and the subcategory chart were in the center. We placed them in the detailed level.
- The line chart depicting the trend of overall sales was at the bottom, although it shows the trend of the entire company's sales. We moved it up to the second level.

In addition to this, we aligned the proportions of the blocks (we'll talk about this a little later).

From the perspective of dashboard composition, we should always follow the levels scheme. However, this is not a strict sequence; the main thing is not to miss anything. You can start from any step because dashboard design is still a creative process. We break down this process into steps so that you consciously think through each one, especially if you're just gaining experience in data visualization.

Step-by-Step Guide for a Dashboard

Here's what we have to do to create a dashboard.

Step 1: Place KPI Cards on Top

This step may seem obvious, but not everyone adheres to it. It may happen that initially you have three to four cards on your dashboard, but then the number increases to six to seven, and you start adding them in another row below or in separate blocks in the workspace. We recommend placing no more than six cards at the top, as they are key indicators, not just all the summary values in a row. If you have around 10 KPIs, prioritize them. It may turn out that you're displaying second-level data as cards.

Figure 10-5 shows a snapshot of a contact center dashboard (the figure displays only its upper half, containing levels 1 and 2). The row of cards contains eight indicators, and it already appears slightly overloaded.

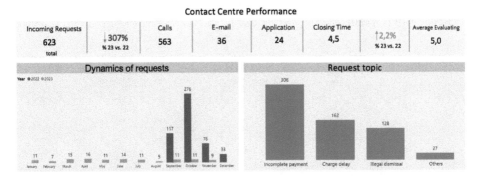

Figure 10-5. Example of an overloaded dashboard with cards

Actually, the total count of calls, emails, and mobile app requests adds up to 623 requests. This represents a detailed breakdown of the cumulative value by the "request source" category, and it should be positioned at the second level of the dashboard, as depicted in Figure 10-6. While we compacted the second level slightly, now incorporating three visuals instead of two, the overall result is more balanced.

Figure 10-6. An alternative and more balanced representation of the same information

Step 2: Define Dashboard Grid

The workspace refers to the page area below the cards, where charts and tables are placed. The grid is the division of the workspace into blocks (modules) where we place visual elements. In the unsuccessful example in Figure 10-1, these blocks ended up with different heights, and their headers were at different levels, creating a sense of chaos. It's important for the modules to be aligned with each other both vertically and horizontally. The KPI cards should also be aligned with the grid, and the cards should be aligned relative to the charts. Ideally, a symmetric grid should be achieved, as shown in Figure 10-7.

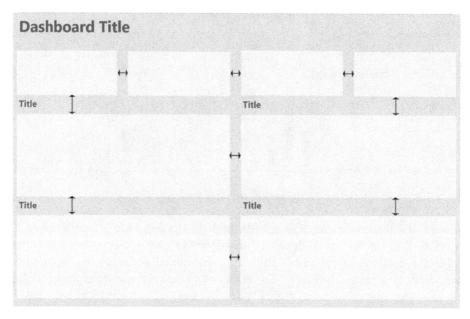

Figure 10-7. 2×2 grid

In practice, achieving a perfectly symmetric grid is rare because there may be an odd number of charts and KPI cards. In such cases, we can accommodate two visual elements in one block, as shown in the example in Figure 10-2: we placed a pie chart of four countries and a bar chart of three categories in one module. Conversely, there may be fewer visual elements than modules, and they themselves may be larger. In this case, you can visually combine two modules into one place—for example, a large table with conditional formatting or more complex visuals, which you'll become familiar with in the next part of the book.

The second most popular grid for a dashboard consists of six modules, which we call 3×2, meaning three columns plus two rows (Figure 10-8). From this grid, various combinations can be obtained by merging certain modules horizontally or vertically.

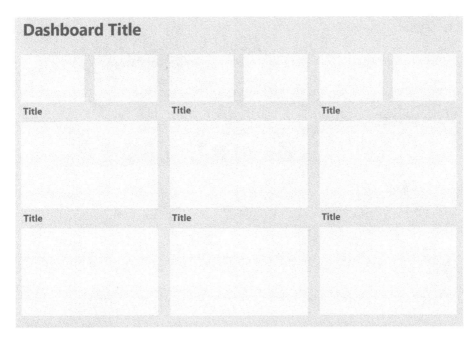

Figure 10-8. 3×2 grid

In Figure 10-9, you can see an example of a dashboard based on a 3×2 grid. There are only three visual elements in its workspace, but the chart on the left is stretched vertically and occupies two modules, while the sales dynamics chart and the table on the right are stretched horizontally and also each occupy two modules. For balance, the KPI cards are also grouped into three blocks; they are positioned according to the modular grid and aligned relative to the chart below.

Figure 10-9. An example of a dashboard with a modified 3×2 grid layout

Let's transform the dashboard from our example (Figure 10-2) using the same principle. In the second level of information, we have three charts. For each of them, we'll assign a block of the same size (a 3×2 grid). At the bottom, we'll shrink the line chart to one-third of the width of the page, and we'll allocate two-thirds to the table. Since there were originally three KPI cards, there's no need to change anything here (we'll remove the additional sales plan indicator). As a result, we get another version of an organized dashboard (see Figure 10-10). Which do you prefer?

Figure 10-10. Dashboard rearranged using a 3×2 grid layout

For visual indication of the modular grid, you can simply place the charts and tables on a white background and separate them with padding, but this requires more attention to aligning the elements (pixel adjustments). Sometimes, such minimalist dashboards without extra shapes and blocks look stylish (especially if there are only a few of them on one page), but more often we still work with backgrounds and substrates. Through them, we not only emphasize the ordered structure but also make the dashboard more expressive and memorable. You can set the background for dashboard objects in several ways.

In the simplest version, we enable the background for each chart. If we want to place two objects in one module, we should place them side by side so that their borders are adjacent to each other, and their height matches (as in the example with KPI cards in Figure 8-16). You can adjust the background in the *General → Effects* section (Figure 10-11). We recommend using the lightest shade possible for the background. To avoid eyeballing it in the color palette, you can use the transparency parameter. In our example, we took the lightest shade of blue in the palette as a base but set its transparency to 80%.

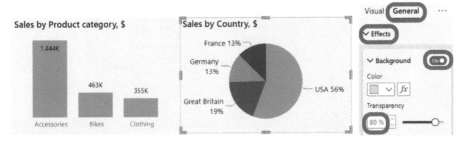

Figure 10-11. Combining two charts with a shared background (background set separately for each object)

Using the background of a visual element alone won't allow for flexible design adjustments. For instance, we can't modify the spacing between the title text and the edges of the shape (in Figure 10-11, the text "sticks" to the left and top edges), or specify rounded corners for the shape. Therefore, as an alternative method, we typically use the insertion of an additional element—a rectangle. We have already discussed this approach for KPI cards (Figure 8-23). Just a reminder: to insert a shape, we need to switch to the *Insert* tab in the menu bar, click the *Shapes* button, and select the desired shape (Figure 10-12).

Figure 10-12. Adding a rectangular block as a background

You can choose either a regular rectangle or a rectangle with rounded corners. For both options, you can specify a custom corner radius. A radius up to 10 px can be considered optimal—the corners look neat and don't distract the user's attention (Figure 10-13).

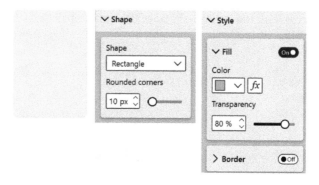

Figure 10-13. Background design—rounding corners and adding the fill

After inserting the shape, in the *Style* section, we can adjust the fill color. By default, Power BI creates bright shapes. We need to change the color to a light or semitransparent one, as in the example of setting the background above. The border, which is also set by default, is not necessary (remember the "one effect at a time" rule), so we either disable it or adjust it to the color of the background. We recommend working with the background rather than borders because visually they appear as separate elements and do not unify but instead delineate objects on the page.

It's also important to disable the background of the shape in the *General* settings. If you don't do this, the background color of the entire shape (rectangle) will protrude beyond the rounded corners.

The third option is to design images with pre-drawn backgrounds for visuals in a separate application and upload them as the page background. We'll look at how to do this in the next step.

Step 3: Adjust the Page Background

To be frank, Power BI is a tool for working with data and visualization, not for advanced UI design. You can add shapes and customize colors and borders, but not as flexibly as in tools like PowerPoint or specialized design applications like Figma. If you want to use a "multilayered" background with overlays, gradients, icons, etc., chances are you have a designer who has created a layout in a separate application, and it would be easier for you to add it as a background image rather than lay it out from separate elements in Power BI.

Let's say you already have a background image made by Midjourney. You are an international corporation and want to emphasize your global presence in reports with a world map (Figure 10-14).

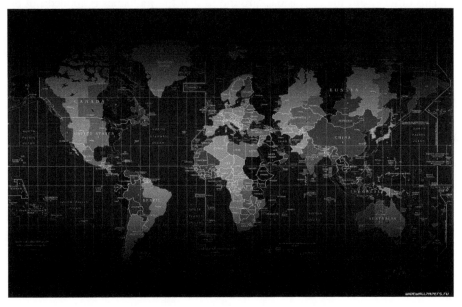

Figure 10-14. Background image for the dashboard

Up to this point, we've been working with the settings panel for individual visual elements. To add an image as a background to the report, we need to adjust the format settings for the entire page. To do this, click on any empty space in the dashboard's workspace and switch to the second tab of the *Visualization* pane—the paintbrush icon on the background of the sheet, not the chart, as it was before (Figure 10-15). Here are the options available for customization:

Page details

Name, page functions.

Canvas options

Size, alignment.

Canvas background

You can upload an image that will fill the canvas background. After that you might be confused, because the page will remain white. That's because the default transparency is 100%. To make your background image visible, reduce the transparency to 0% or an intermediate value.

Wallpaper

This differs from the canvas background in that the wallpaper is applied not only to the canvas, limited to the predefined size, but also the entire report page. Thus, if the width of the report is less than the width of the screen, the background image will fill the entire screen, while the image loaded for the canvas background will only fill the report (the edges of the screen will remain white).

Filter pane area

Customization of the appearance of the filter pane.

Filter cards

Formatting of fields on the filter pane.

Figure 10-15. Using a picture as the background image

We want our background with the map to completely fill any screen (the white background should not remain at the edges), so we'll adjust the *Background Image* settings.

In the *Image* field, click on *Upload* and specify the path to our image. You won't see changes immediately (or only at the edges beyond the workspace) because the canvas background technically sits above the background image and defaults to white with 100% transparency. Move the slider to 0% transparency and you'll see the background image fully.

To adapt visual elements to the new background (as shown in Figure 10-15), you need to follow these steps:

- If previously we set a light blue background color using 80% transparency (Figure 10-11) or manually selected a light shade, here we need to make changes. Set the background color to white with 10% transparency.

- Disable the background for the dashboard title text field, and make the text itself white for contrast against the dark blue background.

The example with the map is not best practice—this is how dashboards looked about 10 years ago. A bright contrasting background distracts from the charts, while the purpose of the report is the opposite—to draw attention to the data. If you reduce the transparency of the background image to 80% or choose another image, the report will look calmer but will still retain its originality (Figure 10-16). Always remember color adaptation for the backgrounds of visual elements and text fonts without backgrounds.

Figure 10-16. Dashboard with a specially designed background

In real-world scenarios, we rarely add maps as background images like in Figures 10-15 and 10-16. Instead, we upload images with pre-drawn backgrounds for visual elements. The page background is usually solid, or with a subtle gradient or semitransparent background image that doesn't distract users from the information. It's important to note that when working with pre-drawn backgrounds, we use the canvas background, and for the background image, we simply adjust the background. Otherwise, all pre-drawn shapes for objects would shift on screens of different widths and heights.

In Figure 10-17, you can see an example dashboard for event visitor feedback. The central part with the nonstandard version of the radar chart (an aster plot) appears to be elevated above the "secondary" parts located on either side of it. We couldn't achieve this volumetric effect using shapes in Power BI, so the designer drew the background separately. We then uploaded it as the *Canvas background* and placed the charts on top of it.

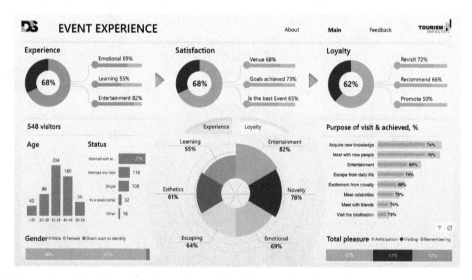

Figure 10-17. Dashboard with a nonstandard designer background

Another point to note here is that when uploading an image as both the canvas background and background image, there are three options for image placement: *Normal*, *Fit*, and *Fill*. For adapting an image of any size, we recommend using the *Fit* or *Fill* options.

Step 4: Customize the Color Theme

In the ribbon, under the *View* tab, you can find various premade color theme options on the left side (Figure 10-18). If you choose one of them, all visual elements on all report pages will automatically adjust to match the selected theme.

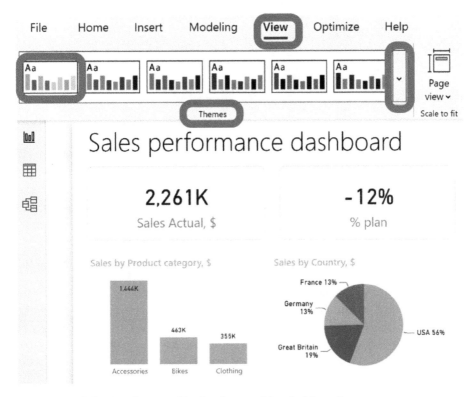

Figure 10-18. Selecting the overall color theme of the dashboard

If this is a company activity report, the corporate colors (brand book) are often used as the working palette. These colors are unlikely to be available in the ready-made Power BI themes, so you'll have to customize the theme manually. However, there's nothing complex about it. Moreover, after configuring the theme once, you can save it and reuse it in other Power BI reports. Let's see how to do it.

On the *View* tab, expand the list of themes (click the arrow to the right of the theme options ribbon). In the drop-down menu below all the preset options, there are several actions available. We choose *Customize current theme* (Figure 10-19).

Figure 10-19. Creating a customized color theme for the dashboard

The first step in the opened window is to set the name of the new theme. Then, we proceed to adjust the main colors. Since we took an existing theme as a source, we will not configure the colors from scratch but rather modify the existing ones. To do this, we sequentially expand the palette next to each color using the arrow (Figure 10-20). To avoid manually selecting shades, there is an option at the bottom of the block to specify the color in hex or RGB format. Usually, the company's brand book specifies color names in one of these formats. If you don't have the brand book at hand, you can "extract" colors manually. To do this, insert an image containing the desired colors (logo/screenshot from the website or other reports, etc.) into any graphics editor (Photoshop, Figma, or even Paint). You can extract the color using the "eyedropper" tool.

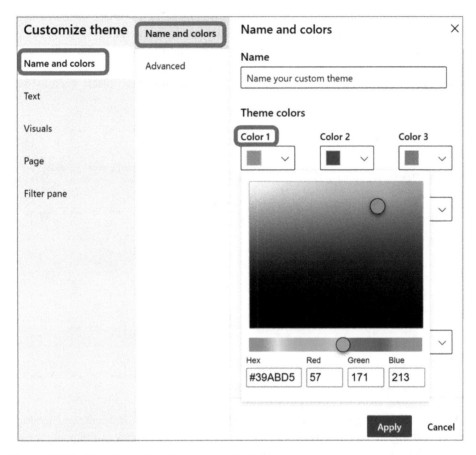

Figure 10-20. Choosing colors for a customized theme

As for the main colors of the theme, choose two to three. All visual elements will be based on them. If you need more colors (for example, for segments of a treemap), work with shades of the existing colors. They are automatically generated from the basic palette, and you can always see them by expanding the settings of the element. You also can add neutral gray as another color.

An exception here is conditional formatting for deviations in cards or tables. A negative deviation is always strictly red, and a positive one is green. Even if you really want to make it blue or another corporate color—you shouldn't. Red and green are commonly associated with bad and good, respectively, for people in most Western cultures. By looking at familiar colors, the user will perceive the information more quickly. For the same reason, try to avoid pure red and green as the main colors so that the user does not instinctively perceive the data as negative or positive.

The next section of theme customization is *Text* (Figure 10-21). Here, we can change the font settings for the entire report or individually for headings and cards. We rarely change the font style (Segoe UI is universal), and the size is usually adjusted in each element. Therefore, there is no need to change anything here except for the font color if you understand that you will use something other than black, such as dark blue.

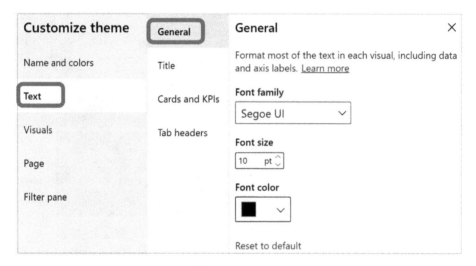

Figure 10-21. Font settings for the customized theme

In the *Visuals* settings, you can specify background, borders, headers, and tooltips. The only thing we recommend changing here is the transparency of the background. Set it to 100% so that you don't need to manually disable or modify the background of visual elements (including text labels and shapes) later on.

In the *Page* section, you can set the background or background image for all pages of the report at once. This is convenient if you use the same background and don't need to customize it for each page separately.

We usually hide the *filter pane* from report users—it's our working tool, and designing a special layout for it is necessary.

That's it, the theme is ready. Select *Apply*, and the dashboard will automatically adjust according to the specified settings.

As we mentioned, you only need to customize the corporate theme once. Now you can save it and apply it to any Power BI files. To do this, select *Save current theme* from the drop-down menu of the theme list (see Figure 10-22). Then, in each new Power BI file, choose the *Browse for themes* option from the same menu and specify the path to your theme.

Figure 10-22. Saving the customized theme

But just setting up a theme is not enough—you also need to apply it correctly. Let's highlight the main rules to help you with this:

- All titles of visual elements should be the same color (including cards). It's important to note that the table header is not considered its title, hence:
  - The text color in the table header may differ from the colors of titles.
  - The font size should not be as large as the titles.
  - Besides the header, the table should always have a title (and it should follow the style of all titles in the report).
- The same indicators or categories on different visualizations should have the same color. For example, if you're showing sales figures by product category on a bar chart and the same data's trend on a line graph, it's important that both the bars and the line share the same color. This simplifies comprehension.
- Backgrounds of objects or the overall background (when used) should be consistent in style (shape, color, transparency). Additionally, pay attention to their alignment.
- Fonts across all elements in all objects should be consistent, as well as the font sizes of identical elements (titles, KPI card values, category labels, etc.).

Step 5: Check Cross-Filtering

The key benefit of a dashboard is its interactivity, allowing data to be filtered based on selected categories with a simple click on chart columns or table rows. In Chapter 9, we familiarized ourselves with the filtering and highlighting principles. By default, many visuals come with highlighting activated, and we suggested switching it to the filter mode. Hence, during the last step of configuring the entire dashboard, ensure that all filters are set up accurately.

To do this, select a visual element (in Figure 10-23, we selected a bar chart in the bottom left corner), then go to the *Format* tab on the top menu and click on the *Edit interactions* button. Icons showing the type of interaction with the selected chart (filter, highlight, or disabled) will appear for all objects on the dashboard. Go through each visual element that can influence others and check the specified type of cross-filtering.

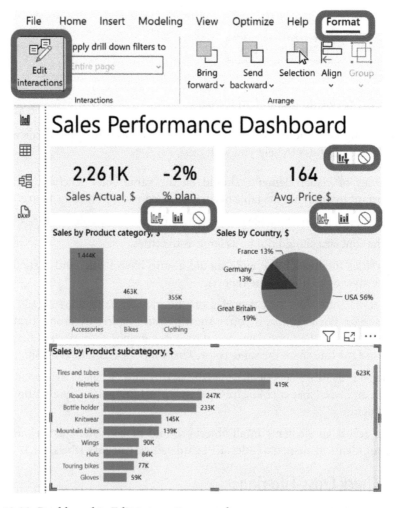

Figure 10-23. Dashboard in Edit interactions *mode*

On this note, we conclude the dashboard assembly. Of course, we've explored only a small portion of Power BI's capabilities for working with colors and styles, but it's time for us to move on to advanced visualizations.

Tips and Notes

A report page is usually divided into several zones, each designated for specific purposes and charts. These zones are arranged from top to bottom, descending from the general to the specific:

Header (level zero)
> This includes the title, navigation buttons, drop-down slicers, and compact buttons.

The first level—KPIs
> The rule is that we always start the dashboard with cards at the top, and only with cards.

The second level—visualized subtotals, trends
> Below the cards, in the upper half of the workspace, we place high-level visualizations. These visuals also serve as filters.

The third level—details
> Here, we present more granular data, usually in tables with conditional formatting. However, belonging to the third level is determined not by the form (chart or table) but by the content.

Step-by-step guide for a dashboard:

1. Place KPI cards on top.
2. Define the workspace grid and configure backgrounds.
3. Adjust the background.
4. Customize the color theme.
5. Check cross-filtering.

Download the *.pbix* file with customized visuals (*https://oreil.ly/n7LlI*).

---

1. On the timeline, both the y-axis labels and the data labels are displayed. Which of the following statements is correct?

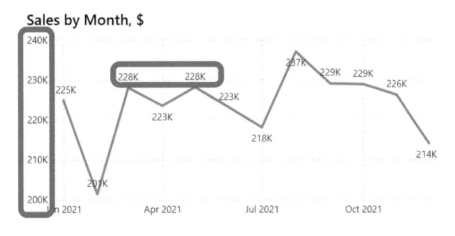

Sales by Month, $

A. The y-axis is unnecessary; it needs to be removed.

B. The data labels are unnecessary; they need to be removed.

C. No errors; the axis and labels are needed.

2. The category labels don't fit on the bar chart. How do we fix this?

Sales by Product category, $

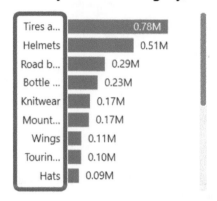

A. Increase the size of the chart so that category names are fully visible.

B. Expand the y-axis, increasing the maximum width to 50%.

C. Adjust word wrapping to multiple lines.

3. Where should the legend appear on a pie chart?

A

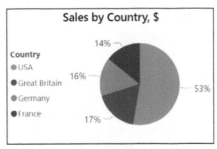

B

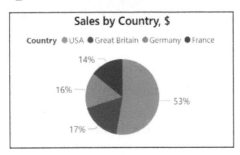

C

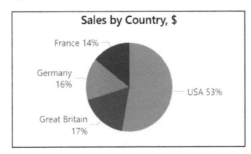

A. On the left, as we read the chart diagonally from left to right and top to bottom.

B. At the top, as we have a rule that we read from top to bottom.

C. Disable the legend and move the category labels to the chart.

4. Find the error in the treemap chart.

Sales by Month and Product category

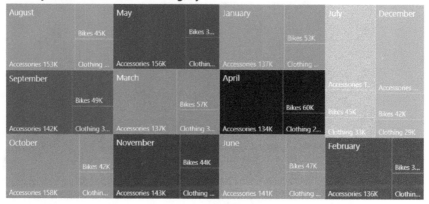

A. The months are arranged incorrectly; they need to be ordered.

B. The data labels should be converted to percentages because the treemap shows structure.

C. The treemap is chosen incorrectly; in this case, we need a different type of chart.

5. The table has too many indicators in the Sales column. How can we quickly convert values to thousands?

Product category	Sales, $
⊞ **Accessories**	1,719,415.00
⊟ **Bikes**	557,955.00
Mountain bikes	165,261.00
Road bikes	288,769.00
Touring bikes	103,925.00
⊞ **Clothing**	404,748.00
Total	2,682,118.00

A. Create a new measure where the value is divided by 1,000.

B. Expand *Specific column* → select the column in *Apply settings to* → change *Value decimal places*.

C. There is no option for this. We should divide this value in the data source.

Answers

1. **The correct answer is C.**

   Answer A is incorrect because, in this case, the axis scale has been adjusted so that it starts at 200K instead of 0. The y-axis should be displayed so that the user understands that the increase and decline on the line chart do not correspond to the actual scale.

   Answer B is incorrect because, for a timeline, it is preferable to display data labels for ease of perception. Without them, one has to mentally draw lines to the y-axis, which is inconvenient.

   Answer C is correct because in this case, both types of labels are necessary. The y-axis is necessary because it does not start at zero, and data labels are necessary for ease of perception.

2. **The correct answer is B.**

   Answer A may be a particular solution, when we have space to enlarge the chart. Usually the workspace on the dashboard is limited, and a defined grid may restrict us from changing the size of the chart.

   Answer B is correct. By increasing the maximum width of the y-axis, you can provide more space for displaying text inside the column chart, which can be useful in the case of long category names.

   Answer C is incorrect because splitting the category names into two lines will alter the thickness of some bars and make the chart look messy.

3. **The correct answer is C.**

   Answer A is incorrect because it is hard to correlate the pie slice with a small colored dot in the legend.

   Answer B is incorrect for the same reason, even if the legend is placed on top.

   Answer C is correct. A more efficient option would be to disable the legend and display category labels next to their respective sectors on the chart. This reduces the need to match the legend and the chart, making the information perception more intuitive.

4. **The correct answer is C.**

   Answer A is irrelevant because a treemap chart is not used for timeline visualization. There is no point in improving an incorrectly chosen chart.

   Answer B is also irrelevant for the same reason.

   Answer C is correct. For timeline visualization, we always use a line chart, which displays the flow of time in the most familiar way. Remember: time always flows from left to right.

5. **The correct answer is B.**

Answer A is too complex; it can be simplified.

Answer B is correct. Splitting the indicator in the table settings will provide a convenient data display in thousands without actually changing the original data.

Answer C is incorrect because such an option exists in Power BI, and using it is quite straightforward.

Trusted Advanced Visuals

As you'll recall, we worked with simple bar charts, pie charts, line graphs, and tables in Part I. In Part II, we'll introduce you to more sophisticated visuals, which we use extensively in our corporate reporting. In Part III, we'll discuss even more complicated visuals that, while having a wow factor, also have the potential to be confusing for or misunderstood by the audience.

Let's start by looking at simpler visuals and gradually move to more complex ones, which will require meticulous data preparation:

- Funnel charts
- Maps
- Tornado charts
- Waterfall charts
- Bullet charts
- Gantt charts
- Sankey charts
- Advanced KPI cards

Some of these charts are relatively easy to build, which is why beginners often find them appealing. However, it is crucial to understand the specific purposes of each chart and use them accordingly. For example, beginners commonly make the mistake of using a funnel chart to display data rankings, which is incorrect as it distorts the true meaning of the data.

Other visuals require the user to prepare data in a specialized format designed exactly for that visualization. It requires time and effort to ensure the data table is structured appropriately for constructing particular charts in Power BI. For instance, while a waterfall chart in Power BI may visually resemble its Excel counterpart, the underlying data must undergo a distinct transformation process.

There are three ways in Power BI to add an advanced chart to a report:

Use the default set of visuals.
Some of the charts in Part II can be added to the report directly from the *Visualization* pane. Unlike classic bar charts and line graphs, they differ in configuration parameters and source data requirements. We will show you how to make such charts clear for every business user.

Download a custom visual from the AppSource gallery.
Some items will be downloaded from the Microsoft visuals marketplace. In these cases, we will talk about the differences between variants of the same chart to help you understand the benefits and drawbacks of each and learn how to choose the right one for your task and how to configure specific parameters.

Design your own custom visual.
You can develop custom visuals if there are none in the gallery for your task. Actually, we try to adapt existing solutions instead of reinventing the wheel. As you'll see in our example of Multi-Target KPI in Chapter 18, our team developed a new visual, because existing charts didn't meet project requirements. And we will show you how to do it.

Maybe you have already used some of the charts in this list intuitively in your reports, and you were doing well. For example, you can skip the step-by-step setup of the map (it is really quite easy) and read only about the drawbacks and limitations of this visual. As a result, this will help you avoid making logical mistakes.

Each chapter goes from simple features to more complex ones, and at the same time from the most commonly used to rare, more exotic visuals. You can read them in any order and use this book as a manual in the future. When a new task arises, take it and find the right chart and remember the right fine-tuning steps.

OK, ready? Here we go.

CHAPTER 11

Funnel Chart

For the practice, please download a special dataset (*https://oreil.ly/a0X2H*).

The funnel chart is extremely popular in business reports. For years it was unavailable in Excel, so having it in a report could mean that you were using advanced business intelligence tools. Today it is available in the latest versions of Microsoft Office, and we can publicly use it, but Power BI has more options for creating brilliant reports with it.

The funnel chart displays sequential processes, where at every step the quantity is reduced. In Figure 11-1, you'll see a good example of how the sales process progresses from initial contact with the client to presentations and negotiations prior to the deal, and finally to signing a contract.

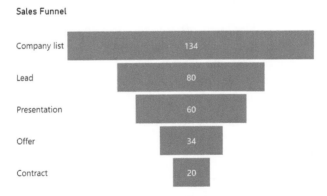

Figure 11-1. Sales process displayed on the funnel chart

You can see that out of 134 clients on the list, our sales department has signed contracts with 20 of them; in other words, the conversion rate is around 15%. For such a simple chart, we can manage without Power BI. However, Power BI provides a more interactive way for us to look deeper into this data.

In Figure 11-2, you'll see a section of the dashboard where we have a column chart with the number of contracts by salespersons, with the funnel underneath it. If we click on a certain salesperson's column, the funnel will be filtered by their data.

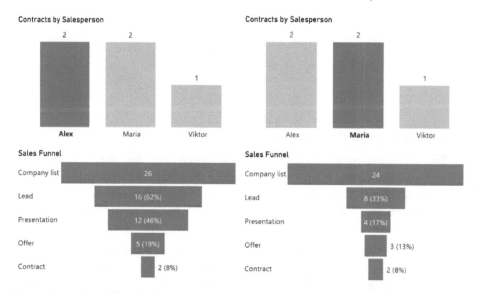

Figure 11-2. Cross-filtration between column chart and funnel (filtering by Alex on the left and Maria on the right)

At first glance, Alex and Maria's scores are the same: give or take 25 companies on the list and 2 contracts—but there is a significant difference in conversion at the intermediate sales stages. Alex can generate leads from 62% of companies, whereas Maria gets only 33%. We can see "bottlenecks" in her sales funnel. And we realize that we would boost sales if we increase her conversion rate at the lead stage.

In this example, we got such insight, first, because we used cross-filtering charts, and second because the conversion markers were displayed on the funnel at once, instead of estimating it by eye.

Although it is easy to build a funnel in Power BI, you can still make mistakes in the design. We'll provide checklists to show how to correctly set up your funnel chart.

Step-by-Step Guide for Funnel Chart

A funnel chart is also commonly used to show the recruitment process, from initial responses to interviews and finally through to recruitment (Figure 11-3). Similar to sales, it is important to track conversion rates at stages and realize where we are losing applicants.

From this example, we'll break it down step-by-step and show how to improve the default selection funnel chart. Building a funnel generally lies in setting the correct sizes of the chart and data labels—all inscriptions should be completely visible. Figure 11-3 shows how this visual will look in Power BI by default and after five setup steps.

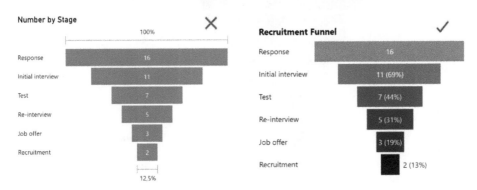

Figure 11-3. A comparison of funnel charts: default (left); after configuring (right)

In the left picture, which is automatically built by Power BI using the data we have entered, the percentages are shown only for the first and last element (100% and 12.5%); the other ones do not have this data. Furthermore, the category labels are too small and hard to read. In the step-by-step guide we are going to fix these shortcomings, add color-coding, and learn how to make the version on the right.

Step 1: Set the Conversion Display

The funnel chart in Power BI displays two conversion rate labels by default: 100% at the first stage, and the result of the entire process on the last. But it is unclear what happened in the transition from one stage to another. To see conversion at each stage of the process, we will add it to all values in data labels.

There are two options: a percentage of the first or a percentage of the previous one. Either the share of the test is from the first-stage response, or the share of the test is from the primary interview of the previous stage. The choice depends on what is more important for you to understand: what percentage of customers or employees have reached the current stage of the funnel, or what the conversion rate is between stages. We will choose a percentage of the first because it is important for the recruiting process to understand the proportion at each stage of the initial number of applicants.

Open the section *Data labels → Options* and choose *Data value, percent of first* in *Label contents*, as in Figure 11-4.

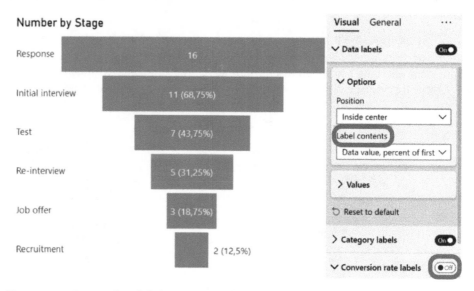

Figure 11-4. Setting data labels options and turning off Conversion rate labels

Conversion labels appear by default. Now they have become redundant, as we added the value of conversion at each stage to the data labels. We will turn off their display by turning off a tick in the relevant section (*Conversion rate labels*).

Step 2: Set Values

Go on to the *Data labels* section and move on to *Values*, then adjust the following components to suit your needs:

Font
    As usual up to 12 pt.

Color
    We don't usually recommend changing the default color. The point is that if the data label does not fit in the short column (as it does with the job offer), it is displayed on the right side with a white background. And the color automatically changes from white to gray. If we make it light blue, for example, in this situation it would be hard to read on a white background. But if we have a light column color, the dark text will appear universally.

Display units—Auto

In our case we don't change anything, but if you have thousands or millions, then convert to those units.

Value decimal places—0

Likewise, we have integers here, but, for thousands and millions, you may need to add some. For example, if 12.5K goes into the funnel, that leaves 0.7K on the way out.

Percentage decimal places

This option will appear when *Label contents → Data value, percent of first* (or *previous*) is on. By default there will be two digits, but we will remove all of them by specifying *0* (see Figure 11-5). Of course, excess is never good. But since we already have two indicators in the data label, every extra digit will be more difficult to read.

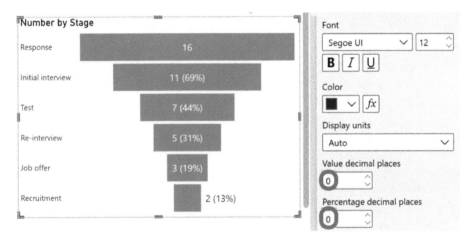

Figure 11-5. Displaying conversion label (in the parentheses) with zero decimal places

Step 3: Display Category Labels Without Shortening

According to the general checklist from Part I, we increase the category captions to 12 pt. However, for long captions, we cut off the words. In our case this is not critical, as we get the idea, but sometimes it is important.

We will remind you that for bar charts in Chapter 3, we solved this problem with the "maximum width" parameter, where we set the space for the category block to 50% of the width of the chart area. Unfortunately, there is no such parameter for the funnel. We have three ways of solving this problem:

Stretch the chart by width

This is the simpler way, and appropriate if you have enough space on the dashboard.

Reduce the category names

Sometimes titles contain three to four words, and you can keep the one key word that conveys the idea. Or you can combine several words into an acronym (but only if it is clear to your audience).

Use a text box for category labels

If the first two ways don't work well for you, there is a third, more radical option: disable category labels and replace them with a text box. *Caution!* This will work only if the number of stages will not change when you filter the data.

Press the *Text box* button on the *Insert* block of the *Home* tab in the top menu, seen in Figure 11-6. The text box will then appear in the working area.

Figure 11-6. How to insert a text box

Then fill the text box with the names of the funnel steps, as shown in Figure 11-7. Format the text using the rules we discussed in step 1: set conversion display. The settings window of the text box will appear near the visual when you highlight it. Set the text color by pressing button *A*.

Pay attention: settings are applied only if the text is highlighted.

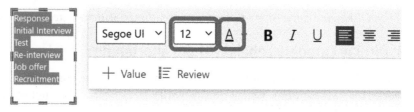

Figure 11-7. Font configuration in text box

Next you can turn off the tick at the section *Category labels*, as shown in Figure 11-8. Now the labels will duplicate information in the text box, so they aren't necessary.

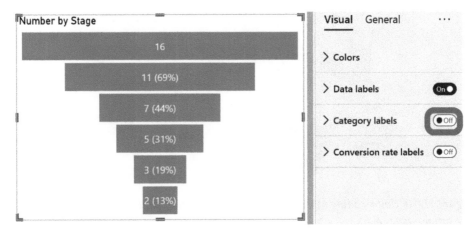

Figure 11-8. Disabling category labels

Now we will combine the text box with the chart, where category labels correspond to funnel lines (Figure 11-9). As a result, the visual becomes more compact, but category labels are displayed completely and without shortening at the same time.

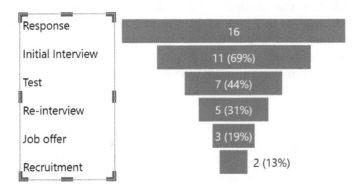

Figure 11-9. Category labels by text box

Step 4: Set Color-Coding

Color-coding is an optional step—most often all stages of a funnel chart are designed in a single color. But sometimes, on a dashboard, we need one indicator to be the same color everywhere. For example, in the dashboard in Figure 11-10, we use color to see how the client "matures" (like a tomato in the garden), as the green lead gradually "warms up" to a red contract. And in this case, the number of contracts is shown in red in the column chart, in the funnel stage, and in the corresponding trend graph on the right. This is an exception from the general rule (using red only for negative), but it's acceptable in this specific context.

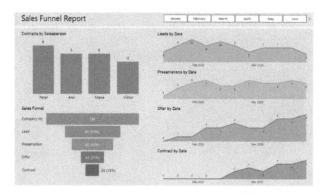

Figure 11-10. Color-coding at the dashboard: column chart and line charts correspond to the funnel stage colors

But be careful using a lot of bright colors! It may overload your report. It is better not to paint the funnel with all the colors of the rainbow; instead, colors should correspond to indicators on the other charts (leads – green, presentation – yellow, etc.). A compromise may be a gradient scale within a single basic color.

Activate a tick near the inscription *Show all* in the setting section *Colors* to set colors for each stage, as in Figure 11-11. You may manually use a method of color "intensifying" from light tone to dark or vice versa: select the intermediate colors from the palette. This will visually highlight the result. Be careful when selecting shades, so that you don't end up with a too-light color that blends with the white of the data labels.

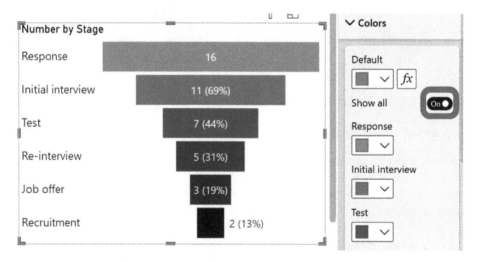

Figure 11-11. Customizing funnel element colors

Step 5: Title and "Text Box Trick" Again

Recall that we are renaming the title of the chart according to its meaning. And instead of the default *Number by Stage* (Figure 11-11), we write `Recruitment Funnel` and align it on the left side as shown in Figure 11-12. But there are some nuances for perfectionists at this stage, too.

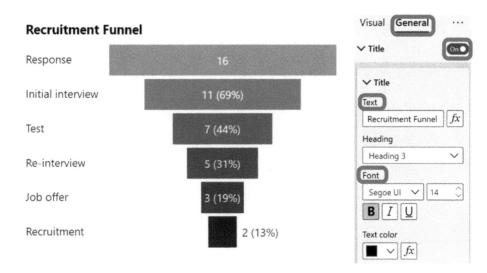

Figure 11-12. Chart title formatting

If you increase the chart size so that category labels fit completely, it will take a lot of space on a dashboard—there is not always an opportunity for this. If you are limited to available space, use the life hack: category labels of a funnel chart can be taken out of chart limits and placed in a text box (Figure 11-9).

Category labels are placed as necessary, but another problem appeared—the chart title moved down, and now it isn't aligned to the left or the center (Figure 11-13).

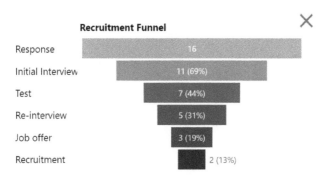

Figure 11-13. Chart title is not aligned to the left or in the center

We will turn off a tick at the section *Title* to fix it. Instead of the standard title, we will add one more text box in which we will type the title `Recruitment Funnel`. Now we need to set it by already known rules: size 14, alignment on the left.

As always, it was not without problems—there is no Segoe UI Semibold among the available fonts for the text box. Therefore, we will turn back on the tick for the *Title* section by highlighting this field, on the *General* tab on the side, and set up this title, as for any other chart. (Figure 11-14).

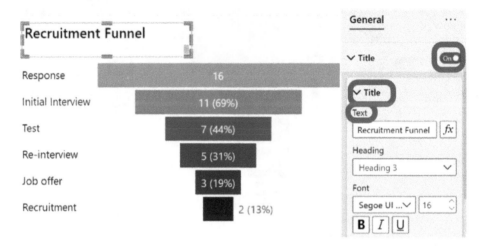

Figure 11-14. Chart title through the Title *section of the text box*

It remains only to align all three blocks with each other: the chart title, the category labels, and the visual. So we get a compact version of the funnel chart, which does not take up much space on the dashboard (Figure 11-15).

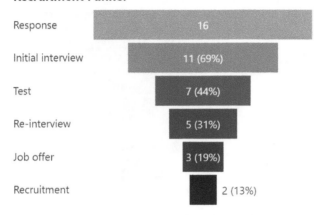

Recruitment Funnel

Response	16
Initial interview	11 (69%)
Test	7 (44%)
Re-interview	5 (31%)
Job offer	3 (19%)
Recruitment	2 (13%)

Figure 11-15. Final customized funnel

Possible Mistake

So, this is a beautiful funnel. New analysts are often tempted to use it as soon as possible in a report, to show advanced visualization. Eventually, the funnel is used to show an ordinary ranking. But there is no conversion process from one product to another, which distorts the meaning.

Figure 11-16 shows two options for displaying the signed deals, depending on the advertising channel those clients came from. But the case with the funnel is not correct, because the logic of its structure lies in the fact that each successive element follows from the previous one and is part of the funnel. According to the chart on the top, 19 deals by radio advertising are a part of the 25 deals made by TV. And the 16 direct mail deals are part of the same 19, which came from radio. It's not so! You should show classic rankings here, and the best option for that is a typical bar chart, as shown on the bottom in Figure 11-16.

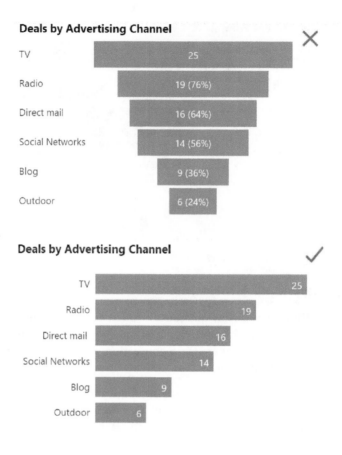

Figure 11-16. Incorrect display of ranking with the funnel (on the top) and correct display using the bar chart (on the bottom)

Keep in mind that our aim is to show the data clearly, removing everything redundant. Less is more.

Tips and Notes

A funnel chart is a comprehensive visual used to show a process that includes several stages, when there is an elimination at each stage. Do not use this visual if you need to display the structure or rating—this is a common mistake.

Checklist for setting up a funnel chart:

1. Set the conversion display in the data labels. Switch off "default" conversion rate labels.

2. Adjust the font: increase to 12 points. Convert to thousands or millions for larger values. Remove decimals from the conversions in parentheses.

3. Increase the font size for the categories. If the names won't fit, try one of the following: stretch the width of the chart, shorten the category names, or display them as a separate text box.

4. Specify colors for funnel bars (process stages). Be careful with the graphic palette so that the diagram does not appear too mottled.

5. If you have used the text box trick for the categories, you need to apply it to the chart title as well.

Download the *.pbix* file with customized visuals (*https://oreil.ly/-TBXW*).

CHAPTER 12

Map

For this chapter, use the same practice dataset (*https://oreil.ly/DataViz_dataset*) as for Part I.

Dashboards often contain information about sites on different continents or in different countries, regions, or cities. With maps, managers can control, for example, the geography of sales, deliveries, or purchases. There are several maps in the standard set of Power BI visuals; of the simple ones, there are two options:

Map (bubble map)
This displays values as bubbles; the higher the value, the larger the bubble.

Filled map
This displays regions and countries that have data filling their area. But there is no qualitative difference in filling.

There are also options for integration with Azure Maps and ArcGIS, but this is mostly for corporate projects. AppSource has many other maps with different capabilities and adaptations for certain regions (for example, provinces of China).

The map in Figure 12-1 illustrates how sales are spread across the regions of Europe. As you can see, there is a focus of sales around Paris, but there are almost equal sales across the regions of the country. Shipments to England stand out in terms of scale compared with the rest of the European regions, but there are no sales in the UK. Sales in Germany are uniform and have a few dispersed centers throughout the country.

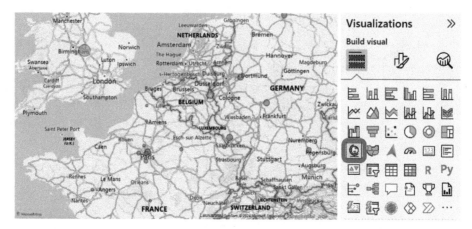

Figure 12-1. Map to illustrate sales in different regions of Europe; the bigger the bubble, the more sales in the region. Bubble color represents different product categories.

You can use a map to show their results if your company has many sales outlets, warehouses, or call centers in different geographical locations. Below, we will explain how to allocate data fields in Power BI for scaling and design this visual intelligently.

Step-by-Step Guide for Setting Up a Map

You can create a map on the dashboard in Power BI and design it visually. To do this, simply follow the five-step instructions.

Step 1: Allocate Data Fields

To ensure that the data on the map is displayed correctly, make sure that the fields with them are positioned correctly. Add fields on the *Create visual element* tab:

Location
> Here we move the field with the names of the cities, regions, or addresses (in our example, it is *State*).

Legend
> Here we place the field with the data of the top level of the geographical hierarchy (in our case, it is *Country*).

Bubble size
> This is for the numerical value (in our case, it is *Sales fact*).

In general, if you get something strange instead of a map (an empty map or incomprehensible pie charts), it is often due to mixing up the *Location* and *Legend* fields. Delete them and start over:

- Put the field with the names of the cities, regions, or addresses into *Location*.
- Then add the numerical value into *Bubble size*.
- *Legend* is optional; your map may have no legend.

In Figure 12-2, you can see the proper placement of the data fields.

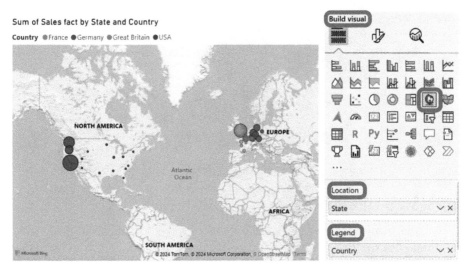

Figure 12-2. Proper placement of the data fields will show classic bubbles on the map instead of pie charts

Step 2: Add and Set Up Category Labels

This map can be zoomed, and it is not always clear what the bubbles refer to. To fix this, you can add the names of the regions to the bubbles. For this purpose, activate the check box for the *Category labels* section and adjust their appearance (Figure 12-3):

Font
> Increase to 10–12 pt.

Color
> Leave it white by default, because we use a dark gray background.

Background
> Leave it on, so that the labels do not get lost in the colored background of the map and bubbles.

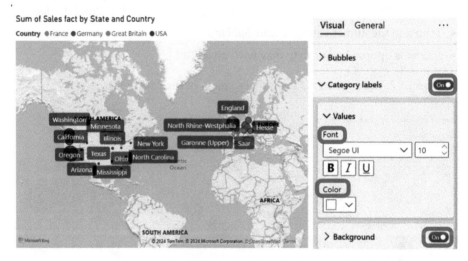

Figure 12-3. Region names can be configured under the Category labels *section*

Step 3: Set Up the Bubble Size

When a user is zooming the map, small bubbles often get lost. To avoid this, increase their minimum size from the default 10 points to 12. You can do this in the *Bubbles* section (Figure 12-4).

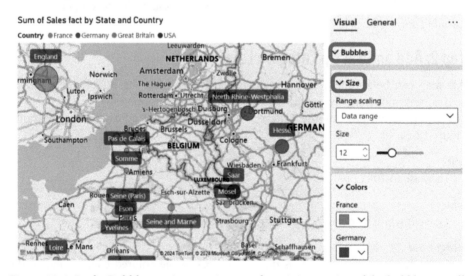

Figure 12-4. In the Bubbles *settings section, set the minimum size of the bubbles as well as their colors*

It would be enough in our example to make the bubbles visible at any scale. In your own projects, you should find the golden mean on your own. All other bubbles will automatically be enlarged based on the given indicator (in our case, it is the revenue volume).

In the section *Colors*, you can change the color for the conditional formatting to achieve a greater visual distinction between countries. For example, France is blue, Germany is purple, and Great Britain is orange.

Step 4: Set Map Parameters

For business dashboards, avoid choosing maps in saturated colors—it detracts from the data. Select the style of the visual element in *Map settings* → *Style*, as you'll see in Figure 12-5. In our case, we will select *Light* from the suggested options.

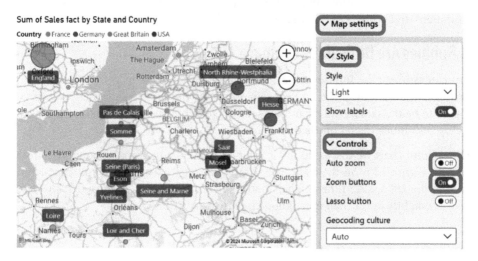

Figure 12-5. Select map style and add zoom buttons under Map settings

If you have worldwide sales, in the *Controls* section you can leave a tick near *Auto zoom*—so you will see the full map at any updates.

If you need to track only a part of the map—for example, Europe—you should uncheck *Auto zoom*. Once you zoom the map view to Europe, it will remain on your dashboard; you won't need to zoom it again. However, even after autoscaling is switched off, you can still drill down and move to other sectors of the map as required. Some users are not aware that the map can be zoomed in using the mouse wheel. You can add zoom buttons for easy usability by ticking the box next to the relevant item.

Step 5: Give a Clear Headline

Your map is almost ready; one final touch remains. Now, give the chart a clear name and set it up in the same way as you have already done with the other charts:

1. Under *Name*, replace the automatic wording with an understandable title.
2. Leave the default font size of 14 points.
3. Specify left alignment.

Your bubble map setup is complete!

Possible Mistakes

Before you start creating and setting up a map on your dashboard, review the limitations and options of this visual element that can cause mistakes.

1. Bubbles Are Difficult to Compare

You can estimate the indicators on the map only by the size of the bubbles, but this estimate will not always be correct. For example, bubbles with similar values may appear to be the same. And even if we see a large bubble next to a small one, we don't realize how much bigger one is than another.

The column chart we discussed in Chapter 1 could do a better job than a map in this case. In Figure 12-6 on the right, the data is perfectly clear. There, you can see that sales in the US are 2.5 times higher than in Germany or the UK, and that in France they are slightly lower than in neighboring European countries.

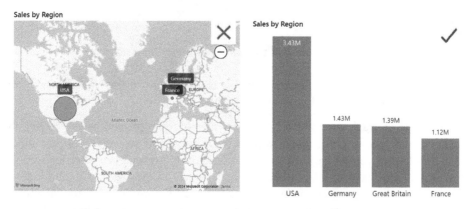

Figure 12-6. On the left are sales volumes in different countries on a map; on the right is the same data on a column chart in a more accurate format for comparison

2. Data Labels Don't Display Values

Maps also lose out to other visuals in informativeness. You can add only the category names (countries, regions, cities), but you cannot display numerical values. In Figure 12-7, you can see that there is not even a *Data labels* option in the settings panel.

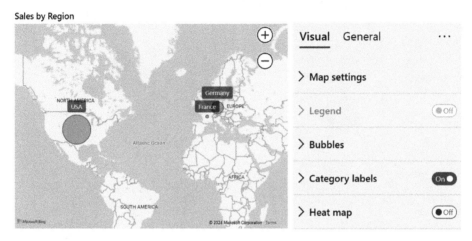

Figure 12-7. Power BI does not allow exact numerical values to be displayed on the map

3. Appearance of Unnecessary Pie Charts

If you place data fields in Power BI incorrectly, the program will add pie charts to the map. Many people are happy about it and try to display the sales structure like this. We do not recommend using this technique in interactive dashboards. Pie charts are overlapping in Europe (Figure 12-8), so all this turns into a color mess.

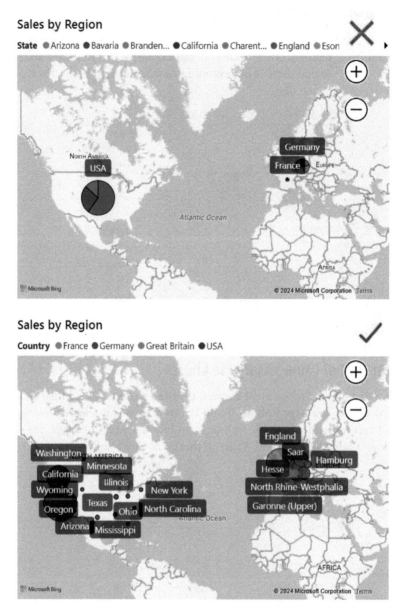

Figure 12-8. On the top is a map with incorrectly positioned data fields; on the bottom is a more informative version with classic bubbles

As you can see in Figure 12-8 on the top, the legend of the pie chart is placed above the map instead of next to it. As a result, it is not clear which region belongs to which sector. Decide on classic bubbles in the same colors as the top-level geographical data (in our case, it's the country).

4. Mistakes in the Placement of Objects

Due to the similarity of names, the map does not always correctly relate the region to its location. Therefore, for instance, some regions in France may be located in Romania, or Washington may be listed south of California. To avoid this, it is better to add geographical coordinates as well as the names of the regions to the data to avoid distorting the representation. Figure 12-9 shows how to add coordinates to a map.

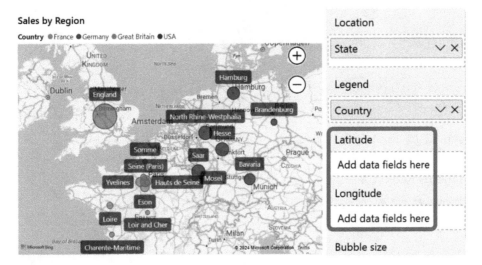

Figure 12-9. You can add the exact coordinates of objects in the settings panel, in the Latitude *and* Longitude *rows*

Now that we're acquainted with the features of the visual element, let's move on to the building and design. In Figure 12-10, we can see the map default. But in Figure 12-11, the map is quite different after adjustment.

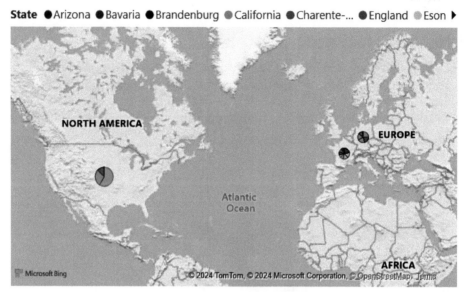

Sum of Sales fact by Country and State

State ●Arizona ●Bavaria ●Brandenburg ●California ●Charente-... ●England ●Eson ▶

Figure 12-10. The default map

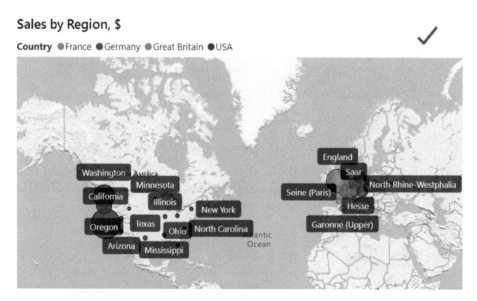

Sales by Region, $

Country ●France ●Germany ●Great Britain ●USA

Figure 12-11. The map after configuration

Tips and Notes

We confess that we don't like to use maps on dashboards. They tend to take up a lot of space and are usually not very informative for financial reporting and executive dashboards. But it might be effective for operational delivery monitoring and customer location correlations.

When choosing a map for your dashboard, keep the real business need in mind; don't choose the map option just for the visual variety.

Checklist for setting up a map:

1. Correctly position the fields for the map construction.
2. Add and set up the category labels.
3. Set the minimum size of the bubbles so that they are visible at any map scale. Adjust the colors of the bubbles.
4. Select a simplified map base and neutral style, and adjust the scaling.
5. Edit the name of the chart to make it clear and easy to understand.

Download the *.pbix* file with customized visuals (*https://oreil.ly/ZkBSR*).

CHAPTER 13

Tornado Chart

For the practice, please download a special dataset (*https://oreil.ly/KUB6h*).

A tornado chart looks similar to a funnel divided into two parts. One indicator is displayed on the left, and another one on the right. A tornado chart provides a comparison of two indicators, with an emphasis not within a category but on the correlation as a whole. Tornado charts help you to compare the values of two indicators and visually evaluate the impact of one of them on the other.

In this chapter we will analyze sales data by managers and cities:

- Revenue (synonym of sales actual)
- Sales target
- Profit (synonym of margin actual)
- Quantity (units sold)

In Figure 13-1, you can see that the bigger the profit, the bigger the revenues.

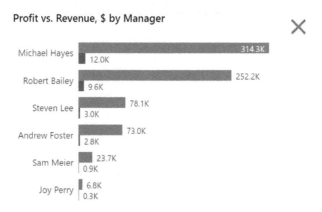

Profit vs. Revenue, $ by Manager

	Profit	Revenue
Michael Hayes	12.0K	314.3K
Robert Bailey	9.6K	252.2K
Steven Lee	3.0K	78.1K
Andrew Foster	2.8K	73.0K
Sam Meier	0.9K	23.7K
Joy Perry	0.3K	6.8K

Figure 13-1. Tornado chart displays correlation between profit and revenue

We could show the same data on the bar chart (see Figure 13-2), but when comparing data of different scales, the bars with smaller indicator values (in our case, profit) can almost disappear, and the true meaning of the chart gets lost.

Profit vs. Revenue, $ by Manager ✕

Michael Hayes	314.3K	12.0K
Robert Bailey	252.2K	9.6K
Steven Lee	78.1K	3.0K
Andrew Foster	73.0K	2.8K
Sam Meier	23.7K	0.9K
Joy Perry	6.8K	0.3K

Figure 13-2. Comparison of two indicators of different scales with the bar chart could be misleading

The tornado chart has the advantage of allowing us to compare indicators with different units of measurement, such as sales in dollars and in units (refer to Figure 13-3). When we need to compare data with vastly different orders of magnitude (for example, millions of dollars and a relatively small quantity of product units), it can be challenging to do so with standard bar charts. However, the tornado chart can be customized in a way that visually compares seemingly incomparable numbers, making the comparison intuitive.

Figure 13-3. Comparison of two indicators with different units

The tornado is always sorted from larger to smaller by one of the indicators; in Figure 13-3, it is units. This chart looks like a funnel, but it is a bit asymmetrical, and that's why it is called the tornado. The chart in Figure 13-4 represents the margin actual and quantity by managers, but it looks totally asymmetrical. This means that there is no direct correlation between indicators.

Manager	Margin Actual, $	Quantity, units
R. Hayes	29,929	327
M. Bailey	24,022	1,319
N. Lee	7,440	259
A. Foster	6,950	551
S. Meier	2,260	132
J. Perry	650	12

Figure 13-4. There's no direct correlation between margin and quantity

The chart you see in Figure 13-4 is technically correct; there are no mistakes in sorting. Margin is just weakly dependent on the number of units sold. Bailey is the first in the quantity of units sold, but second in revenue, while Hayes earned $29.9K by selling only 327 units.

Possible Mistake

You may feel a strong urge to quickly incorporate a custom visual into your report and showcase the comparison between the actual sales (*Actual*) and the target set by the company for the sales manager (*Target*) using the tornado chart. However, this approach could lead to a semantic error. Take a look at Figures 13-5 and 13-6, where we attempted to replicate such an approach.

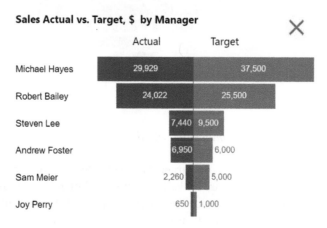

Figure 13-5. Don't use tornado charts to compare Target *and* Actual

Figure 13-6. Correct representation of Target *and* Actual *sales value comparison*

Of course, we can see a general trend that the bigger the plan, the bigger the fact (will it always be so?), or even recognize (by comparing the numbers in the data labels) an outlier where Foster has fact values that are bigger than targets. But is the tornado the correct chart selection there?

Tornado charts allow us to make a visual analysis of sensitivity between two indicators, answering the main question: are the changes in one indicator leading to the corresponding changes in another? Usually it is not the question we ask about plan/fact performance. Generally, we need to compare fact versus target values for each manager to answer two main questions about the data:

- Which manager achieved target values?
- Which manager performs better (is close to the target)?

We can't do that visually with the tornado chart because the fact and target bars are in opposite directions and it is very difficult to compare the size of the bars by their length only. That's why we recommend you use an ordinary bar chart in this case. Although less glamorous, Figure 13-6 displays the meaning of the data correctly, without distortion.

Therefore, don't try to use a tornado chart to make a comparison between two indicators for each category, "point by point." It is misleading and very difficult to use. However, there is an advanced alternative for plan-fact comparison: the bullet chart. You will learn more about it in Chapter 15. Until then, let's see where we can get tornadoes and other nonstandard charts.

AppSource Gallery

In Chapter 11, about the funnel, we used a chart from the basic set in the *Visualizations* panel. This time we'll go beyond and take it from the AppSource gallery—a marketplace extension for Power BI.

To download a new visual from the AppSource gallery, as you'll see in Figure 13-7, click the button with three dots under the list of chart icons and select *Get more visuals* from the drop-down menu on the *Build visual* tab.

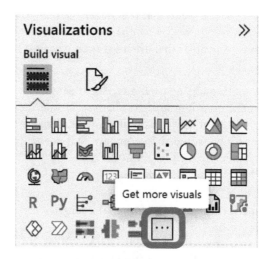

Figure 13-7. Adding a new visual from the gallery

Power BI will require authorization to connect to the gallery. You will need an account. These options are available as part of the Power BI free license. You will be redirected to a window with a lot of charts. It has a list of headings at the top (for time, comparison, etc.), but it's easier to use the search on the top right. Type **tornado** in the search bar (see Figure 13-8) and you'll get the only option available today (new tornadoes may be available by the time you read this chapter).

Click on the icon and choose *Add*; then, a new icon appears in the bottom row of the *Visualizations* section. Other charts you would add to your report will also appear there.

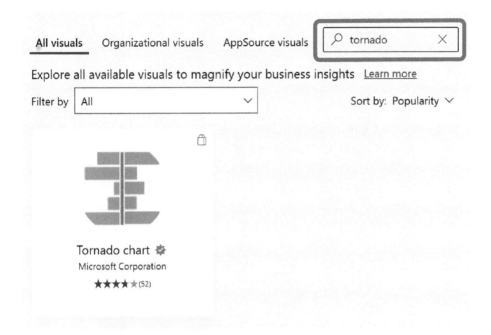

All visuals   Organizational visuals   AppSource visuals   🔍 tornado   ✕

Explore all available visuals to magnify your business insights Learn more

Filter by | All ⌄   Sort by: Popularity ⌄

Tornado chart 🏅
Microsoft Corporation
★★★★☆(52)

Figure 13-8. Search for **tornado** *in the list of custom visuals*

Step-by-Step Guide for Tornado Chart

We have two ways of creating a tornado: using the custom visual we just downloaded from the gallery, or turning an ordinary table into a tornado using conditional formatting. First, let's design using a ready-made template from the gallery.

To create a tornado, you need a category and two measures; select them from the *Build visual* section in the *Visualizations* panel, as you'll see in Figure 13-9, and move them to the empty rows below the chart icons.

Group

The field of values that we will analyze; this will be the y-axis. In our case this field is *Manager*, i.e., the names of employees whose results we want to analyze.

Values

Add *Sum of Margin Actual* and *Sum of Turnover* fields. Only two indicators can be placed here, since the point of a tornado is to compare two values.

You get the primary version of the chart (see Figure 13-10), which we will design and edit.

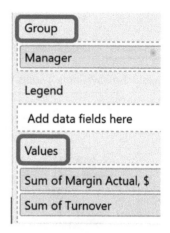

Figure 13-9. Data fields for tornado

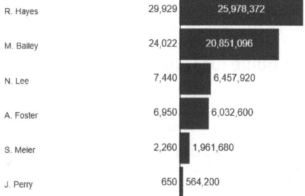

Figure 13-10. Default view of the tornado chart custom visual by Microsoft

Step 1: Set Up Data Labels

As is the case with most other charts, these parameters are configured in the *Data Labels* section, as you'll see in Figure 13-11:

Text size
    Increase to 12 pt.

Decimal Places
    Specify the number of places after the decimal point.

Display Units
    If you select *None*, the system determines the digit capacity by itself. We will choose *Thousands*.

Fill (inside/outside)
    This is the color of the numbers font. For the values inside we choose white, for outside, black.

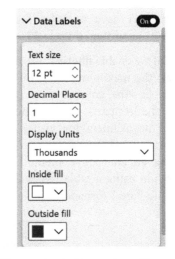

Figure 13-11. Customizing Data Labels

Step 2: Adjust the Values Axis

The *Margin Actual value* on our chart is much smaller than the *Turnover*, so the bars with margin are completely invisible. To fix it, we need to change the scale of the axis (Figure 13-12).

Figure 13-12. Default (left) X-Axis *settings must be fixed to show correct data scale (right)*

Go to the *X-Axis* section and set the maximum value for the indicator that has a smaller value. In our case we have *Turnover* in millions and *Margin* in thousands. That is why we set the maximum for the *Margin Actual* field as you'll see in Figure 13-13.

You don't have to enter the exact value of 29,929, just round it up to 30,000.

But if we enable filtering, e.g., choose data for a year, the maximum value we set earlier won't help us—the column *Sum of Margin Actual* (on the left part) will become too short again and inconvenient for visual comparison (see Figure 13-14). To solve the problem, we suggest using an alternative method of building the tornado using a table (we will talk about it in "Table-Based Tornado Chart" on page 209).

Figure 13-13. Setting maximum for X-Axis

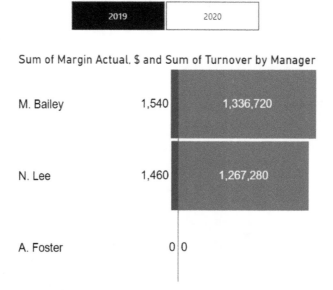

Figure 13-14. Even after applying a fix to axis scale settings, filtering of data could lead to unwanted results

Step 3: Set Up the Y-Axis—"Group" Parameter

The list of categories, or groups, placed vertically in a tornado chart can be referred to as the y-axis. This parameter is called *Group* for tornado, as you'll see in Figure 13-15. Let's set it up:

Color
Leave it black (or choose a color for the best legibility for your chart).

Text size
Increase to 12 pt, an optimal readable size for the chart labels.

Position
Leave it on the left (this is the recommended option for business dashboards, but other solutions are also possible).

By default, the tornado is always built in descending (or ascending) order of one of the values. If you want to change the sorting order, select the *Additional parameters* button marked with three dots above the upper right corner of the chart. Select *Sort axis* in the drop-down menu, where you specify the desired parameter and the type of sorting (see Figure 13-16).

Figure 13-15. Configuring Group parameters

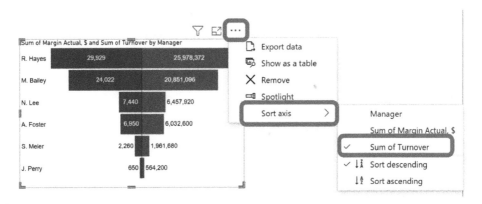

Figure 13-16. Setting up sorting order for the tornado chart

Step 4: Customize Legend and Title

There is no option to set up a legend on the tornado chart visual, and this creates some difficulties. Even if we type both indicator names in the title, it wouldn't be obvious which one is revenue or profit. Therefore, we have to create the legend manually.

The easiest way is to add a text box above the relevant elements. But this place on the chart is taken by its title. We have to disable it and create it manually using the same text box.

To create a new title and legend, switch to the *Formatting a visual element* section. On the *General* tab, disable the checkbox in the *Title* field (Figure 13-17).

Figure 13-17. Disable the visual title

In the top menu bar on the *Insert* tab, select the *Text box* item (Figure 13-18).

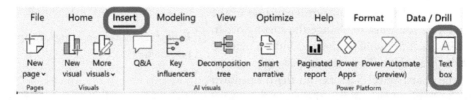

Figure 13-18. Insert a text box on the page

You will see a window where you can enter the text you want. We want to make three text boxes: two for bar headers, *Margin* and *Turnover*, and the field with the chart title. We manually place each text box in its proper place, simply by dragging and dropping:

- Block with the name of the chart—top left
- Margin block—above the columns with *Margin*
- Turnover block—above the columns with *Turnover*

To customize each text box, select it and specify the necessary parameters in the pop-up window:

Font
   Choose a font type. It is recommended to use a consistent font for all elements across all charts on the dashboard.

Size

Use 14 pt for titles and 12 pt for data labels. These are the recommended font sizes for standard dashboards, as they are the most readable.

Color

Leave it black by default.

Horizontal alignment

Leave it by default at the left edge.

After all settings are applied, we get the result you see in Figure 13-19.

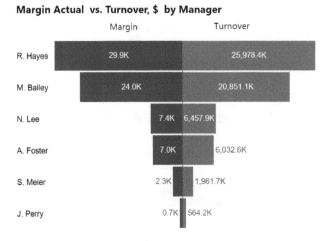

Figure 13-19. Tornado chart after all settings are applied

Limitations of Tornado Chart by Microsoft

We have managed to create an informative chart, but unfortunately, this is not always possible. This visual has limitations that can hinder obtaining a clear result in some cases. Let's explore these limitations and learn how to overcome them.

One data display unit for both parts

If we compare millions of dollars and the amount of sales in units, we have to show the data labels on both the right and left sides of the chart. As a result, we get huge nine-digit numbers separated by commas in the left-hand columns (see Figure 13-20).

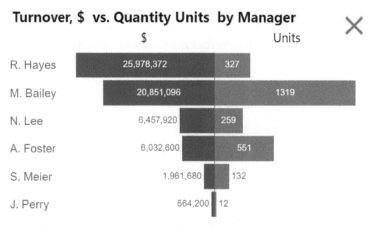

Figure 13-20. Too-long data labels for the Turnover, $

Violation of proportions

If we use a filter on the chart, initial settings of the maximum values of indicators can become too big or too small for the correct display of data. For example, the bars on the side with smaller values become unreadable (see Figure 13-21).

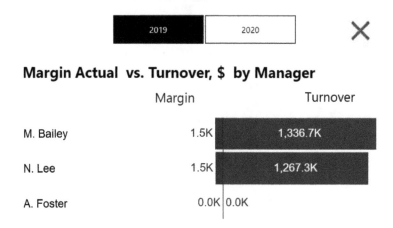

Figure 13-21. Too-short bars for Margin

Lack of legend

There is no such element for the tornado chart, although it is clearly necessary. We solved this problem by adding a text box. In the next part of this chapter, you will learn another way to display a legend.

Table-Based Tornado Chart

Another way of visualizing data in the form of a tornado is based on a conventionally formatted table. It will help you avoid the disadvantages mentioned in the previous section. In Chapter 7 we told you how to add a bar chart to cells, and now we'll show you how to take this idea further.

We will create a table on the page with the necessary data and edit it step-by-step. For the analysis, we will take the actual margin and the quantity of the units sold (Figure 13-22).

Manager	Sum of Margin Actual, $	Sum of Q-ty, units
A. Foster	6,950	551
J. Perry	650	12
M. Bailey	24,022	1,319
N. Lee	7,440	259
R. Hayes	29,929	327
S. Meier	2,260	132
Total	**71 251**	**2600**

Figure 13-22. Base table to be formatted as a tornado chart

Step 1: Set Conditional Formatting

In the *Cell elements* menu, activate the *Data bars* checkbox for each row of data. Enable sorting by one of the elements (in the example, by *Sum of Margin Actual, $*) by clicking on the column header in the table, as in Figure 13-23.

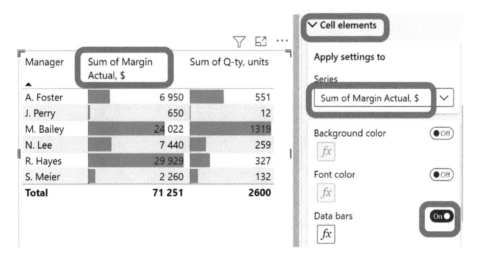

Figure 13-23. Set conditional formatting (Data bars) for the table columns

Step 2: Change the Left Bar Direction and the Bar Colors

In the same *Cell elements* section, select the column of data that is on the left (*Sum of Margin Actual, $*, in our case), and under the enabled *Data bars* parameter, click the *fx* button. In the new window, we can change the color of the columns and specify bar direction *Right to left* (see Figure 13-24).

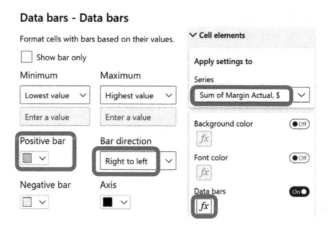

Figure 13-24. Set bar colors for the data column on the left—Sum of Margin

Do the same for the column of data that is on the right (*Sum of Q-ty, units*): select the column, and under the enabled *Data bars* parameter, click the *fx* button. We don't need to change bar direction: it is the default *Left to right*. One thing we should do: change the positive color to lighter, so that the values are easier to read. Finally, you will get a table with data bars in the cells. The bars spread out in opposite directions and look like a tornado (Figure 13-25).

Manager	Sum of Margin Actual, $ ▼	Sum of Q-ty, units
R. Hayes	29,929	327
M. Bailey	24,022	1,319
N. Lee	7,440	259
A. Foster	6,950	551
S. Meier	2,260	132
J. Perry	650	12
Total	**71,251**	**2,600**

Figure 13-25. Table with conditional formatting applied

Step 3: Change the Table Style and Remove the Grid

Now we should remove all unnecessary table formatting to make it look like a tornado chart and not a table, as you'll see in Figure 13-26:

Style presets
> Select *Minimal.*

Grid
> Disable horizontal and vertical gridlines.

Border
> Disable all checkboxes.

Totals
> Disable the box next to the *Values* field.

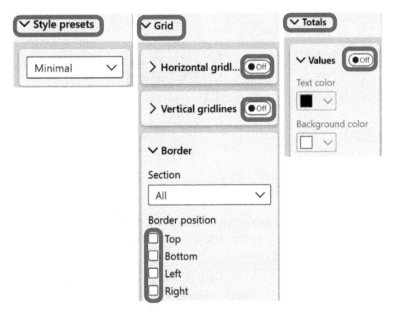

Figure 13-26. Clearing unnecessary table formatting

Step 4: Format Data Labels

As the data is presented in table cells, its formatting must be done for each column separately in the *Specific column* settings section.

Select the desired column in *Series*, switch *Apply to values* on, and customize the contents of the *Values* section as in Figure 13-27:

Alignment

> Left column (Margin Actual, $) align to the right; visually it will be aligned to the center of the tornado. The same for the next column (Quantity, units), but align it to the left.

Display units

> Here we can choose the order for each data series. For the *Margin Actual* row, we'll keep units default (*None*).

Value decimal places

> Specify the required number of decimal places (for *Margin Actual*, 0).

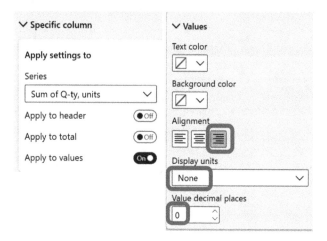

Figure 13-27. Formatting data labels

We get the final result of the table, which looks exactly like a tornado chart, as you'll see in Figure 13-28. To keep it symmetrical, you can simply stretch the last column of the table to the desired proportions.

Manager	Margin Actual, $	Quantity, units
R. Hayes	29,929	327
M. Bailey	24,022	1,319
N. Lee	7,440	259
A. Foster	6,950	551
S. Meier	2,260	132
J. Perry	650	12

Figure 13-28. Table-based tornado chart, final result

Benefits of a Tornado-Style Table

As you'll see in Figure 13-29, the version of the chart we've just created (on the right) is more functional than the ready-made visual on the left. Here are a few of its main advantages.

Benefit 1

The tornado-style table works correctly with filters and shows the data proportionally. While in the classic tornado chart one of the columns (in Figure 13-29, left, it is quantity in units) can shrink to an unreadable minimum on the custom visual when filtered; the tornado-style table shows the data correctly.

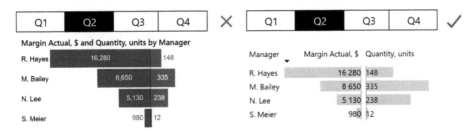

Figure 13-29. Tornado chart custom visual (left) versus table-based tornado chart (right) with filter applied

Benefit 2

We are working with a table, and therefore you can add another column of data to it, which will be located next to the tornado or before it and carry additional information. For example, let's display the indicator of margin target execution (a column with a short title of *vs. Target*), as in Figure 13-30.

Manager	vs. Target		Margin Actual, $	Quantity, units
R. Hayes	80%	◯	29,929	327
M. Bailey	101%	◯	24,022	1,319
N. Lee	78%	◯	7,440	259
A. Foster	116%	◯	6,950	551
S. Meier	45%	◯	2 260	132
J. Perry	65%	◯	650	12

Figure 13-30. Display additional information along with the tornado chart in the table

Benefit 3

When working with the custom visual, we can change the width only for the entire chart. When working with the table, we can change the width of the columns separately, just like in Microsoft Excel. And we are able to sort columns the same way, just by clicking on the desired column name.

Benefit 4

We can just use column headers as legend items without messing with text boxes and their formatting. The name of each indicator is above each column with a data bar. It's clear enough!

Until Microsoft developers or their partners create a truly functional visualization of the tornado, we recommend using a table-based approach for this purpose. This approach gives more options for making a comprehensive visualization.

Tips and Notes

The tornado chart is used to visualize the relationship of indicators reflecting rankings. Its analog can be considered a clustered bar chart, but in some cases the tornado is better:

- If you want to display indicators in different units on one graph; for example, on one side, pieces or kilograms, on the other, currency
- If you want to emphasize the correlation between the parameters; for example, to show that the sales manager has more real deals with fewer calls

Checklist for Setting Up a Tornado

To design a tornado chart from ready-made visualizations, you need to take four steps:

1. Set up data labels by specifying the displayed units and the number of decimal places.
2. Adjust the scale of the x-axis by setting the indicator or smaller range to the maximum value.
3. Format the y-axis, specifying a font size of 10–12 pt, color black, position on the left, and sorting by the desired row.
4. Manually set the legend and name of the chart, disabling the default name and adding text boxes with the desired content.

To create a tornado-style table, there are more steps, but the result will be more functional:

1. Create conditional formatting for the table columns by enabling the *Data bars*.

2. Change the direction of the bars on the left side in the additional column settings and change the bar colors.

3. Change the table style to *Minimal*, disable totals, and remove all grid lines.

4. Format the data labels for each column: set the displayed units, specify the number of decimal places, and align the data in the cells (left column to the right edge, the right column to the left).

Download the *.pbix* file with customized visuals (*https://oreil.ly/Mm7PP*).

CHAPTER 14

Waterfall Chart

For the practice, please download a special dataset (*https://oreil.ly/8WjRv*).

In this chapter, we will begin with the default visual provided by Microsoft and discuss its features and limitations. We will pay attention to data preparation and introduce you to Power Query. Finally, we'll end with a simple waterfall and explain its benefits.

To make informed decisions based on data, it is not sufficient to merely compare target versus actual values. In certain processes, such as manufacturing, finance, or enterprise sales, it is crucial to understand the specific factors that contributed to the deviation from the plan. If you possess detailed data on the influencing factors, the most effective way to visualize them is through a waterfall chart. Although it is included in the basic set of Power BI visuals, we consider it an advanced option due to the intricacies involved in its construction. Further, we will explore alternative variations of waterfall charts available in the AppSource gallery.

Let's begin with a straightforward example of Apple sales. Suppose that sales in 2022 and 2023 turned out to be roughly the same, with a growth rate of less than 1%. However, as you'll see in the waterfall chart in Figure 14-1, iPhone and iPad sales have declined, while accessory sales have shown the highest growth.

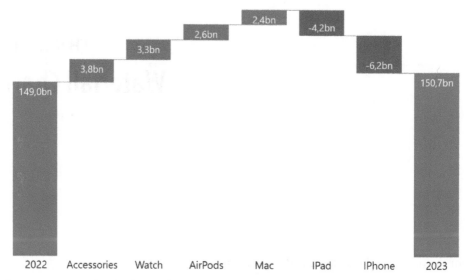

Figure 14-1. Apple sales by product 2022–23, $ billions

The data provided in Figure 14-1 is fictitious and intended to illustrate the factors influencing the sales growth or decline of each product. Instead of showing absolute data for each product in every year, the focus is on the difference between the two years' results. Positive differences are represented by upward green segments, while negative differences are indicated by downward red segments. The resulting visual resembles a cascading waterfall, with distinct steps reflecting the changes in sales.

Let's explore another case of comparing the factors that influenced the attainment of the profit goal. A manufacturing company set a target of $140 million in profit, but ended up reaching $160 million, as you'll see in Figure 14-2. What were the factors that led to this outcome?

- The company's profit increased as a result of changes in currency exchange rates.
- The growth in production outputs had a positive effect on profitability.
- However, expanded production led to the need for urgent procurement of materials at higher prices, which had a negative impact on profit.
- Staff costs also increased due to the increase in production volume, reducing profit by $8 million.
- Several other, less significant factors influenced profit growth, which we grouped under "Others."

Financial analysts are familiar with such data; for them, all these insights are clear in spreadsheets. But managers appreciate waterfall charts—thanks to them, they really see what drives their business!

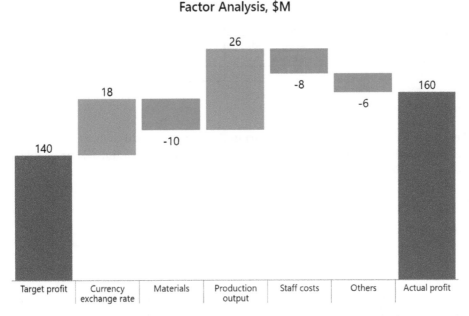

Figure 14-2. Analysis of the factors influencing the formation of actual profit compared with planned profit

Data Preparation

In this chapter, we will focus on data preparation. Unlike classic visuals, the waterfall chart in Power BI doesn't handle the source data in an obvious way. Read on to learn how it works. For practice, you have two tables—"as Excel" and "as Power BI"—so you can understand the difference between them.

Many people start by preparing their data in a table format similar to Figure 14-3, which we refer to as the "as Excel" table. It appears simple at first glance: the factors are supposed to be plotted on the x-axis, and their corresponding values on the y-axis.

Factor	Value
TARGET	3200
Sales	-24
Materials	39
Production	-110
Marketing	-145
Distribution	-66
Others	-42
ACTUAL	2852

Figure 14-3. Data table "as Excel"

Let's see if we can create a waterfall chart in Power BI using this dataset. *Value* should be placed on the *Y-axis*, representing the numerical values, and *Factor* should be assigned to *Category* (Figure 14-4).

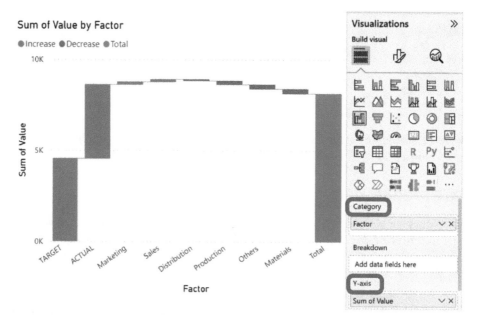

Figure 14-4. A meaningless waterfall chart based on "as Excel" data format

As you can see in Figure 14-4, we end up with a confusing picture: the actual value is placed above the target value, followed by the factors, and, at the end, the sum of value. This visualization fails to convey any meaningful message.

Don't worry, it's not your mistake. It's just that Power BI requires the data to be formatted in a different way.

In Figure 14-5, you can see the table with separate columns for target and actual. Even though we are only displaying the changes for each factor on the chart, we still need the original values for the plan and actual data to construct it. The program will calculate the difference between them automatically. No separate rows are required for the plan and actual totals—they will be computed automatically as the sum of the column.

One more thing to note is that we can have only one numeric field on the y-axis. However, we still need to differentiate between the plan and actual values, which will be indicated by a separate column called *Version*.

Factor	Target	Actual
Sales	500	476
Materials	550	589
Production	600	490
Marketing	650	505
Distribution	700	634
Others	200	158

Figure 14-5. Table with separate columns for target and actual

In Figure 14-6, we end up with a "flattened" table structure that has twice the number of rows. It can be inconvenient to manually prepare such data. An alternative option is to use Power Query transformations to achieve the desired format from the previous table (Figure 14-5). However, delving into those details exceeds the scope of our visualization guide.

Factor	Version	Total
Sales	TARGET	500
Materials	TARGET	550
Production	TARGET	600
Marketing	TARGET	650
Distribution	TARGET	700
Others	TARGET	200
Sales	ACTUAL	476
Materials	ACTUAL	589
Production	ACTUAL	490
Marketing	ACTUAL	505
Distribution	ACTUAL	634
Others	ACTUAL	158

Figure 14-6. Data table "as Power BI"

Now let's create a chart using the correct data. The following fields are highlighted in Figure 14-7:

- For the *Y-axis*, we place the numerical field *Sum of Total*.

- For the *Category*, we need to move the field *Version*, which contains the indicators for plan and actual.

- For the *Breakdown*, we place the field *Factor* with the list of factors. They will appear on the x-axis between the plan and actual values.

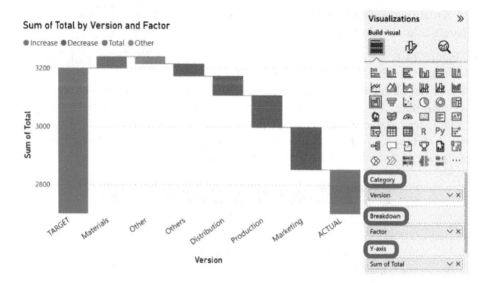

Figure 14-7. Default waterfall chart built on appropriate data fields

Now everything is logically correct: profit target is displayed first, followed by the growth factors, then the factors that caused a decrease, and finally the actual value. On the chart, it may seem that the actual profit is several times smaller than the target, even though the original data does not show such a significant difference. This is because the *Y-axis* automatically adjusts its scale to highlight the breakdown factors.

 Power BI automatically sorts the categories (*Version*) based on the descending order of the *Y-axis* values. In our case, the sum of the target is greater than the sum of the actual, but if it were the other way around, the pillars would be arranged differently. We will explain how to adjust the sorting settings in "Simple Waterfall" on page 228.

As always, it is necessary to go through the steps of fine-tuning to ensure that this visualization accurately represents the data and is easily understandable. We want it to convey the intended meaning at a glance.

Step-by-Step Guide for Default Waterfall

The default chart in Figure 14-7 has a lot of things to be improved, so let's fix them step-by-step.

Step 1: Adjust Data Labels

As always, our first step is to enable data labels (*Format visual → Data labels*). Take note of the units of measurement: by default, Power BI selects them in the *Auto* format. For our example, this works well, as the plan and actual values are four-digit numbers, while the factors are two- and three-digit numbers, making them easily understandable without the need for decimal places. However, data can vary, so you have the option to choose the units of measurement that best suit your data.

That is why we keep *Auto* units and reduce decimal places in Figure 14-8. We need to strike a balance depending on the data order, and it's impossible to guess it perfectly since the data on the dashboard is updated, and next time the miscellaneous expenses may not be 23 million but 0.8 million. But in our case, the *Auto* format fully meets our requirements.

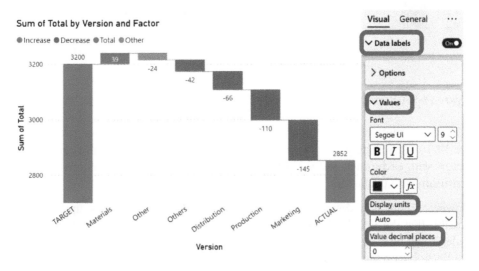

Figure 14-8. Data labels *configuration*

Step 2: Scale Y-Axis

After enabling data labels, we deviated from the general rule of "either data labels or the y-axis scale" for other charts. However, this time we will make an exception and include both the data labels and the y-axis scale on the chart.

In Figure 14-8, we can observe that the y-axis doesn't start from 0 but from about 2,800. And it becomes evident why the blue bar representing the actual value of 2,852 appears the same as the adjacent red *Marketing* bar at –145. If we want to show the real proportions, let's adjust the *Y-axis* settings as shown in Figure 14-9: change the minimum value from *Auto* to *0*. Afterward, we can choose to hide the axis. However, to be honest, this worsens the visualization. In the context of the larger target and actual values, our bars depicting the change factors have transformed into thin stripes that fail to effectively represent the data.

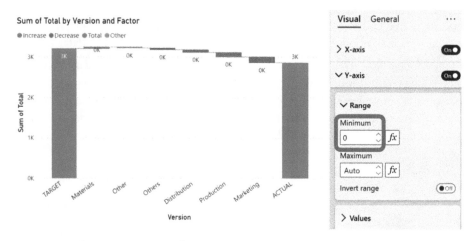

Figure 14-9. Chart view starting from 0 at y-axis

What's the solution? Find a compromise based on the range of your data. In Figure 14-10, we set the y-axis to start at 2.5K. This way, you can visually compare the factors with each other, and the plan and actual bars will stand out enough to avoid confusion with the factors.

However, there is a downside to this approach. When the data is updated, it is possible that the actual value may be smaller, for example, 2.6K, and with a fixed axis scale, it will once again appear as a short bar. Even worse, if it falls below 2K, it will not be visible on the chart at all.

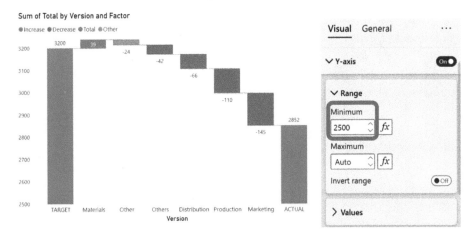

Figure 14-10. Chart view starting from 2,500 at y-axis

In this chapter we have reached a challenging level of data visualization, so it is not always possible to provide accurate instructions for all use cases. For optimal scaling of the y-axis, there are three options, each with its own pros and cons. The choice is up to you, depending on the data range:

- Keep automatic scaling and display the axis.
- Set the axis start at zero and hide the axis.
- Adjust the axis start in a way that preserves the proportions of the category and breakdown without distortion.

For any of these options, we recommend that you turn off the grid lines. With data labels enabled, there is no need for additional lines to guide the viewer on the scale. It is also advisable to disable the axis title to avoid overcrowding the chart.

Step 3: Configure the X-Axis and Determine the Number of Columns

As with traditional bar charts, we disable the axis label and maximize the size of the value labels. Keep in mind that people are accustomed to reading text horizontally rather than at an angle. In Figure 14-11, we demonstrate the importance of horizontal text. Therefore, you'll need to find a balanced solution: it's preferable to reduce the font size and present the labels horizontally (right) rather than using a large font that becomes difficult to read (left).

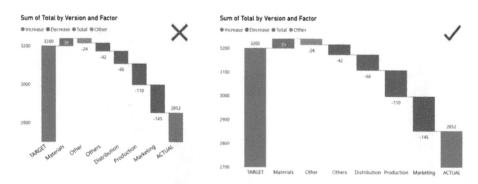

Figure 14-11. Wrapped text (left) and horizontal text (right) on the x-axis

Pay attention to the yellow column labeled *Other* on the chart and the same element in the legend. The concept behind the column is that if you have 10 or 15 factors, it would be impractical to visually represent all of them. Therefore, Power BI recommends by default to display only the top five, while grouping the smaller values and showing their cumulative positive and negative deviations in the yellow column. In Figure 14-12 shows another specific parameter, *Breakdown*, for the waterfall chart that pertains to the x-axis.

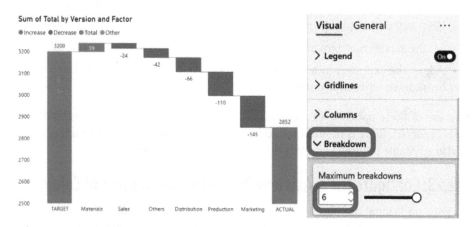

Figure 14-12. Choosing the number of factors displayed on the chart

In our dataset, it happens that we have six factors, and within the yellow column, there is actually one (red for sales) that is significant. So there is no point in hiding it. To address this, you need to expand the *Breakdown* menu and adjust the right slider to set the maximum value to six.

Now the legend is unnecessary. When there was a yellow column, it was necessary to clarify that it represents *Other*, but the color codes "green = increase" and "red = decrease" are self-explanatory.

In practice, the grouping into "Other" is not based on a predefined "top five" or "top seven" principle, but rather on the specific business context. Even if a factor has a small deviation, it is still considered relevant and included in the chart. Likewise, miscellaneous revenues or expenses can exhibit significant deviations. The selection of significant factors is typically determined by the client or user based on their specific requirements.

In this guide, we have focused on the nuances of working with data labels for the x- and y-axes. The final step is to replace the placeholder text in the title with meaningful content, as we do for all charts. That is how it finally looks in Figure 14-13.

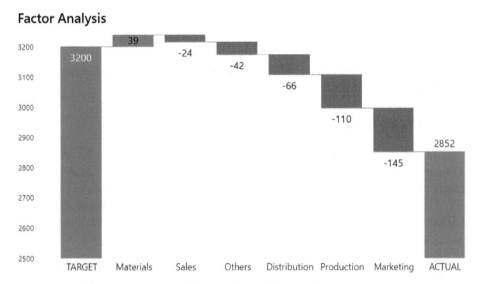

Figure 14-13. The revised waterfall chart after all the configurations

Limitation of Standard Waterfall Chart

The breakdown points are typically arranged in descending order by default: starting with the positive green bars and followed by the negative red bars. However, factors often have a logical sequence, such as materials, production, and sales. We would like to arrange them in the same order as they appear in the data source.

There is no specific parameter in the *Visualization* panel for that. However, we can utilize the default ellipsis icon in the top right corner of the chart (Figure 14-14). But if we change the sorting direction, it will affect only the actual and target blue bars, which doesn't make any sense. (Nevertheless, we can use the sorting settings to arrange the *Version* field in the desired order, ensuring that *Target* always appears first. To do this, we just need to apply descending sorting based on the *Version* field.)

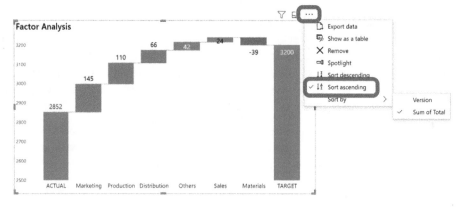

Figure 14-14. Wrong ascending sorting by category (starts from actual)

To overcome this limitation, we will once again turn to the gallery for nonstandard charts. Let's tackle that now.

Simple Waterfall

If you search for the term "waterfall," you'll find numerous options, as you can see in Figure 14-15. We will focus on the Simple Waterfall visual because it is truly straightforward and solves the aforementioned issue with the sequence of breakdown points. Furthermore, it offers several other advantages. We don't have any particular favorites among the other waterfall chart variations, as they all have their own unique features and some may require a premium version.

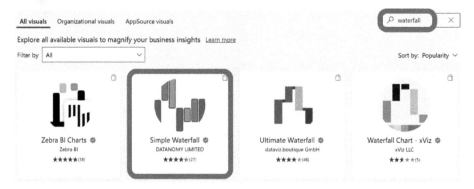

Figure 14-15. Waterfall chart variations at the AppSource gallery

To build it, we utilize a table in an Excel-like format (Figure 14-3). The chart fields are self-explanatory: we have *Values* for numerical data and *Category* for the text field containing factor names. However, the outcome in Figure 14-16 is messy again: the actual value is annotated above the plan, factors are added and subtracted from it, and a redundant total is displayed.

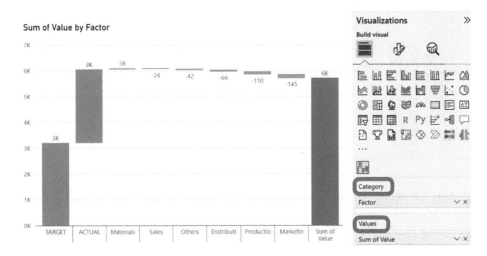

Figure 14-16. Meaningless default simple waterfall

Let's explore the formatting options of this waterfall chart and understand its "simplicity." Expand the *Define Pillars* section and disable the *Show Cumulative Total* option (Figure 14-17). This will remove the pointless blue column, and most importantly, it will allow you to specify which column should serve as the starting point and begin from zero.

Figure 14-17. Disable Show Cumulative Total

In the list that appears in the *Define Pillars* section (Figure 14-18), enable the checkboxes for *TARGET* and *ACTUAL* to make them the reference points.

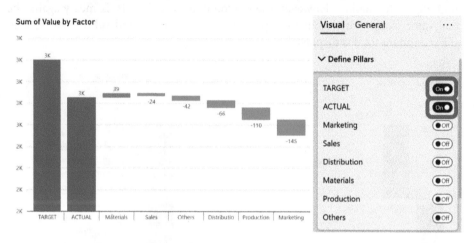

Figure 14-18. Define TARGET *and* ACTUAL *as pillars*

Unfortunately, the desired outcome did not occur. The data is still sorted in descending order, with the blue columns appearing consecutively, followed by the positive green column, and finally the negative red columns at the end.

Don't despair! This waterfall chart has the option to sort the *x-axis* in alphabetical order, as you'll see in Figure 14-19. If you rename the category labels so that they align in the desired logical order, you will achieve the desired result. You can assign prefixes such as a-b-c or 1-2-3 to them.

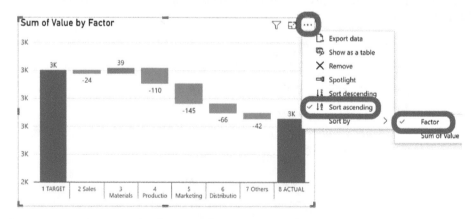

Figure 14-19. Custom order for x-axis by assigning prefixes

However, we do not recommend such an approach as best practice. There is a more reliable solution, although it lies beyond the parameters of the chart. We were hoping to avoid complex technical aspects in this book, but we will have to delve into transforming the raw data in the Power Query Editor.

This is an advanced level of working with data, and it's a topic that merits entire books and dedicated training courses. In this guide, we will devote just a few pages to this powerful tool, but it will enable you to proudly claim that you have performed multidimensional transformations using Power Query. If you're already familiar with Power Query, you know that we'll be executing the "pivot column" step. So, feel free to proceed to the step-by-step guide and follow along.

So, let's embark on this journey to explore the power of Power Query and unlock the true potential of your data within Power BI. Get ready to elevate your data visualization game to new heights!

Transforming Data with Power Query

On the *Home* tab, find the *Transform data* button, which is situated in the center. Depending on the size of your screen, you may see the button directly or in a drop-down menu, similar to what is shown in Figure 14-20.

Figure 14-20. How to launch Power Query Editor

Next, you will see a separate window called the Power Query Editor. Its interface resembles the data view in Power BI, but it has its own unique features. Here are the main components, numbered in Figure 14-21:

1. At the top, there is a ribbon with tabs such as *Home, Transform, Add Column,* and others. Each tab contains various action buttons.

2. On the left side is the *Queries* panel. Here, "queries" refer to the same concept as tables in the data model, but they are located on the left side instead of the right. You will see familiar table names such as *For Excel* and *For PBI*.

3. In the center is the workspace with a data preview table of the selected query. In Figure 14-21, the *For Excel* query is selected on the left, and the central area displays the columns of this table.

4. On the right side is the *Query Settings* panel, which includes the *APPLIED STEPS* section. This section serves as a log of operations, allowing you to view all the transformation steps, go back to any step, make adjustments, or undo previous actions.

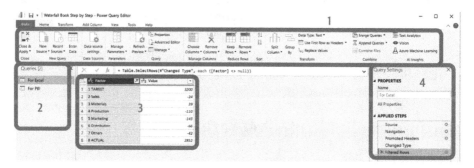

Figure 14-21. Key elements of Power Query interface

Remember our task: we need to change the order of factors on the x-axis arbitrarily. Currently, this is not possible because within the *Indicator* column, sorting can only be done in ascending or descending order. However, if each factor is represented as a separate column instead of as a row within a single field, we will be able to arrange them in any desired order.

If we were working in Excel, we could use the transpose function or manually rearrange the cells. However, we will follow the approach of not modifying the data source directly and instead transform it in Power BI, while keeping a record of the changes in the operation log.

Step 1: Execute the Pivot Column Function

On the ribbon, go to the *Transform* tab and find a small button called *Pivot Column*. Select the *Factor* column and click on this button, as you'll see in Figure 14-22.

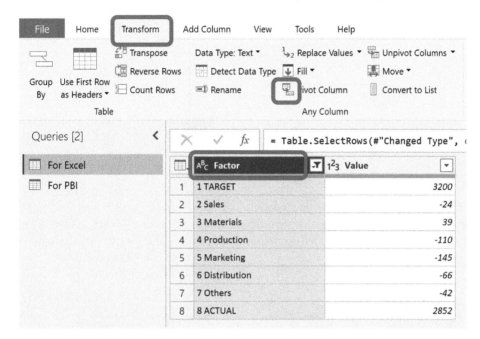

Figure 14-22. Steps for the pivot table

Step 2: Select Values Column

After clicking the *Pivot Column* button, a pop-up window (Figure 14-23) will appear. In the *Values Column* section, select the field containing numerical data that you want to pivot from rows to columns. In our case, it's straightforward—the field is named *Value*.

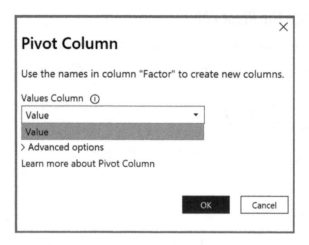

Figure 14-23. Selecting the Values Column

Click *OK*, and the table will be updated. The factor names, which were previously listed as rows in a column, are now individual columns: *Target, Sales, Materials*, etc. Since we are using a simplified example, there is only one row left in the table, as you'll see in Figure 14-24.

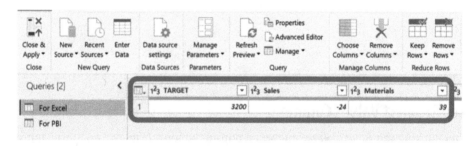

Figure 14-24. The result of the data transformation

In real projects, there are dozens of columns and thousands of rows, making it impractical to move them manually. The *Pivot Column* function becomes an indispensable tool for analysts and managers, enabling efficient data transformation.

Step 3: Close & Apply

We have finished the transformations and now we want to go back to Power BI. You might be surprised that you don't find a *Save* button, and indeed it is not here. Instead, in the top left corner, you will find *Close & Apply*, as in Figure 14-25, which serves the same purpose. So go ahead and click on it without hesitation.

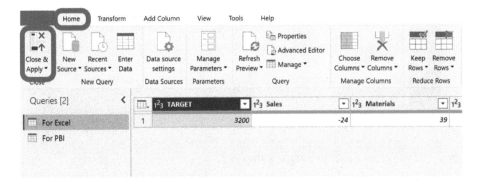

Figure 14-25. Close & Apply *button*

We have looked at a simplified example to solve a specific task. Of course, in industrial projects, many more transformation steps are involved. However, let's now shift our focus back to visualization.

Step-by-Step Guide for Simple Waterfall

We have finished data transformation, so now let's go back to the chart. As always, we use these steps to make it visually clear.

Step 1: Reposition Fields

Now, in the *For Excel* table, we have not just two fields but eight, each in numeric format. When updating the data, the default simple waterfall from Figure 14-16 would result in an error, so we'll build the waterfall chart from scratch. In Figure 14-26, you can see that this process is quite easy: we leave the *Category* field empty and populate the *Values* field in the desired order. We sequentially drag and drop all the fields from *Data* in the desired order. However, if you make a mistake or decide to change the order of the factors, you can always rearrange them by simply dragging and dropping within the *Values* field.

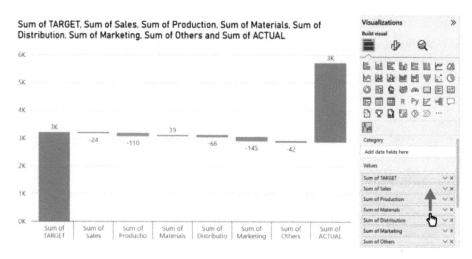

Figure 14-26. Values fields for simple waterfall

Step 2: Define Pillars

As you can see in Figure 14-27, we can select the reference columns:

- Expand the *Define Pillars* section.
- Disable the *Show Cumulative Total* mode.
- Enable the columns *Sum of TARGET* and *Sum of ACTUAL*.

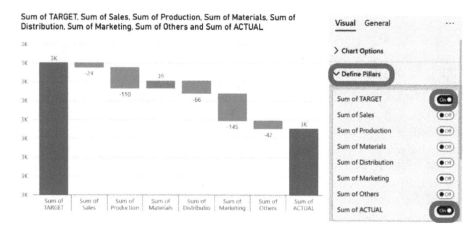

Figure 14-27. Define TARGET and ACTUAL as pillars

Step 3: Configure Data Labels and Y-Axis

Data labels and axis formatting are adjusted in the same manner as we have done multiple times before. Data labels are turned on, and we set a larger font size. We select appropriate units of measurement and determine the number of decimal places. Grid lines are turned off. We do not disable the y-axis, as our reference columns do not start from zero. For the x-axis, we choose a font size that ensures all labels are visible and horizontally aligned, and we edit the title for clarity.

Step 4: Adjust Category Labels for the X-Axis

Please pay attention that on the chart (Figure 14-27), the factor names appear as "Sum of..." because the system highlights that it has aggregated all the data within that column. This can be visually distracting. To remove unnecessary words or rephrase the factor name, you can follow the steps shown in Figure 14-28:

1. Within the *Values* field group, select the chevron on the right of the desired measure, and in the pop-up menu, choose *Rename for this visual* (Figure 14-28), or simply double-click on the measure name in the visual.

2. Delete the extra words or rephrase as desired. This same method can be used for any chart.

Figure 14-28. Rename data fields for this visual

Upon completing all the configurations, we obtain the final version of the waterfall chart (Figure 14-29).

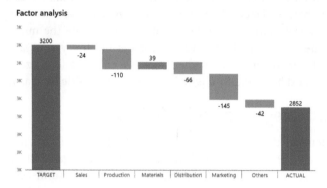

Figure 14-29. The final clear view of the simple waterfall

Benefits of the Simple Waterfall

Why we prefer the simple waterfall:

- Instead of three fields (category, breakdown, value), we only have two: numeric value and text category. It's really simple!
- The scale is automatically adjusted, creating a visually appealing representation.
- We can arrange the categories in any desired order.
- It has a horizontal orientation (Figure 14-30)! In our case, there is no need to display it horizontally—eight vertical columns are displayed properly, and the data labels fit well.

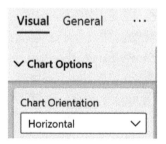

Figure 14-30. Chart Orientation *option*

However, if we have more than 10 factors, especially with names consisting of two to three words, the horizontal waterfall chart will be our salvation.

How to turn it on:

- Go to the first point in the *Chart Options* section → *Chart Orientation.*
- Choose *Horizontal.*

That's all!

Take a look at Figure 14-31, which shows another advantage: you can designate not only the starting and ending pillars but also intermediate values. This doesn't occur frequently, but in this example, we emphasize the intermediate production costs and then demonstrate how the final cost is formed through administrative and distribution expenses.

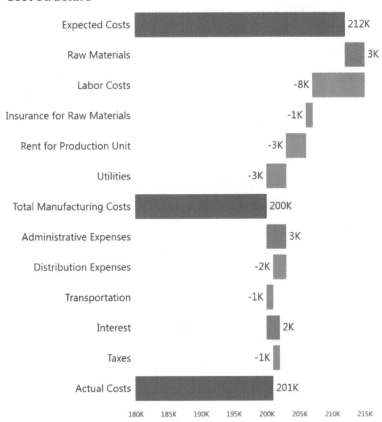

Figure 14-31. Horizontal waterfall for a long list of factors

Some drawbacks of the simple waterfall include:

- The requirement to convert the source data into a "wide" table format.
- When changes in the factors affect the result, we have to manually modify the set of fields used in the visual.

Let's summarize. Waterfall is one of the most complex charts. Business users often require more and more features for fine-tuning, but all these nuances are really needed for financial analytics (and not only). This chart, properly prepared, answers important questions: not just showing that actual value is less than target, but why this deviation occurred. There are many versions in the gallery, but there is no ideal solution. The most advanced version, in our opinion, is Zebra BI Charts, but it is also the most expensive and complicated. So you need to find a compromise that works for your business context.

Tips and Notes

Waterfall is one of the most complex diagrams commonly used. It has many nuances related to data preparation and transformation. Despite the difficulty, the result is worth it.

Checklist for setting up a default waterfall chart:

1. Enable and adjust the data labels.
2. Scale the y-axis to make the difference between factors visible.
3. Adjust the category axis named *Breakdown*; group factors of small values to *Other* (if needed).

Checklist for setting up the simple waterfall chart:

1. Reposition field order, setting *Target* first and *Actual* last.
2. Define *Target* and *Actual* values as pillars.
3. Enable and adjust the data labels, scale the y-axis to make the difference between factors visible. Shorten category labels for the x-axis.

Download the *.pbix* file with customized visuals (*https://oreil.ly/Bubup*).

CHAPTER 15

Bullet Chart

For the practice, please download this dataset (*https://oreil.ly/2ymPY*).

A bullet chart is an advanced version of a bar chart with a target and actual value, as in Figure 15-1. The idea is simple: we combine the bars so that the actual value is inside the plan bar and goes like a bullet in a barrel to the target level. In other words, we see how our sales channels "fire" (exceed the target), or if they just remain in the gun.

Figure 15-1. Bullet chart displaying target and actual margin by sales channels

Bullet Chart Options

Figure 15-1 illustrates the simplest approach to displaying target versus actual. But there are different options, which depend on business context. For example, it is important not only to understand the degree of achievement of performance targets but also to determine in which permissible zone the deviation falls.

In Figure 15-2, we marked zones with colors: light red (which may look pink) is under 80% of execution, yellow is between 80% and 100%, and green is above 100%. Also, the target is shown with a vertical graduation mark, to avoid overloading the chart. In Figure 15-2 you see the case of a company where each manager has a $100 million sales target:

- Michael Hayes fulfilled his sales target by 110% and will receive a bonus.
- Robert Bailey fulfilled his plan by 90%, but still will get a bonus, although at a discount.
- Steven Lee reached only 75% of his goal—it is in the red zone—and he won't receive a bonus at all.

Actual Sales vs. Target, $M

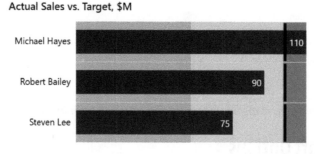

Figure 15-2. Sales target execution, shown on the "good-bad" color scale

In the corporate world, the KPI calculation system may be quite sophisticated; there may be both reduction and raising factors, for exceeding the plan. You can increase the number of color zones to show it and replace dangerous red with neutral gray for more positive motivation, as in Figure 15-3.

Actual Sales vs. Target, $M

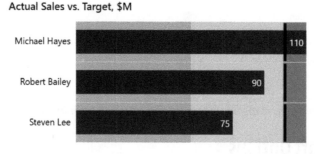

Figure 15-3. Sales target execution, shown on the "neutral-good" color scale

Typically, corporations don't care solely about "who can sell the most" but instead set different goals for each manager based on their product portfolio, market, etc. It may be that Lee (Figure 15-4), who looked like an outsider with his $75M in the first case, has exceeded his plan of $70M, while Hayes has a plan of $120M and hasn't accomplished it yet.

Actual Sales vs. Target, $M

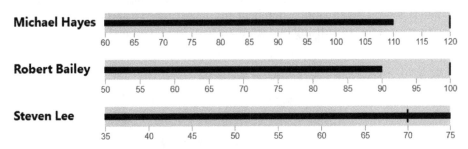

Figure 15-4. Actual sales by managers with individual targets

Bullet charts can be useful for many types of businesses, not just for corporations with a complex KPI system. Let's return to the binary question of whether or not the target has been achieved and depict the diagram from Figure 15-3 more briefly:

- In Figure 15-5, only the finish line is left of the target bar.
- The bar with the actual values is colored entirely according to the status of the plan's implementation.
- Data labels show not only the actual value but also the percentage deviation from the plan.

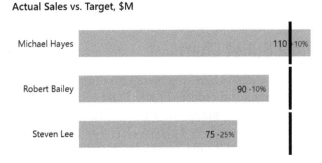

Figure 15-5. Simplified bullet chart, showing target as a vertical marker and the data labels as a percentage deviation

Figure 15-5 looks better than the charts in Figures 15-2 to 15-4 because we don't draw a lot of color bars and we focus directly on the actual value. The only thing missing is that we don't see the cutoff where the yellow or red zone border begins. However, if all you want to know is whether or not the plan is fulfilled, then Figure 15-5 shows an obvious result.

In addition, it also is worth paying attention to the fact that some examples may have an inverted logic. For example, in some cases, exceeding the target is bad and a shortfall is good. This situation often happens in cost analysis scenarios. For instance, if you overspent the advertising budget, that's bad, and if you met the limit, that's fine (Figure 15-6).

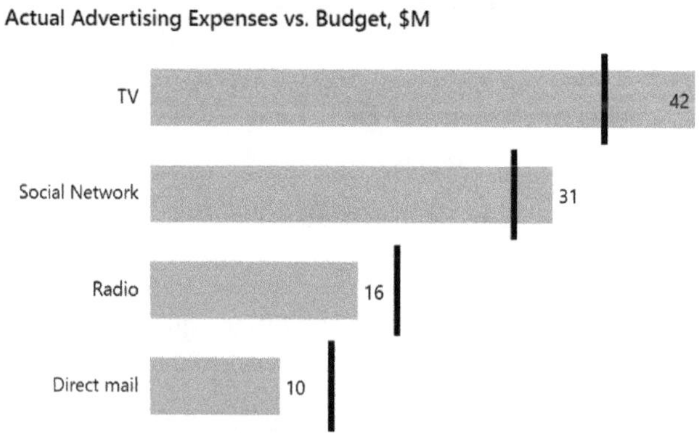

Figure 15-6. Bullet chart with inverted logic: overfulfillment is marked red and under-fulfillment is green.

We've looked at ready-made, designed charts. But as you might guess, the default version will look quite different, because it always requires additional customization. You need to properly place the data fields, remove extraneous information, and configure the signatures. We'll discuss this in the next section.

How to Build a Bullet Chart

In Chapter 13 on the tornado chart, you were introduced to the AppSource gallery. Here we'll follow the same procedure. In the *Build visual* section, under icons of available charts, we choose the button with three dots (ellipsis) and select *Get more Visuals* from the drop-down menu (see Figure 13-7). In the opened window, we write **bullet** in the search box, and this time we get a lot of options from different developers (Figure 15-7).

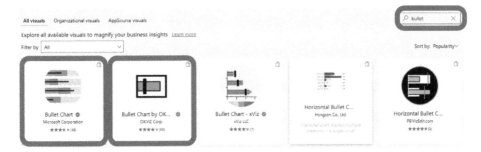

Figure 15-7. Search results for "bullet" in the AppSource gallery

What is the difference between these charts, and which one is the best to choose? The fact is that initially the gallery only had visuals from Microsoft. Over time, with the ability to offer paid versions, third-party developers began to add their products here. Microsoft's visuals are free, but, as basic introductory samples, they are limited in functionality. The really sophisticated charts are the products of Microsoft's partner developers. They have separate paid options, but the free versions are cooler than the standard Microsoft visuals. We will use the free features in the book, but we will also touch upon the paid options in an introductory way.

However, let's start with Microsoft's default bullet chart, because it is created by the authors of Power BI and serves as the foundation for this program, and all its options are free. For practice, we will use data in the structure of target and actual sales by managers.

Bullet Chart by Microsoft

Figure 15-8 illustrates the only option that can be built in this visual, which allows you to create a bullet chart with a scale. However, for readability and aesthetics, it needs to be configured.

Figure 15-8. Default view of the bullet chart by Microsoft

Unfortunately, Microsoft doesn't offer as much in the way of editing this visual element. All we can do is set the color-coding of the scale.

This visual allows us to set the value (percentage) and color for five preset zones. We will use only three of them, to avoid overly colorful designs.

Select the *Format Visual → Data Values* tab to set the terms (Figure 15-9):

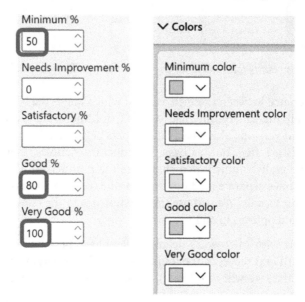

Figure 15-9. Setting the percentage and color scale to highlight the minimum to very good zones

Minimum
    Fifty percent of the plan fulfillment.

Good
    Eighty percent of the planned indicator.

Very Good
    Includes exceeding the plan, i.e., 100% or more.

After configuring the data values, set their color coding. Let's define in the *Format Visual → Colors* tab:

- *Minimum*—red
- *Good*—yellow
- *Very Good*—green

Figure 15-10 shows the results after these simple adjustments.

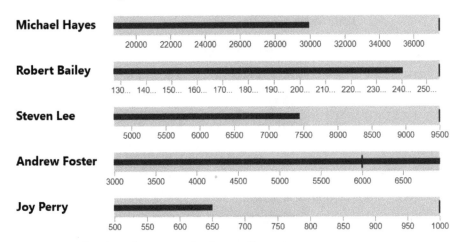

Actual Sales vs. Target, $M

Figure 15-10. Bullet chart by Microsoft after configuration

An advantages of Microsoft's default chart is that it's quite suitable to compare target execution by categories with individual targets (managers, regions, products) because it is already normalized on a scale. This chart already has preset colors with clear names, and it can be picked up and customized in a few clicks.

But there are some disadvantages:

- There is no "display units" parameter for data labels. It becomes messy with repeating zeros, especially when we have millions (Figure 15-10).
- You cannot set the scales to the same size, so it is complicated to compare data when each element has its own scale with multidigit numbers.
- You cannot change the font of category labels.

That's why we won't give you a checklist on how to make it pixel-perfect. For that purpose we'll look at another visual, the bullet chart by OKViz.

Bullet Chart by OKViz

From the visuals available in the gallery, I prefer the product by OKViz, as it offers a good set of options to create a clear and informative chart.

There are two options for displaying the data in this visualization, as you'll see in Figure 15-11. If you add the target to the *Comparison Value* field, you get a bullet chart of two joined columns, resembling a bar chart with grouping (Figure 15-11, top). If you move the target value to the corresponding *Targets* area, it will be indicated by marker, and you can immediately see whether or not the plan is fulfilled (Figure 15-11, bottom). This option is more compact.

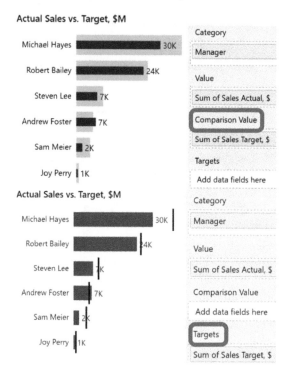

Figure 15-11. Sales target displayed by a background bar as a comparison value (top); sales target placed in the Targets *field and displayed by a vertical marker (bottom)*

These are the final results after applying the desired layout. As always, the default chart is not well designed, so let's move on to a more detailed checklist to get a perfect result.

Step-by-Step Guide for Bullet Chart by OKViz

With the default settings, we obtain the result shown in Figure 15-12, which is unlikely to meet our needs because it is difficult to understand the values of the parameters and the meaning of the gray gradient in the background.

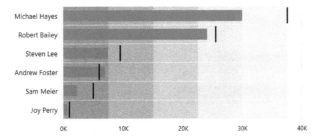

Figure 15-12. Default view of the bullet chart by OKViz

Step 1: Switch Off the X-Axis and Switch On Data Labels

Data Labels in this visualization are displayed only for the indicator that is located in the *Values* field; there is no option to display data labels for the target value (Figure 15-13).

Turn off the *Values Axis* checkbox, turn on *Data Labels*, and configure them in the usual way:

Text size
Increase to 12 pt.

Display unit
Auto, it's displayed in thousands.

Value decimal places
We have a range from 29.9 to 0.7, so it is correct to show *1* decimal digit for this data.

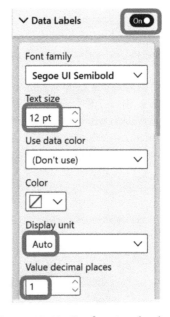

Figure 15-13. Configuring the data labels

Step 2: Adjust or Turn Off the Color Coding on the Scale (States)

Initially, the bullet chart is supposed to show values against a "bad-normal-good" scale. The gray gradient of the default chart in Figure 15-12 shows exactly this scale.

But this is not quite true, because each manager has a different target, and the condition markings are the same for everyone. So in our case (and in any case where the plan values are different for each item) we disable *States* and get our minimal bar chart (see Figure 15-14).

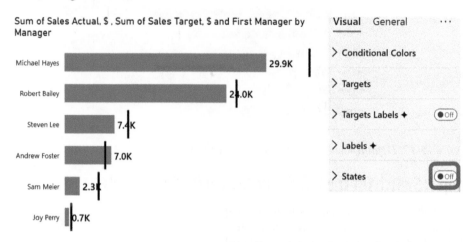

Figure 15-14. Turn off the States field to remove the background gradient scale

If the normative scale is relevant for your data (if you have one chart element or if the target is the same for everyone), you can select colors for it in the *States* section. Turn "States" back on, adjust the size of each scale zone as a percentage, and set the color for each zone (Figure 15-15). In this case, it will be immediately visible in which color zone the actual indicator fits and how far it is behind or ahead of the target.

Figure 15-15. Configuring the States field for the color coding of the bad-normal-good background scale

Step 3: Setting Up the Y-Axis

Y-axis in this visualization is called *Category Axis*. With our chart here, everything is simple. Increase the font size to 12; you are unlikely to have any trouble with this. In addition, this visual has a handy built-in feature—it automatically enlarges the area for category names, so that in any case the names would fit completely.

Step 4: Setting Up Conditional Formatting

The key information in this chart is whether the goal is met or not met. You should emphasize this with the adopted color coding: an unfulfilled plan in red and an over-fulfilled one in green. In the free version, only two options are available for column colors, default and conditional, and that's enough for our goal.

In the *Data Colors* settings, set the base color of the columns (*Default color*) to red (Figure 15-16, left).

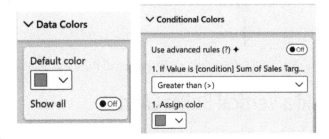

Figure 15-16. Conditional Colors *setting (left: choose default color; right: choose conditional colors)*

Then go to the *Conditional Colors* section (Figure 15-16, right):

- In the field *If Value is [condition]*, set the condition *Greater than (>)*, so it will check if it is greater than the target value.
- In the field *Assign Color*, set the color to green.

Next, you only need to set the name of the chart. On the *General* tab, in the *Formatting* of the visual element, set the *Name* parameter.

After all these steps are applied, we can see a light, clear bullet chart in Figure 15-17:

- State colors are replaced with conditional formatting.
- Data labels are informative and correspond with the data values.
- We can visually estimate the gaps between actuals and targets.

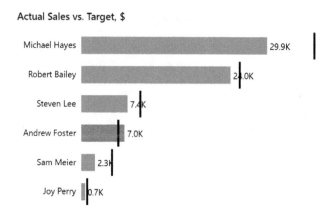

Figure 15-17. The final bullet chart from OKViz after all the adjustments

How to Build a Vertical Bullet Chart

This chart can also be displayed vertically. Sometimes, for the overall style of the dashboard, a vertical version is visually preferred, although in essence, it doesn't differ from the horizontal one. The same rule applies here: if the category captions are placed horizontally (there are very few, short names, or you have enough dashboard space to stretch this visual), then you can make a vertical bullet chart (Figure 15-18).

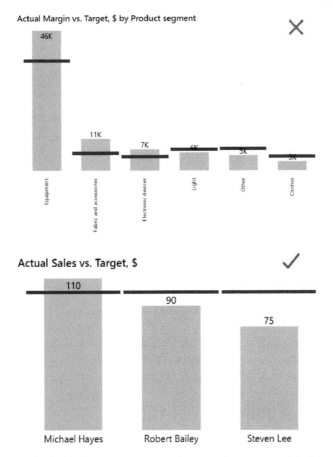

Figure 15-18. On the top is the incorrect case, because the category labels are written vertically, which is unacceptable; on the bottom is the correct one

To point the columns up and down, in the *General* section of the settings, set the vertical orientation (*Orientation* → *Vertical*).

Pay attention: following the columns, the category captions will also be rotated (Figure 15-19, left), but this is very inconvenient for users. Let's turn them back to horizontal.

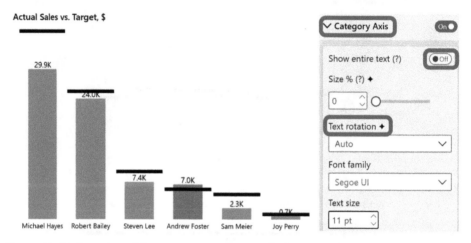

Figure 15-19. Location of the category captions in the horizontal position

In the *Category Axis* section, we turn off *Show entire text*, and in the *Text rotation* box we can set the rotation angle to 0 degrees (but this option is paid) and decrease text size so that all captions are fully readable (11 pt in the example; Figure 15-19).

Paid Version of Bullet Chart by OKViz

The paid version provides advanced design options. For example, we can display variances, different target labels, advanced color rules, or different types of borders, shapes, and shadows (Figures 15-20 through 15-23).

Variances

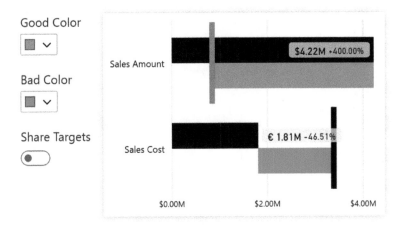

Good Color

Bad Color

Share Targets

Sales Amount $4.22M +400.00%

Sales Cost € 1.81M -46.51%

$0.00M $2.00M $4.00M

Figure 15-20. Variances *paid option*

Variances allow you to emphasize the values of under- or overfulfillment of the plan, i.e., the color is highlighted not by the scale, which may overload the image, but only by the delta between the plan and the reality. At the same time, the actual value is also shown.

Target labels allow you to display multiple targets (e.g., intermediate and final), as well as change the position of the data labels (e.g., show values above the chart graduation mark) as in Figure 15-21.

Target Labels

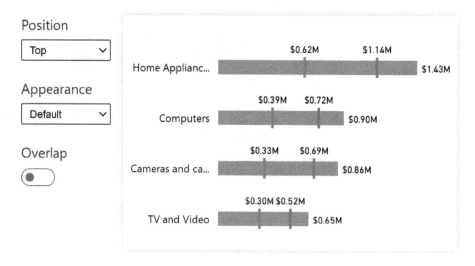

Figure 15-21. Target Labels *paid option*

Advanced color rules allow you to change the colors of the bullet to show more conditions. While in the free version we can use only two colors—default color and conditional color—in the paid version we can set additional colors that show the variability of approaching the plan. For example, the higher the actual value, the more saturated the color will be, as in Figure 15-22.

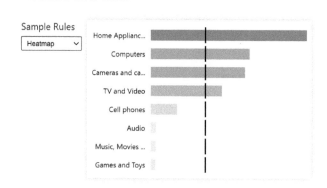

Figure 15-22. Advanced Color Rules *paid option*

In the paid version you can even experiment with the shape of bullets and their boundaries, and make volumetric shadows. But in practice, we don't advise messing around with these, because they interfere with understanding and are rather old-fashioned, as you'll see in Figure 15-23.

Borders, Shadows and Roundness

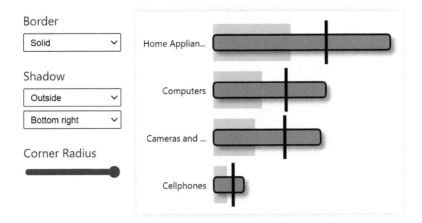

Figure 15-23. Borders, Shadows and Roundness *paid option*

To display the meaning of values, these options are not critical. They are more common for projects where you need to be exactly in line with a nonstandard design, a brand book. If you really need it, you can buy the paid version to take advantage of the full range of visual features. All settings that are available only in the paid version are marked with a rhombus (see Figure 15-24).

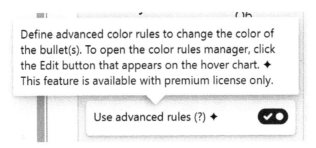

Figure 15-24. Paid option labeling

In this chapter you were introduced to the bullet chart, one of the most reliable nonstandard visuals. It is always appropriate when comparing a company's plan to the outcome. And you can use the color scale or conditional formatting of the columns to emphasize deviations from the plan, whether positive or negative.

Tips and Notes

If you want to start using custom visuals, the bullet chart is one of the most reliable. And if someone makes a trivial bar chart with a plan and fact bars in their report, you can make a cool bullet chart and get a better visualization result. This has been proven time and again by our clients who don't reject it (as they might with exotic charts).

Checklist for setting up a bullet chart:

1. Turn off the *X-axis*, and turn on and configure the data labels: select the font type and increase the size to 12 pt. Also specify the units, the number of digits after the decimal point, and the position of the labels.

2. Switch off the color coding of the scale (background) in the *States* field, or adjust it.

3. Set up the *Y-axis* (category axis), and set its options.

4. Create a conditional formatting for data bars: red as the base color, green for values above the target.

Download the *.pbix* file with customized visuals (*https://oreil.ly/j3_-7*).

CHAPTER 16

Gantt Chart

For the practice, please download this dataset (*https://oreil.ly/QZ9dS*).

This chart is highly appreciated by project managers, as it provides a valuable tool for tracking the progress of individual tasks and overall project timelines. It offers a visual representation that enables efficient monitoring of project milestones and deadlines.

On the left side (Figure 16-1), there is a list of projects or tasks associated with this diagram. The upper part of the chart represents the time axis. Each individual task is represented by a separate bar, the length of which is proportionate to the duration of the corresponding task. Inside each bar, there is a fill that indicates the completion of the respective task. A vertical dashed line serves to mark the current date, signifying a temporal reference point on the chart.

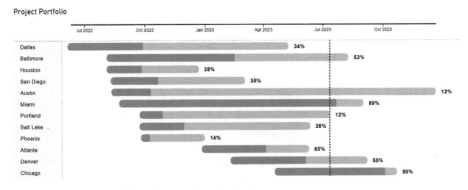

Figure 16-1. Sample of Gantt chart by Microsoft

Figure 16-1 shows a rather concise visual summary. However, typically Gantt charts contain a substantial amount of data: hundreds or even thousands of rows with tasks and subtasks, including their corresponding relationships and dependencies.

Figure 16-2 is a more complex sample by the xViz vendor, closely resembling the interface of a professional project management system, like Microsoft Project and other similar platforms. You may have seen project network graphs printed on dozens of pages, so fitting all that information onto a single screen can be quite challenging.

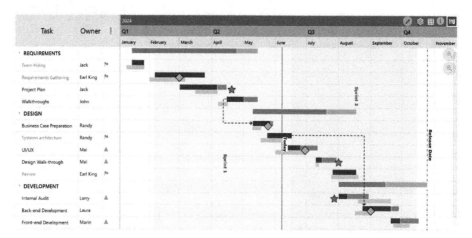

Figure 16-2. Sample of Gantt chart by xViz

The dashboard should provide a brief overview and answers to additional questions at the same time. Figure 16-3 is an example of a medium-complex Gantt, built with visual by MAQ Software.

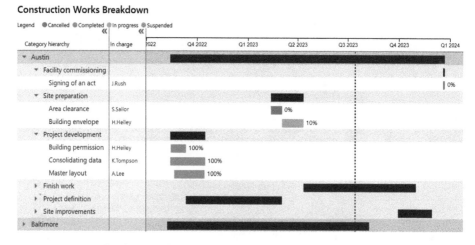

Figure 16-3. Sample of Gantt chart by MAQ Software

There are more than 10 different versions of the Gantt chart in the AppSource gallery, and in this chapter, we will familiarize you with two of them. As usual, we will begin with the visual provided by the Power BI developer itself, Microsoft. Then, we will explore a more intricate one from MAQ Software. They have common principles that we will illustrate with our guides. Based on this information, you will understand how to work with other versions of Gantt.

Gantt Chart by Microsoft

Unlike the waterfall chart, which had its share of complexities and limitations, Microsoft's Gantt chart is the simplest, most straightforward option, and, of course, it's free. We have divided it into two options: simple and hierarchical. Technically, these are the same visuals; they just differ in the settings of fields and source data. We will start by exploring the simple option and then move to the more sophisticated one.

Simple Gantt Chart

To create the simplest Gantt chart, you only need a table with four columns (Figure 16-4):

- Name of the project or task. In our case, we will label projects by cities.
- Start date (required in date format).
- End date (required in date format).
- Task progress, indicated as a percentage of completion (required in number format).

Project	Start	End	Completion
Baltimore	08/09/2022	08/09/2023	53%
Atlanta	01/01/2023	06/10/2023	60%
San Diego	08/15/2022	03/04/2023	35%
Austin	08/16/2022	12/23/2023	12%
Dallas	06/10/2022	05/10/2023	34%
Chicago	04/23/2023	10/23/2023	90%
Houston	08/09/2022	12/23/2022	38%
Miami	08/28/2022	09/01/2023	89%
Denver	02/14/2023	09/07/2023	55%
Portland	09/28/2022	07/12/2023	12%
Salt Lake City	09/28/2022	06/12/2023	26%
Phoenix	09/30/2022	01/01/2023	14%

Figure 16-4. Simple Projects *table*

We will name this table *Simple Projects* and upload it to the data model. Next, we will obtain the Gantt visual from AppSource and select the appropriate fields, as their names are quite clear (Figure 16-5):

- For the *Task* field, select the field with the *project name (city name)*.
- For both the *Start Date* and *End Date*, choose the corresponding fields (they typically have a calendar icon).
- For *% Completion*, select the field *Completion*, containing the task progress. You will see it as a bright color fill against a pale background.

Figure 16-5. Default view of Gantt chart by Microsoft

Now, as always, we need to polish our draft. Currently, we can see only the initial stages of the projects, and we have to scroll the horizontal scroll bar to the right to access the remaining tasks. However, our goal is to create a visual summary that can be quickly understood at a glance.

This problem can be solved easily once you know where to click. Let's jump straight to the last item (Figure 16-6), *Date type*, and expand the drop-down menu. By default, it was set to *Week*, causing our long-term projects to stretch across several screens to the right. For this planning horizon, it would be optimal to choose *Quarter*. Now, we can indeed see the entire project portfolio and the progress of each project.

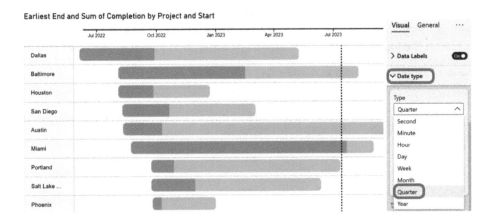

Figure 16-6. Scale is adjusted to quarters

This chart has some areas for improvement, but before we proceed with a step-by-step guide, let's first introduce you to another variant of the Gantt chart: the hierarchical Gantt chart.

Hierarchical Gantt Chart

We created a basic Gantt chart to familiarize you with its functionality. However, in practice, our clients often require more. You are probably eager to delve into the details and observe the progress of individual stages within projects, and even specific tasks.

Let's examine the *Hierarchical Projects* table (Figure 16-7). In this table, each project is accompanied by a stage. It is important to note that the source data should be in a flat format, meaning that the project name is duplicated for each stage entry.

Project	Stage	Start	End	Completion
Baltimore	Project development	08/09/2022	09/12/2022	100%
Baltimore	Project definition	09/12/2022	09/26/2022	100%
Baltimore	Site preparation	09/26/2022	12/20/2022	100%
Baltimore	Finish work	12/20/2022	04/01/2023	100%
Baltimore	Site improvements	04/01/2023	07/01/2023	100%
Baltimore	Facility commissioning	07/01/2023	08/09/2023	53%
Austin	Project development	08/16/2022	09/12/2022	100%
Austin	Project definition	09/12/2022	09/24/2022	50%
Austin	Site preparation	09/24/2022	01/01/2023	0%
Austin	Finish work	12/30/2022	04/30/2023	0%
Austin	Site improvements	04/14/2023	06/26/2023	0%
Austin	Facility commissioning	06/26/2023	12/23/2023	0%

Figure 16-7. Hierarchical Projects table

We create the chart using the same principles (Figure 16-8): *Start Date* and *End Date*, *% Completion*. However, we place the project name in the *Parent* field, which represents the top level of the hierarchy, while the stage is placed in the *Task* field.

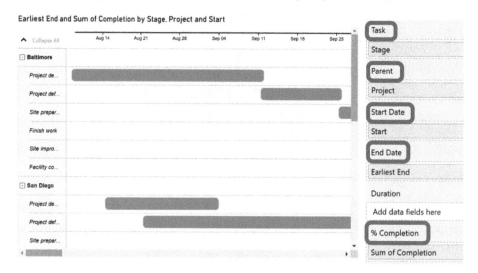

Figure 16-8. Default view of the Gantt chart with project stage hierarchy

This is what it will look like: the left column contains the parent category—project name, highlighted in bold, and next to it is an icon "+" or "−" to expand or collapse the list of tasks (displayed in italics). You might want to stretch this column to the right to fully read the stage names. However, even this adjustment needs to be made through formatting settings in Power BI. Now, let's move on to your favorite guide.

Step-by-Step Guide for Microsoft's Gantt Chart

This guide applies to both options: simple and hierarchical. Gantt charts have their own distinct logic, so we will adjust the sequence of steps accordingly.

Step 1: Adjust the Date Type

Just like in the simple chart (Figure 16-6), we will switch date type from weeks to quarters. This change will allow us to visualize the entire planning horizon.

Step 2: Expand the Category Area

In the default view (Figure 16-8), we noticed that the column containing project and stage names would benefit from being stretched to the right. Short city names fit well, but multiword stages require full visibility to be read easily.

In the *Category Labels* section, you have the option to modify the font color (referred to as *Fill*) and *Font Size*. Let's keep the default values and proceed to the next parameter—*Width*. The current column width is set to only 110 pixels, but we can increase it to 180 pixels, which should be enough (Figure 16-9). We don't recommend exceeding a width of 300 pixels, even if your stage names consist of four to five words. It is preferable to choose concise names and utilize the chart space for visual representation rather than extensive text.

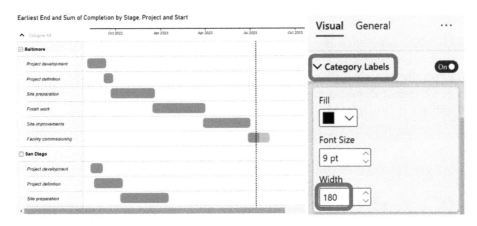

Figure 16-9. Adjusting the Category Labels

Step 3: Add Data Labels

This visual doesn't include the concept of data labels, but it does include a *Resource* field. While originally intended to display the person responsible for the task, such as a human resource or contractor, this field can be used to show the project progress value (or other significant information) instead. The *Completion* field is already being used on the chart to display the same parameter, but we can simply repeat it in the *Resource* field (Figure 16-10).

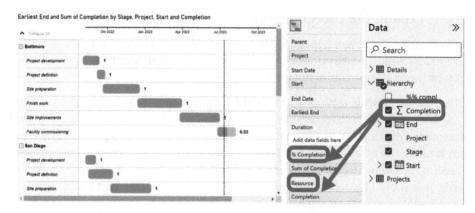

Figure 16-10. Displaying data labels using the Resource *field*

We have *task completion* in a number format; it is important to display progress on a bar. It is currently displayed in decimal format, such as 0.35, but we prefer to see it in percentage format, like 35% (especially when seeing just 1 instead of 100%). However, even if we adjust the field parameters to change the format, the percentages still might not be displayed correctly due to a bug.

Unfortunately, there is no simple hack to fix it. We may resolve this issue by creating a duplicate of the *Completion* column in the source table with the same data, but in text format. For example, with the FORMAT function:

```
Completion Label = FORMAT('hierarchy'[Completion], "0%")
```

Then, put this new calculated column in the *Resource* field, and you will get percentage data labels (Figure 16-11)! Of course, this way requires you to be familiar with DAX calculations. If you are not, just skip this point and use decimal number format; it is not crucial.

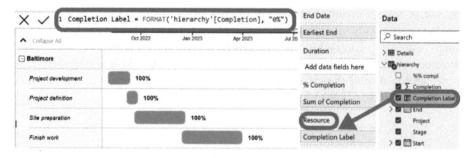

Figure 16-11. Calculated column for percentage format

Step 4: Adjust Bars: Colors and Height

There is nothing critical about the default green color; it is simply from the old color theme of Power BI and might not fit well with your current one. You will not find the *Data Colors* option in the formatting settings; instead, it is located within the *Task Settings* (Figure 16-12). We will change it to the blue that was used for other charts.

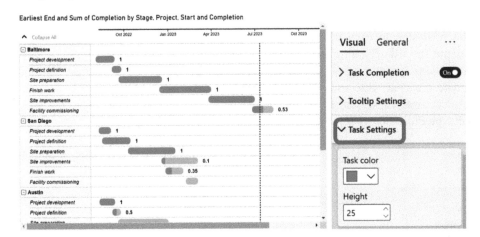

Figure 16-12. Modifying the color of data bars

Another interesting parameter to consider is the height, which defines the overall height of the row and, consequently, the bars within it. If we want to make the chart more compact, we can reduce it in the *Height* field (Figure 16-12), in our case to 25, which should provide a good visual appearance.

Step 5 (Optional): Remove Gridlines

We can also include the item about grid lines here. In Figure 16-1, the task bars are displayed on a plain white background without horizontal grid lines. You can disable the grid lines in the first section of *General* (Figure 16-13).

However, it is up to personal preference if no specific instructions are given. When viewing the collapsed list of projects by cities, grid lines may not be necessary. But when expanding a project, the short bars representing stages may be far away from their respective labels, and grid lines can assist in aligning them.

The final step in each of our checklists is to rename the title. There is no specific requirement—simply go to the *General* section and update the chart title to a more succinct one that captures the essence (Figure 16-14). We will type *Project Portfolio* as the new title.

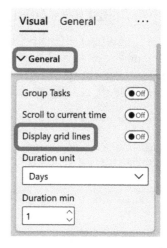

Figure 16-13. Disabling grid lines

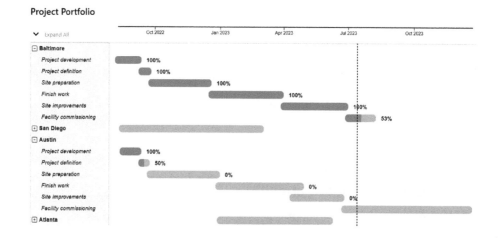

Figure 16-14. Final view of hierarchical Gantt chart by Microsoft

Limitations of the Gantt Chart by Microsoft

During step 3, we faced challenges in displaying the task progress in percentage format, although as noted there, this is not critical.

Another bug you may see in Figure 16-14 in the *San Diego* row: project hierarchy is collapsed and the total bar is displayed with light blue color, as if completion is 0%. But really there are completed tasks. If you collapse *Baltimore*, you will get the same color. We don't have any calculations to fix it.

But the main limitation lies in the number of tasks in the hierarchy, which is limited to only two: *Parent* and *Task*. However, stakeholders often desire the ability to drill down into subtasks. Unfortunately, there are no tricks or workarounds to add more than two fields in this case.

At the same time, it is worth acknowledging Microsoft for creating a Gantt chart that is truly straightforward and easy to understand, making it perfect for becoming familiar with this type of visualization.

Gantt by MAQ Software

In the AppSource gallery, there are more than 10 different variations of Gantt charts, and many of them can help you achieve similar results. We will consider the example of Gantt by MAQ Software (hereafter, we will call it MAQ for short), because its functionality is similar to the Microsoft Gantt visual (Figure 16-15).

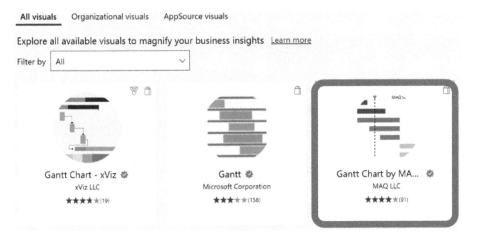

Figure 16-15. Choosing the Gantt chart visual by MAQ

Here is an example of a Gantt chart that resembles project management system interfaces (Figure 16-16):

- Multiple task levels
- Additional column indicating task ownership
- Color-coded tasks based on their status: green for completed, yellow for in progress, and red for cancelled tasks

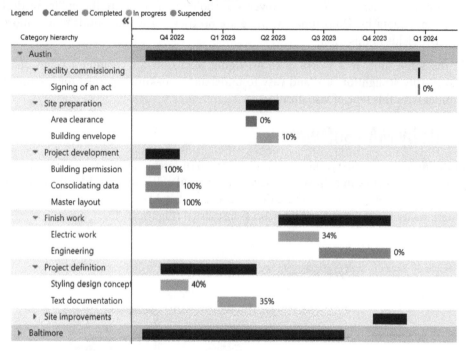

Figure 16-16. Gantt chart by MAQ with advanced options

In the source data, we have included the stage, task, responsible individual, and status (completed, in progress, etc.) for each project (Figure 16-17). It is crucial to store these fields in separate columns.

Project	Stage	Task	In charge	Status	Start	End	Completion
Baltimore	Site preparation	Area clearance	S.Sailor	Completed	04/01/2023	04/19/2023	100%
Baltimore	Finish work	Electric work	J.Rush	Completed	05/09/2023	06/15/2023	100%
Baltimore	Finish work	Engineering	A.Lee	Completed	05/15/2023	07/04/2023	100%
Baltimore	Finish work	Painting	P.Laider	Completed	06/28/2023	07/20/2023	100%
Baltimore	Site improvements	Residential landscaping	S.Camper	Completed	06/10/2023	06/22/2023	100%
Baltimore	Facility commissioning	Delivery of keys	G.James	In progress	07/22/2023	08/09/2023	53%
Austin	Project development	Building permission	H.Heiley	Completed	08/16/2022	09/12/2022	100%
Austin	Project development	Master layout	A.Lee	Completed	08/22/2022	10/15/2022	100%
Austin	Project development	Consolidating data	K.Tompson	Completed	08/15/2022	10/16/2022	100%
Austin	Project definition	Styling design conception	S.Camper	In progress	09/12/2022	11/01/2022	40%

Figure 16-17. Data table for building Gantt chart by MAQ

Next, we will add the Gantt by MAQ Software visual to the report canvas and start visualizing this dataset (Figure 16-18):

Category
    Here, we place the fields *Project*, *Stage*, and *Task*, in that order.

Legend
    We move the *Status* field here for coloring the bars.

Start and End
    These are the familiar fields representing the task start and end dates.

Data label
    This controls the display of data labels. We will show the completion percentage by dragging the *Completion* field.

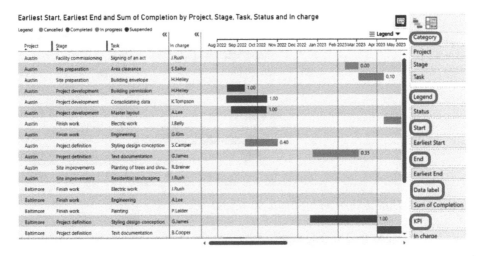

Figure 16-18. Default view of Gantt by MAQ

Pay attention to the *KPI* field. Usually we use this term for total numbers, but for the Gantt chart it is used for text categories, comments, and other additional information. In our case, we will put an *In charge* field there. It will appear as another column; the meaning of this field will become clear in a few steps.

Currently, it may resemble an Excel spreadsheet rather than the polished example depicted in Figure 16-16. However, we will now systematically transform it to achieve a neat, professional appearance suitable for sharing with stakeholders.

Step-by-Step Guide for Gantt Chart by MAQ Software

This chart offers more capabilities, which means we will need to adjust more items. Our checklist consists of six steps.

Step 1: Configure Category Hierarchy

To display the task hierarchy within the project and demonstrate nesting, go to the *Format* tab and expand the *Category labels* section (Figure 16-19). Enable the *Hierarchy layout* option. By default, the three columns will collapse into a single column labeled *Category hierarchy*. You can use the arrows to expand the projects and tasks. Let's expand the *Austin* project and, within it, the stages *Site preparation* and *Project definition*.

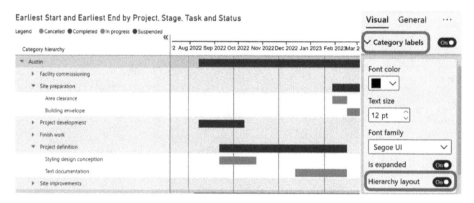

Figure 16-19. How to turn on the hierarchy layout

Here you can also find text formatting parameters, but we can leave them at their default settings.

Step 2: Adjust Area Proportions

You may notice that the column with the category hierarchy is quite wide, with half of it being empty. On the other hand, the task visualization doesn't fit properly. To fix this, expand the *Display ratio* option, which determines the proportion between the tabular and visual parts (Figure 16-20). By default, 40% of the space is allocated for tables, but in our case, we can reduce it to 20% so that the visualization occupies 80% of the overall visual area.

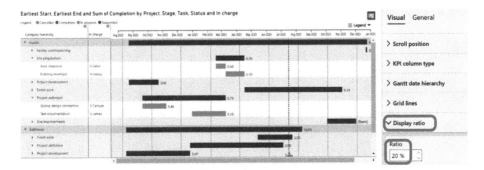

Figure 16-20. Adjusting the width of the category column

We prefer this approach: using proportional values instead of fixed values like in Microsoft's Gantt chart. It provides more flexibility and universality.

Step 3: Customize the Time Axis

Here, the default value is also better than in the Microsoft Gantt chart—it is set to months instead of weeks. But you can still modify these values according to your preference.

Let's do this in the *Gantt date hierarchy* section (Figure 16-21): in the *Hierarchy* field, select *Quarter* from the drop-down list. Leave the *Show today indicator* option enabled, which controls the display of a dashed line indicating today's date.

We will also set the scroll position to the current time. In the *Scroll position* section, choose *Today* in the *Position* field. This way, when we add new periods to the chart, we will by default see the progress up to the current date.

Figure 16-21. Date hierarchy and scroll position

Step 4: Configure Data Labels

It's great that the problem with the percentage format is easily solved—if we set the field itself to be in a percentage format, it will be displayed as such on the chart.

We also observe that the completion percentage is shown for parent tasks as well, which is inaccurate, as in some cases these values exceed 100% (Figure 16-22). To remove those labels, we need to adjust the settings on the *Data labels* tab. At the end of this section, you can find the *Parent Data Labels* option. It controls the data labels for parent tasks, in our case, the *Project* and *Task* columns. Since summing or any other form of aggregation would be incorrect, we need to disable this option.

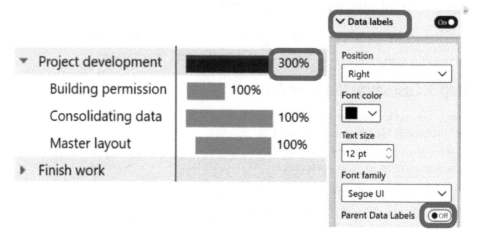

Figure 16-22. Disable the Parent Data Labels

Step 5: Customize Colors for Bar Formatting

To make the task bars change color based on their status, navigate to the *Bar formatting* section and assign colors to each category (Figure 16-23). By default there are blue, violet, and other standard colors (it depends on your current color palette). Let's adjust them due to the meaning:

- *In progress* = yellow.
- *Completed* = green.
- *Cancelled* = red.
- *Suspended and Default* = we will leave the default shades of gray; they look appropriate.

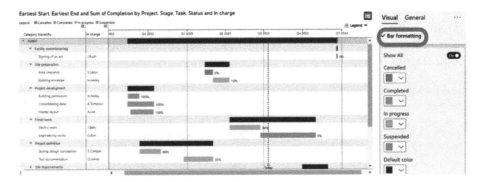

Figure 16-23. Color coding of bars

Step 6: Remove Unnecessary Elements

And a couple of final touches for perfectionists. To enhance the clarity of information on the chart, we disable unnecessary elements.

We uncheck the *KPI Legend* option to remove the unnecessary pop-up window on the right (Figure 16-24). It displays the color indicators of the *KPI* field, but in this particular example, we are not using that functionality. In the *Grid lines* section, we can customize the color and thickness of the vertical lines. We can disable this feature as the current-date markers are sufficient.

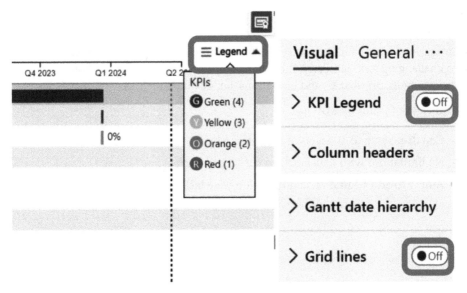

Figure 16-24. Disabling the KPI Legend *and* Grid lines

Additionally, we need to adjust the title on the *General* tab. We replace the default chart title with a clear and concise statement: Works Execution on *Construction Projects*. Here we can also customize other elements such as font, color, and size of the title (Figure 16-25).

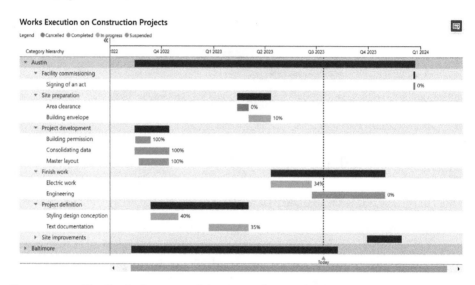

Figure 16-25. The finished version of the Gantt chart with all the desired modifications

Comparison of Gantt Charts

Configuring Gantt charts in Power BI to meet the specific requirements of users can be a challenging task. Similarly, the other six options available on AppSource also have their own bugs, drawbacks, and limitations. Let's explore their key characteristics.

Advantages of Gantt by MAQ:

- Can display up to 10 levels of task hierarchy
- No limitations with data labels in percentage format
- Ability to add additional columns alongside task names

Limitations of Gantt by MAQ:

- Outdated visual design
- Developer icon for updates
- Inability to sort tasks by identifier or start date
- Bugs related to cross-filtering

Paid features:

Progress Bar
> Show progress bar on tasks based on a measure value.

Task Status
> Show custom-colored task status flags based on a categorical field.

Task Milestones
> Plot date fields as milestones on task bar with custom-colored shapes.

Row Configuration
> Customize the row height and task bar radius.

Among all these charts, there is no clear favorite, as each has its own limitations in the free versions and may still have bugs even in the paid versions. Sometimes, it may be easier to create a custom Gantt chart tailored to your specific needs. In the next chapter, we will show you a custom visual that we developed when we didn't find an appropriate visual in the gallery.

Tips and Notes

A Gantt chart displays project stages and its completion across the timeline. There are more than 10 different versions of the Gantt chart in the AppSource gallery, and in this chapter, we introduced you to two of them: a simple one by Microsoft and a more sophisticated visual by MAQ Software.

Checklist for setting up Gantt by Microsoft:

1. Select the appropriate granularity of the time axis.
2. Expand the category area.
3. Select the granularity of the time scale.
4. Adjust the size and position of the data labels.
5. Customize the color and height of the task bars.
6. Disable the legend and grid lines, and edit the chart title.

Checklist for setting up Gantt by MAQ Software:

1. Set the font for category labels and enable task hierarchy within projects.
2. Increase the chart area for task bars on the time scale and adjust the proportions.
3. Customize column headers (time axis) and increase its font.
4. Increase the font size of data labels and remove completion percentage for parent tasks.
5. Customize the colors for tasks with different statuses and assign colors to parent tasks.
6. Disable the tooltip legend and vertical lines, and customize the chart title.

Download the *.pbix* file with customized visuals (*https://oreil.ly/7o8yc*).

CHAPTER 17

Sankey Chart

For the practice in this chapter, use this practice dataset (*https://oreil.ly/_jKe2*).

The Sankey chart is probably the most impressive visualization. It might seem like only a skilled designer could create something like this, and this level of creativity cannot be templated! Nevertheless, even such a chart can be constructed in just a few clicks if you have the data prepared in the correct format (indeed, this is the most subtle and challenging part).

While some may misinterpret it as "sun key" in the name, it has no relation to sun rays or keys. It is actually named after the 19th-century Irish engineer, Matthew Sankey, who utilized this method to illustrate the functioning of a flow engine. In the 21st century, it is being employed to showcase how money works.

The Sankey chart in Figure 17-1 provides a clear and accessible explanation of financial operations, especially for managers who are not familiar with them. We can see that the company's revenue is composed of three main flows: the majority comes from the sale of goods, around 30% from services provided, and a smaller (insignificant) portion from other sources of income. Subsequently, these funds are allocated to two budgets: operational (Opex) and capital (Capex). Moreover, you can see how expenses are distributed within these budgets and, most notably, where they intersect. For example, the salary mainly belongs to Capex, but a portion of it is also included in Opex.

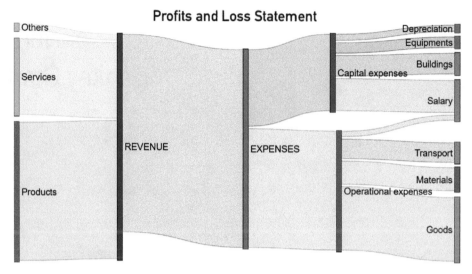

Figure 17-1. Profit and loss (P&L) statement shown in Sankey chart

Of course, the default Sankey chart in Power BI does not look very clear. For this financial example, we will improve it using a step-by-step guide.

Figure 17-2 is another example that will resonate with marketers: the flow of website visitors. The first row of vertical, colorful bars (known as nodes in Sankey charts) represents the sources of traffic: direct, email, Twitter, etc. Then we can see their respective flows (links) following the concept of a customer journey map: the primary flow leads to the blog, with the majority coming from Twitter. However, visitors proceed to the product page mainly from the home page.

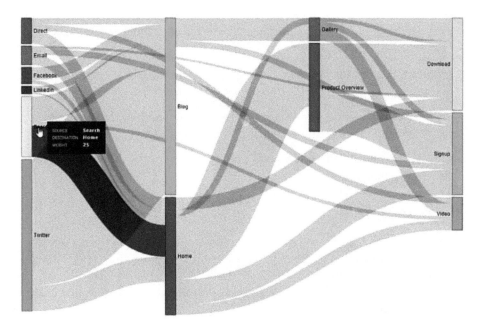

Figure 17-2. Website visitor flows

Here's another example: employee flow (Figure 17-3). In the left chart, we can see the sources from which new employees join our company, and in the right chart, we can observe the destinations and reasons why employees are leaving our company.

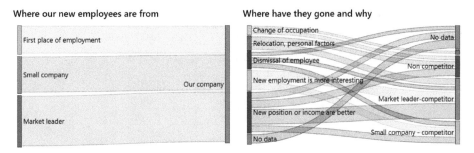

Figure 17-3. Employee flows—incoming (left) and outgoing (right) employees

The uniqueness of the Sankey chart lies in its ability to show both the structure and proportions (regarding cost items, traffic sources, etc.) on one side, while representing the relationships between them on the other. This level of detail cannot be effectively conveyed by a standard bar chart. In essence, Sankey charts provide a comprehensive "big picture" that is particularly valuable for executive-level overview. The main components of a Sankey chart are as follows:

Nodes

These are stages or steps in a process, represented by colored vertical bars.

Links

Lines that connect the nodes, indicating the flow or movement between them.

Weight

A numerical value that determines the thickness or width of the links, representing the magnitude of the flow or quantity associated with each connection.

And our students don't believe that such a thing can be done without coding. But we tell them—it's possible!

Data Preparation

Creating the chart is quite straightforward, and it can be done in just three clicks. However, data preparation in the required format may require some effort. To create it, you need a minimum of two parameters (the source and the destination; additional parameters can serve as intermediate stages) and one measure (the values that will determine the line thickness).

Let's consider the company's budget for income and expenses (budgeted income statement) as an example. Usually, this data is represented in similar tables—for example, as shown in Figure 17-4.

REVENUE			
	Products	490,000	
	Services	272,000	
	Others	29,000	
Total		791,000	
EXPENSES			
Operational expenses	Goods	230,000	
	Materials	89,000	
	Transport	76,000	
	Salary	27,000	
Capital expenses	Salary	120,000	
	Buildings	80,000	
	Equipments	45,000	
	Depreciation	30,000	
Total		697,000	

Figure 17-4. Inappropriate data source "as Excel"

As you already know, for Power BI, data needs to be in a flat format, without empty cells and subtotal rows. However, for Sankey diagrams, there are additional specific requirements.

As we mentioned earlier, for the Sankey chart, we require two parameters: source (where our flow starts) and destination (where it arrives). For each segment between them, there is a numerical value—indicating the amount of money, customers, employees, or other resources that moved from point A to point B. Each of these segments requires a corresponding row in the table to represent it.

For example, revenue as a destination consists of three elements in the *Source* column: *Products*, *Services*, and *Other*. That's why *Revenue* is listed three times in the *Destination* column. However, when revenue flows as a source, it goes to *Expenses* (in the *Destination* column), which only consists of *Revenue* (even though expenses do not account for 100% of revenue). Hence, in the first column (*Source*), *Revenue* appears only once. *Expenses*, as a *Source*, consists of two elements: Capex and Opex. And so on for all elements. The expected outcome is shown in Figure 17-5.

Source	Destination	Value
Products	REVENUE	490,000
Services	REVENUE	272,000
Others	REVENUE	29,000
REVENUE	EXPENSES	697,000
EXPENSES	Operational expenses	422,000
EXPENSES	Capital expenses	275,000
Operational expenses	Goods	230,000
Operational expenses	Materials	89,000
Operational expenses	Transport	76,000
Operational expenses	Salary	27,000

Figure 17-5. Appropriate data source for Sankey chart

Notice that the intermediate nodes act as both *Source* (for their right neighbor node) and *Destination* (for their left neighbor node). That's why *REVENUE*, *EXPENSES*, and *Operational expenses* appear in both places.

Now that we have covered the data, let's move on to the visualization. This time, there are not many options in the gallery, and we will focus on the one visual provided by Microsoft. The other options are not fundamentally different from it.

Step-by-Step Guide for Sankey Chart by Microsoft

For this particular chart, there aren't many variations in the AppSource gallery, and most of them follow a similar working principle (Figure 17-6). Therefore, we will focus on one example, the Sankey chart by Microsoft, to understand its functionality, and we won't explore other alternatives further.

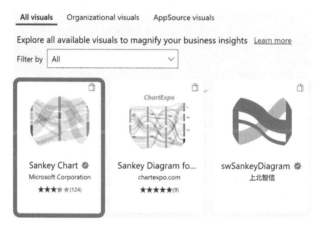

Figure 17-6. Choosing the Sankey chart visual by Microsoft

Step 1: Allocate Data Fields

In the fields area, we input the relevant data as follows:

Source
> Corresponding to the *Source* column, this signifies the left boundary of the bars.

Destination
> Representing the *Article* column, this designates the right boundary of the bars.

Weight
> Aligned with the *Amount* column, this signifies the width of the bars.

Great! We've successfully created the visualization of the P&L statement as described in Figure 17-1. So far it has a poor design but the same business meaning (Figure 17-7). It commences on the left with the revenue sources: products, services, and a slender bar representing other income. All of these combine into the red category of revenue, and from there, almost everything flows into the yellow expenses category. The flow of expenses then begins to split into two budgets, forming separate "streams" for various expenditure items.

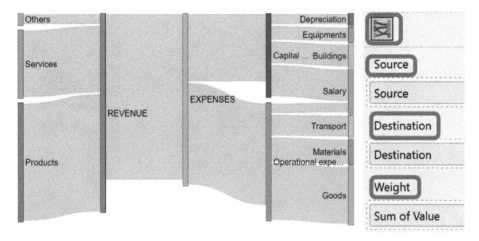

Figure 17-7. Default view of Sankey chart by Microsoft

Step 2: Adjust Node Positions

When critically examining the visualization in Figure 17-7, one can observe a dispro-portion in information density: the last quarter of the chart displays numerous small flows from budgets (Capex, Opex) to expense items. At the same time, the flow from revenue to expenses occupies the same amount of space, appearing as a single continuous gray bar.

To address this imbalance and allocate more space to the branching flows of income and expenses, we can easily make a simple adjustment. You won't find a parameter for this in the settings. Instead, all you have to do is select the node and move it freely to reposition it, as in Figure 17-8. By doing this, we can create ample room for the diverging revenue and expense streams and improve the overall clarity of the visualization.

Indeed, in Figure 17-8, you can see how we move the node *Salary*, and as a result, the linked flows are highlighted. While this method is straightforward, manually moving each node can become cumbersome, especially when dealing with a larger number of nodes, such as 20 or 30. It can be time-consuming and challenging to achieve pixel-perfect alignment.

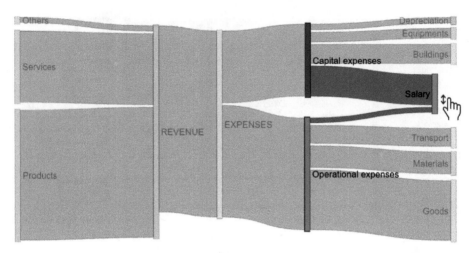

Figure 17-8. Dragging to change the position of links and nodes

Step 3: Adjust Colors for Nodes and Links

The colors of the nodes in Power BI are set according to the default palette. However, the colors of all the links between them are gray, which looks somewhat dull. Let's create a color scheme: shades of green for revenue items and shades of red for expenses. To do this, we'll open the *Nodes* parameter and set the color for each node (Figure 17-9).

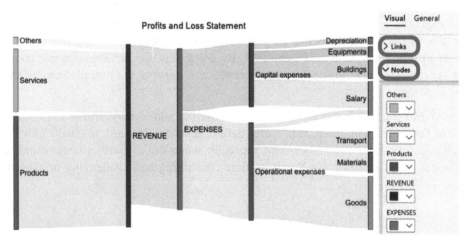

Figure 17-9. Setting the color palette

Similarly, we can adjust the *Links* parameter:

- For revenue items with "revenue" on the right, we'll recolor them using various shades of green.
- The link between revenue and expenses will remain a neutral gray, but we'll make it lighter.
- Next, we'll recolor the links from expenses to budgets (Capex, Opex), and then to specific items, using a soft shade of red and an orange hue, respectively.

Similar to step 2 for node positions, the downside of this approach lies in its being a completely manual configuration. For example, we would like to set a red color for all the links related to capital expenses at once, but we have to go into each one individually to change the color. And considering that during the coordination process with the client, we often have to adjust category colors, this all can turn into hours of routine work.

Limitation for Data Labels

Incorporating data labels is a crucial step we follow in all our checklists. However, in this particular case, we'll make an exception and treat it as a limitation. Although the chart settings offer an option called *Enable link labels*, it doesn't quite live up to our expectations. The link labels serve the purpose of displaying both data values and category labels on both ends of the link. However, this approach often results in lengthy strings that can extend beyond the available space on the link (Figure 17-10).

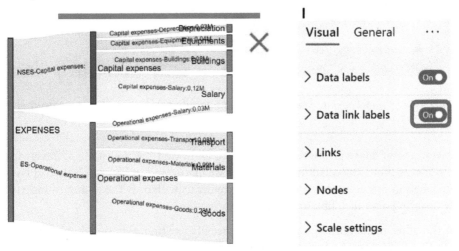

Figure 17-10. Unreadable data link labels

Consequently, the data values, which are the most crucial information, can get obscured and become difficult to distinguish amid the clutter of overlapping and repetitive category labels. Unfortunately, this undermines the effectiveness of data labels, making it challenging to access the actual data values directly from the visualization.

Due to these readability and presentation issues, we advise against enabling data link labels. In a Sankey diagram, the primary focus should be on portraying the big picture rather than inundating it with cluttered text flows. Instead, we suggest the standard approach of hovering over the link to view data values in a pop-up tooltip. While this may not be the best practice, it represents an acceptable compromise to balance the need for information with visual clarity.

Common Mistake

The Sankey diagram is primarily designed to showcase intricate, multistage processes, where data flows from one stage to another, branching out along the way. However, when you have only two categories of data—source and destination—it's tempting to construct a Sankey diagram, which is easy to do and can yield a striking visualization. Novices often choose this approach, celebrating the apparent ease of achieving such results (see Figure 17-11, left).

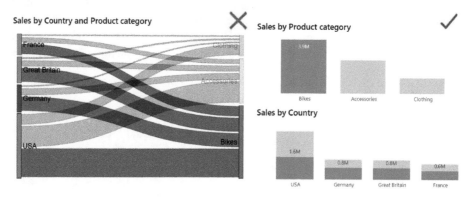

Figure 17-11. Inappropriate Sankey (left) and two column charts with cross-filtration (right)

However, what do we ultimately see in Figure 17-11 (left)? A multitude of intertwined gray lines without any quantitative data. As we discovered in Figure 17-10, displaying data labels in this context is meaningless, leaving us with only the option of individually hovering over each link to reveal its information.

On the other hand, although slightly less visually exciting, functional column charts offer the advantage of presenting both overall sales and the ability to cross-filter by any element. For instance, in Figure 17-11 (right), we have applied a filter for "Bikes," allowing us to instantly see the specific amount of revenue generated by this category in each country and its proportion to the overall sales in that country.

For this reason, we recommend using the Sankey diagram primarily for high-level illustrations of major multistage flows (typically three to five levels), complementing it with data details provided by other visual elements. When dealing with a large number of nodes, links, and levels in the displayed process, the Sankey diagram becomes less effective, as it loses its visual clarity.

Tips and Notes

Optimally, the Sankey diagram should transcend the appearance of a tangled web of spaghetti and instead captivate the user's attention, guiding it toward the pivotal elements. We highly encourage delving into creative experimentation with data intricacies and visual dimensions, aiming to preserve lucidity and depth in the presentation of information.

Checklist for the Sankey chart by Microsoft:

1. Prepare the data in a meticulously "flattened" format, where each link boasts its separate row, featuring fields such as *Source*, *Destination*, and *Weight* (value).

2. Adjust node positions manually, ensuring the links flow harmoniously with even density.

3. Adjust the colors for nodes and links. Yes, this is also done manually.

Download the *.pbix* file with customized visuals (*https://oreil.ly/2xwm0*).

CHAPTER 18

Advanced KPI Cards

For the practice in this chapter, use this practice dataset (*https://oreil.ly/Huf5z*).

In Chapter 8, we familiarized ourselves with cards designed to display total values, commonly referred to as key performance indicators (KPIs). The easiest way to display a KPI is as a rectangle containing a title (indicator name) and its corresponding value. However, typically, a KPI is associated with a target or baseline against which we compare the actual value. In relation to it, we configure conditional formatting for the data label.

Usually, we want to see the KPI alongside its difference (reference value). This additional value is displayed at a size approximately 1.5–2 times smaller than the KPI. Additionally, it has its own title, smaller in size than the main category label. With some effort, such a visual element can be grouped from two cards and two textboxes (Figure 18-1). For the end user, this will appear as a single element. However, for the developer, such an approach complicates the process of editing and maintaining the report.

Figure 18-1. Single card in a user view (left) and its components in a developer view (right)

Managing a single element is much more convenient, and there are quite a few of them in the AppSource gallery. Each visual has its unique features or, conversely, shortcomings that still need to be compensated for with text boxes. Some options are available in paid versions only. In this chapter, we will showcase the advanced capabilities of various cards, so you can understand the functionality that may be desired. Figure 18-2 shows not just a card and a chart side by side but a unified element with a sparkline (a small line chart without data labels that shows a trend). This option is available in the Card with States by OKViz.

This card looks quite distinctive, almost as if a designer worked on it. This element even has style templates; we chose one and made some adjustments. However, being perfectionists, we notice that the title is positioned below the data value, and there are no options to place it on top. If we needed to implement this in line with design or corporate guideline requirements, we would have to disable it on the card and add a text box on top.

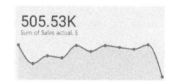

Figure 18-2. Card with States by OKViz with enabled sparkline

Let's consider another example in Figure 18-3: the Ultimate KPI Card. It has the title positioned at the top and even includes three additional measures with arrows, absolute variances, and percentages. It's convenient that we don't need to display these values using additional table cards with a colorless grid. However, we are still limited in text alignment options, arrow styles, and so on. Watermarks are also displayed in the background, so you need to buy a license to make them disappear.

Figure 18-3. Card with arrows from the Ultimate KPI Card

Another example, in Figure 18-4, is the Multi-Target KPI card, which also includes three additional measures and even a bullet chart. Our actual value exceeds the plan by 9%, so the bar crosses the target label. It's convenient that all of this is contained in one element, and when adjusting the overall size, all proportions inside are maintained.

Figure 18-4. Example of Multi-Target KPI card

The AppSource gallery contains several advanced cards, each of which would require a separate chapter to explain configuration:

- Card with States
- Multi-Target KPI card
- Ultimate KPI Card
- Dynamic KPI Card
- Advanced card
- Zebra BI Card

In this chapter we'll focus on the Multi-Target KPI card, but first, let's start by outlining the criteria for the "perfect card" from the standpoint of a self-service business intelligence (BI) developer. It's crucial that all features can be made apparent through intuitive configurations, eliminating the need for intricate calculations. Even if a designer devises an extraordinary layout, we should be able to implement it through card settings rather than combining multiple elements.

Essential Criteria for a Perfect KPI Card

By following these criteria, you will set up a comprehensive and visually appealing card. You can use default cards as a baseline and combine them with other visuals and text boxes, or find an advanced format that will meet all these criteria.

Layout and alignment

We seek the capability to position the title at the top and align it to the left, right, or center, both horizontally and vertically. While recognizing that it's impractical to account for all nuances of creative design, our goal is for 90% of tasks to be resolved through parameter settings and proportions rather than manual pixel adjustments.

Additional indicators

A mere total without context is not adequate for an advanced dashboard. A typical requirement is to visualize the variance from the plan alongside the actual value. However, there's often a need to compare it with the previous period or against a specific benchmark. It's convenient when the card can immediately showcase multiple measures.

Calculation presets

For standard variations (difference versus target, percentage difference), we would prefer not to create measures. For example, if my plan is 50K, and the actual is 40K, I want to explore presets to determine the best way to display the variance: as 80% of the target, as a –20% difference, or simply as the absolute variance of –10K.

Conditional formatting and icons

As you already know, you can establish color rules for any shape. However, it's more convenient when you can adjust everything and observe the conditions right in the formatting panel, instead of in a separate rule-setting window. Users often request traffic light indicators or arrows, similar to conditional formatting in Excel.

That covers the basics, but there are features you might not have considered; different developers have their own tricks, and you might want to use those as well:

Multiplication

You can add not just one card but an entire row at once. This also saves time on alignments when you have not five separate cards but all within one object, preserving all proportions.

Microvisuals

Frequently, we incorporate sparklines (Figure 18-2) on cards to convey trends concisely without value labels. Alternatively, you can use a progress bar or a simplified bullet chart (Figure 18-4). While not essential, it does impress clients with a wow factor.

Style templates

At an advanced level, it's beneficial to have the option to choose from style template variations. This allows not only fitting a specific design but also having the card itself embody design best practices and inspirational ideas that can be customized for your project.

Next, we'll explore these criteria through the example of the Multi-Target. We researched other KPI cards and didn't find a suitable one, so our team developed this visual. Sure, other visuals are also excellent, each with its own unique features. However, sometimes their configurations are quite complex. Using the example of the Multi-Target, we will showcase the settings and the underlying thought process, enabling you to create flawless KPIs in your reports. Perhaps, at the time you are reading this book, new cards with even greater capabilities have appeared in the AppSource gallery. Either way, you can use these steps to check that the visual meets all the criteria of a perfect card.

Step-by-Step Guide for Multi-Target KPI

To build this visual, there are four main fields (Figure 18-5):

Main measure

Place *Sales fact* here.

Category

Field for multiplication by categories. Leave it empty for now; we'll come back to it later.

Additional measures

Here, you can place up to three measures that will display deviations or other additional values on the side. For now, let's place *Sales plan* here, and we'll add more later.

Bullet target

This field is for placing a measure that will be used to build the bullet chart as the target. We'll do this later.

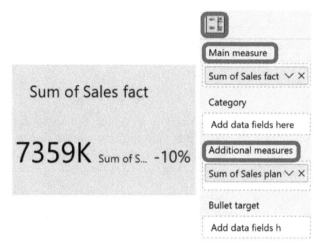

Figure 18-5. Building the default Multi-Target KPI card

The title is centered at the top, with the main measure's prominent figure on the left, and on the right, the name of the additional measure alongside the calculated percentage difference. In this case, our actual figure lags behind the plan by 10%. This is the most common scenario, so we've included it by default, and you can edit all of this in subsequent steps.

The fields were automatically added with the prefix "Sum of," but we don't need it in the title. Additionally, we'll rename the extra measure to better reflect the deviation, calling it "vs. target" (or "vs. plan" if you prefer). You can make these adjustments directly in the field within the *Build visual* section. Now, the name fits perfectly (Figure 18-6).

Let's now include an additional measure. In corporate reports, there could be various target versions, like an annual budget, forecast, or a comparison with the previous year. Although our dataset is straightforward and lacks such metrics, let's assume we want to also visualize unit sales. Instead of creating a separate card, we can conveniently add it here. As depicted in the figure, you can observe it appearing as a second row on the right side of the card (Figure 18-6).

In this case, we observe a side effect of preconfigured calculations for additional measures. We intended to see just the absolute unit value, but we have a deviation in thousands of percentages between units and dollars. We'll need to address this in step 3.

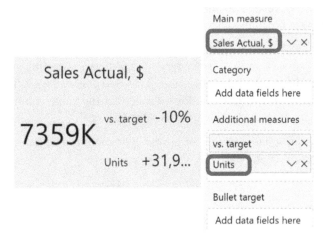

Figure 18-6. Adjusting titles and adding an additional measure

We aimed to have the default card view ready to use without requiring any adjustments. Nevertheless, there are numerous parameters available for detailed customization, enabling you to give your card a completely different look. Let's begin.

Step 1: Define Grid

Visually, the card is split into two sections: one for the main measure and the other for additional measures. The default ratio is 50%, but depending on the content, you may need to adjust these proportions. Let's decrease it to 40%, allocating a bit more space for additional measures—leaving 60% for them (Figure 18-7).

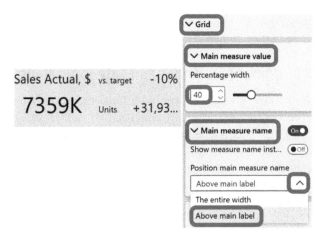

Figure 18-7. Adjusting the ratio of measure areas and the position of main measure name

The next parameter related to this is the position of the *Main measure name*. By default, the name is positioned above both sections, but you can opt to place it solely above the main measure, resulting in a more compact card height.

The next step is to look at the *Layout type* of *Additional measures*, and it's better to consider it with three additional measures. Let's add the average price to the *Build Visual → Additional measures* fields. Please note that the value is not configured yet and is displayed incorrectly; we'll handle its setup in step 3.

In the *Grid → Additional measures → Layout type* section, you can choose between horizontal or vertical (Figure 18-8).

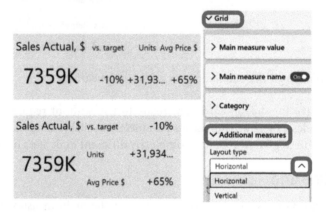

Figure 18-8. Two layout options for additional measures: horizontal (top) and vertical (bottom)

In the vertical option (bottom), additional measures are displayed in a column; in the horizontal one (top), they are shown in a single row, making the card more elongated but allowing for a reduction in height.

Step 2: Adjust Alignment for Values and Category Labels

As a default, the measure is centered, and additional measures somewhat resemble a table grid. In the *Grid → Alignment* parameter, you can select both vertical and horizontal alignment for each element. In our example, we maintained the default vertical centering (hence the element not being expanded in Figure 18-9). Horizontally, we aligned the main elements (*Main measure name* and *Category*) at the center. Additional measure names were positioned to the left of their area, while additional measure values were placed on the right.

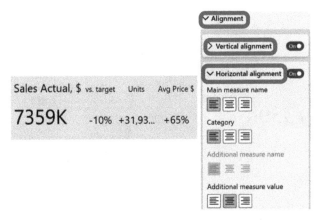

Figure 18-9. Alignment adjustment for values and category labels

These default settings are suitable for the vertical orientation of additional measures (in a single column). Another option is to set a horizontal layout (in a single row) at step 1, which would make the main measure and its title (*Category*) look more aesthetic when aligned on the left.

Step 3: Adjust Values

Now, let's fine-tune the presentation of values on the card. This is achieved through the *Value format* section. We have no concerns with how the main measure is displayed, so we'll keep it as is. However, in *Value format → Main measure value*, you can specify the *Display units* and the number of decimal places.

For additional measures, some adjustments are needed. The *vs. target* parameter is correctly displayed on the card as the *Percentage over Main Measure*, so we'll leave it unchanged. However, *Units* and *Avg Price* are currently displayed inaccurately. In *Value format → Additional measure values → Additional options*, choose *Units* (Figure 18-10), and then, in the *Component type* drop-down, select *Measure*, since we're interested in simply the quantity of units sold. Subsequently, in *Additional options*, select *Units*, and in *Component type*, again choose *Measure* from the drop-down. It's crucial: for the correct display of the average price, the *Avg Price* field at the *Build visual* stage must be labeled as *Average*.

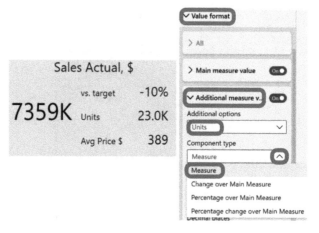

Figure 18-10. Adjusting the display format of values

Step 4: Adjust Fonts

One of the benefits of the Multi-Target KPI card is that you can configure the color, size, and font type for all elements in a single section, with each having its own settings if needed. If certain names are too long, you can enable *Word wrap* (Figure 18-11) to allow words to wrap onto multiple lines.

Figure 18-11. Choosing and customizing fonts for each element of the card

We won't delve into the specifics of font selection options; they are fairly self-explanatory (Figure 18-11).

Step 5: Set Up Conditional Formatting for Additional Measures

Right in the card itself, we can easily set up a conditional formatting to visually highlight deviations in values, either positive or negative.

If you check the *vs. target* option under *Conditional formatting → Additional measure value*, the "traffic light" formatting will be applied by default. In this setup, *Condition 1* assigns a green color if the value of this parameter is greater than 0 (Figure 18-12). *Condition 2* (Figure 18-13) assigns a red color if the value of this parameter is less than 0. In our case, with a shortfall of –10% from the plan, the value is displayed in red. If desired, you can customize all these settings and specify your own conditions.

Figure 18-12. Configuring conditional formatting using the traffic light style (condition 1)

Additionally, for each condition, you can add an icon or even *Emoji* (Figure 18-13). You can specify up to three conditions, but in our case, the third one is not needed, so it is disabled.

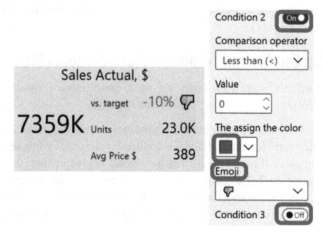

Figure 18-13. Configuring conditional formatting using the traffic light style (condition 2) and adding emojis

Step 6: Multiplication and Background Color

Another highly convenient feature is the replication of cards. We've nearly finished configuring one card. Now, with a single click, we can generate an entire series of such cards. By adding *Country* in the *Build visual → Category* field, we will obtain distinct cards for each country, all with an identical design (Figure 18-14). It's worth noting that all four cards form a single visualization, rather than being separate elements.

Figure 18-14. Multiplication of cards

Returning to step 1, under *Grid*, you'll find the *Category* section. Here, you can indicate the number of cards in a row. In Figure 18-15, we set it to *2*, resulting in a 2×2 matrix. Setting it to *1* will give you a single column; just ensure that you expand the element vertically to accommodate all displayed values.

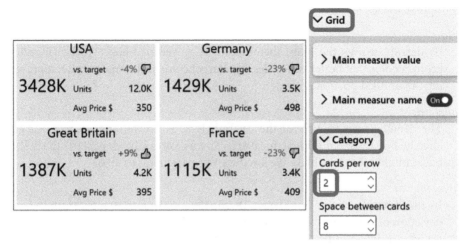

Figure 18-15. Arrangement of cards in a 2×2 matrix

Step 7: Add a "Micro" Visualization—Bullet Chart

Consider this as the finishing touch. Various card options come with additional features to boost visibility, like a sparkline. And here we introduce a bullet chart! To create it, incorporate the field containing the data for comparison with our *Main measure* in *Build visual → Bullet target*. In our scenario, this corresponds to the sales plan *vs. target* (Figure 18-16). Activate the checkbox in *Format visual → Bullet chart* (Figure 18-17) to display it on the card.

Figure 18-16. Bullet chart on the default card

To improve the appearance of this bullet chart, here are the adjustments we can make:

Colors

By default, it uses the main theme color (e.g., red or blue). We'll change it to green, a color that better suits sales. The target color will remain white, representing the unfilled portion.

Bullet height

The default is set to 30% of the card's height. However, considering our card already has three additional measures and is vertically elongated, the default bullet might seem too thick. We'll reduce this parameter to 20%.

Target line

In the example shown in Figure 18-16, the target is not met, resulting in a deviation of –10%, and the bar is filled to 90%. If the target is exceeded, the figure transforms into a bullet, featuring a line that the bar intersects (Figure 18-17). We can customize the color and thickness of this line.

Figure 18-17. Configuring bullet chart parameters within the card

These represent the essential features of the Multi-Target KPI. Additional parameters for detailed customization are described in technical guides. In this chapter, our focus is primarily on presenting ideas for showcasing key metrics at an advanced level. You also can implement these concepts using Excel and PowerPoint.

Tips and Notes

Essential criteria for the perfect KPI card:

- Layout and alignment
- Additional indicators
- Calculation presets
- Conditional formatting and icons
- Card multiplication
- Microvisuals
- Style templates

In the AppSource gallery are several advanced cards that we recommend:

- Card with States
- Multi-Target KPI card
- Ultimate KPI Card
- Dynamic KPI Card
- Advanced card
- Zebra BI Card

Step-by-step guide for Multi-Target KPI:

1. Define grid: area ratio for main and additional measures, vertical and horizontal grid.
2. Adjust alignment for titles and measures.
3. Adjust values, calculation presets.
4. Adjust fonts for values and category labels.
5. Set up conditional formatting, add icons, or even emoji (if needed).
6. Add card multiplication by category (if needed).
7. Add bullet chart (if needed).

Download the *.pbix* file with customized visuals (*https://oreil.ly/HGnyj*).

Part II Quiz

1. Choose the source data table that will allow us to create this waterfall chart.

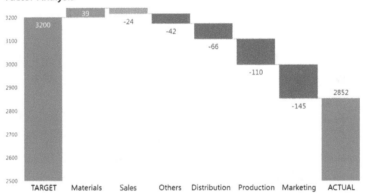

Factor Analysis

A.

Factor	Value
TARGET	3,200
Sales	-24
Materials	39
Production	-110
Marketing	-145
Distribution	-66
Others	-42
ACTUAL	2,852

B.

Factor	Version	Total
Sales	TARGET	500
Materials	TARGET	550
Production	TARGET	600
Marketing	TARGET	650
Distribution	TARGET	700
Others	TARGET	200
Sales	ACTUAL	476
Materials	ACTUAL	589
Production	ACTUAL	490
Marketing	ACTUAL	505
Distribution	ACTUAL	634
Others	ACTUAL	158

C.

Factor	Target	Actual
Sales	500	476
Materials	550	589
Production	600	490
Marketing	650	505
Distribution	700	634
Others	200	158

2. Which waterfall chart is depicted incorrectly?

A

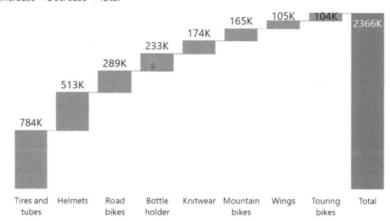

Sales by Product subcategory

● Increase ● Decrease ● Total

B

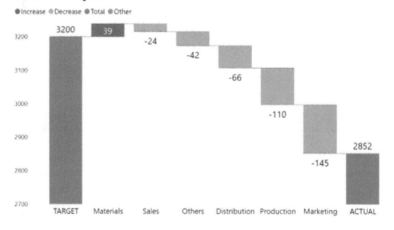

Factor Analysis

● Increase ● Decrease ● Total ● Other

C

Cost Structure

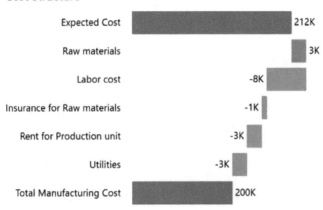

Expected Cost	212K
Raw materials	3K
Labor cost	-8K
Insurance for Raw materials	-1K
Rent for Production unit	-3K
Utilities	-3K
Total Manufacturing Cost	200K

3. Which funnel chart is applied correctly?

A

Sales by Product category, $

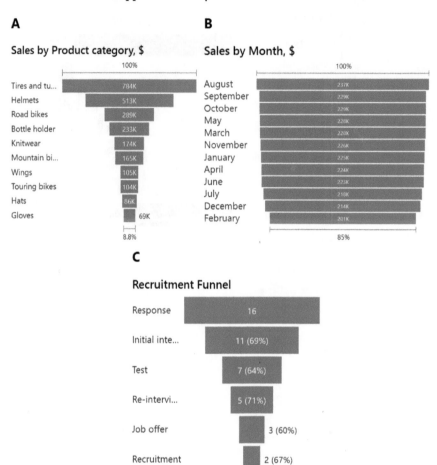

B

Sales by Month, $

C

Recruitment Funnel

4. We have the data in the table. What visualization would be better to create based on this data?

Stage	Number
Response	16
Initial interview	11
Test	7
Re-interview	5
Job offer	3
Recruitment	2

A Recruitment Barchart

B Recruitment Waterfall

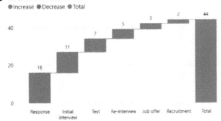

C Recruitment funnel

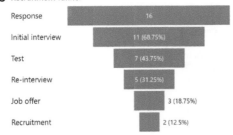

5. Which Sankey chart is used incorrectly?

A

Budget

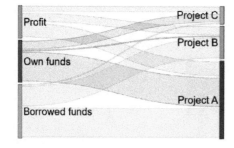

B

Fund distribution

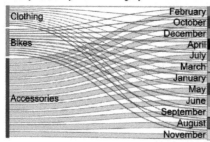

C

Sales by Month by Product category

6. Which tornado chart is used correctly?

A

Sales Actual vs. Target, $ by Manager

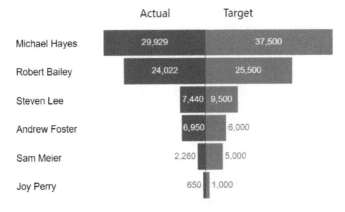

B

Sales Actual, $ vs. Quantity Units by City

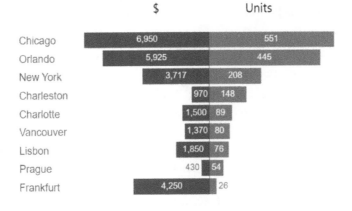

Answers

1. **The correct answer is B.**

   Answer A is not suitable for this kind of visualization (Microsoft waterfall). It is possible to create another type of waterfall (simple waterfall) with this data, but it is necessary to convert this data.

   Answer B is correct. The data in this table is ordered in appropriate mode for creating a waterfall chart.

   Answer C is a standard Excel table. Using it for a waterfall chart, we end up with a confusing picture: the actual value is positioned above the target value, followed by factors, and, finally, the sum of values. This visualization does not convey any meaningful information.

2. **The correct answer is A.**

   Answer A is correct—this waterfall is used incorrectly. There are no positive or negative changes between the start and end points. It is just a sales ranking by product subcategories, which may be clearly visualized with a bar chart.

   Answer B shows the appropriate factor analysis by the waterfall chart.

   Answer C shows the appropriate waterfall chart positioned in a horizontal mode. It depicts factors between expected and total costs.

3. **The correct answer is C.**

   Answer A is incorrect because sales by categories represent a ranking, and for ranking, we use a regular bar chart.

   Answer B is incorrect because it displays the same ranking but organized by months, which is incorrect for a funnel. It's better to display on a line or column chart.

   Answer C is correct. We use a funnel to visualize the sequence of stages, as well as the number of successful actions at each stage, and (most importantly) the overall conversion of all actions. This is why it is correct to use a funnel chart for visualizing, for example, staff recruitment.

4. **The correct answer is C.**

   Answer A is incorrect because Gantt charts are used only for time intervals.

   Answer B is incorrect. For this data, a waterfall chart doesn't make sense as it doesn't provide any information, and these parameters cannot be added together, with each subsequent one being a component of the previous one.

   Answer C is correct. In this case, the data is interrelated, with each subsequent step being the result of the previous one. The funnel chart is ideal for displaying a step-by-step process where one stage flows into another. It visually illustrates the path from the first to the last stage and helps analyze the success of each step.

5. **The correct answer is C.**

Answer A shows the appropriate use of the Sankey chart. It works well for showing proportions and relationships of financial data.

Answer B shows a very simple, straightforward example of a Sankey chart; for several categories it is clear enough. You can see proportions between funds and projects.

Answer C is correct. This chart is not suitable. It depicts sales distribution over the year by product categories, but it's unrealistic to compare category share within a month. A more suitable visualization for this data would be a cumulative bar chart by months.

6. **The correct answer is B.**

Answer A is incorrect; it is not appropriate to compare the plan and the actual using a tornado chart. In this case, a bar chart would be more suitable.

Answer B is correct. It is possible to compare sales in units and dollars to understand the correlation between them.

PART III

Risky Advanced Visuals

In this part, we will continue exploring advanced Power BI visuals but with a different approach. Here, we've gathered charts that might seem exciting at first glance but, in practice, could lead to failure. There's a high risk that these visuals might be too complex and unclear for users without proper explanation.

In this part, there will be seven chapters, each dedicated to a specific type of visualization:

- Gauges
- Scatterplot
- Word cloud
- Decomposition tree
- AI-based visuals
- Radar and aster plot
- Chord diagram

Some chapters will be dedicated to a single visual, while others will explore multiple options. Unlike Parts I and II, we won't provide detailed step-by-step guides for each visual because the settings for many of them are limited. We will explain the constraints and even offer alternatives to present the same data in a simpler and more understandable way using conventional visuals.

Throughout these chapters, there is quite a bit of criticism, but it comes from the perspective of creating business dashboards. All of these creative visuals can be effectively used in presentations, infographics, or data research by experienced analysts. However, if you leave managers alone with such reports, they might end up disappointed and confused. Amid complex figures, they might struggle to find insights.

In areas of potential risk, opportunities also emerge. In our practice, sometimes we take the foundation of a nonstandard chart idea and finalize it by combining various elements. We hope that by reaching this page in the book, you've acquired enough knowledge and experience to make informed choices in visualization.

So, onward—let's continue to enhance your visual literacy and data proficiency!

CHAPTER 19

Gauges and KPIs

For this and further chapters, you can use the same practice dataset (*https://oreil.ly/ DataViz_dataset*) as for Part I.

In Chapter 8, we set up a basic card, and in Chapter 18, we explored advanced cards from the AppsSource gallery. However, the default toolkit includes several other visuals for displaying key performance indicators (KPIs). They look more original than a simple rectangle with a number, but beginners often make mistakes with them. That's why we've moved the information on gauges to the part on exotic visuals. This chapter will explain why.

Gauges

In the early days of BI technologies, gauges were a symbol of high-tech, advanced dashboards. After all, while bar charts and even waterfall charts could be built in Microsoft Excel, such realistic speedometers required specialized software. In Figure 19-1, you can see how those gauges looked.

Figure 19-1. Image with examples of fierce gauges

In every BI application, there is such a visual, and Power BI is no exception. Totals in the form of gauges with arrows, ranges of "good-bad" at first glance look attractive—and you immediately want to put them on the dashboard. In this chapter, we will try to convince you otherwise, showing where they really help highlight the key points and where they only distract from the data.

To create a gauge in Power BI, all you need is a single numerical value (let's choose *Sales fact*), and you'll immediately get an unusual visual. It is designed in a modern, minimalist style. We can see that the sales total is 2.68 million, and the arc is half-filled with blue (Figure 19-2, left). However, if you filter the gauge by product category, nothing changes in the visualization: the arc remains 50% filled, as it was initially (Figure 19-2, right). The only thing that has changed is the final numerical value.

Figure 19-2. Arc fill on the gauge does not change when filtered

It turns out that the visual part of this element does not convey significant information; it merely serves as an aesthetically pleasing frame for the total value. However, on a dashboard, we typically need to save space and highlight key information, and a standard card would be better suited for this task.

Let's see what else the gauge can do. It has a *Target value* field, and we will add that. As a result, in Figure 19-3, we see an additional line on the arc indicating the target. Now, it resembles a bullet chart bent into an arc. If we filter by *Product category*, we get a nearly unchanged image—still 50% of the arc is filled, and the target value line has shifted only slightly. The conclusion remains the same: the arc does not convey useful information; it merely takes up space.

Figure 19-3. Gauges with target; the arc fill remains unchanged when filtered

Is there really no way to shift the arc fill from the 50% mark? There is, if we move *Sales plan* from *Target value* to *Maximum value*. Now the arc fill truly visualizes the ratio of plan to actuals (Figure 19-4, left), and we can estimate that it's about 70%. But what if the plan is exceeded (as in the case of accessories)? In Figure 19-4, right, we don't see how much the actuals exceed the plan; the fill just reaches the end of the arc, which corresponds to 100%.

Figure 19-4. Target value is positioned in the Maximum value *field*

It turns out that such a gauge will incorrectly display the exceeding of the plan: whether it's 120% or 200%, we will still see only 100%. That's precisely why, in Chapter 18, we demonstrated the Multi-Target KPI feature: when the plan is exceeded, a target mark appears and shifts to the left from the right end of the bullet chart (Figure 18-17).

Gauges can be appropriate when we cannot exceed the target or maximum—for example, if we have a rating scale up to 10, 100, or another maximum score. Thus, a gauge is often used in customer and employee feedback analysis. It can look impressive if there are not too many gauges; otherwise, the first level of the dashboard can become overloaded. In Figure 19-5, you can see a fragment of a dashboard on product customer feedback.

Figure 19-5. A row of gauges with a maximum value of 100 points

In the AppSource gallery, you can find numerous variations of gauges. However, we want to clarify that at the time of writing this book, we didn't find a "good enough" gauge that we would use in our Power BI implementation projects. We'll demonstrate this with an example of one visual.

Advanced Gauge by xViz

Advanced Gauge by xViz is another visual that we will test. It uses the same fields as the default gauge. However, it comes with an additional set of features to create a second arc inside the first one (this option is not available in the free version).

Let's place the *Sales plan* data in the *Target value* field. We can see that the arc is unexpectedly three times longer than the planned value (Figure 19-6, left). The only acceptable option is to place it in the *Maximum value* (Figure 19-6, right). If we enable axis labels, we will see not only the initial and final values on the arc but also intermediate ones. This overloads the visualization.

Figure 19-6. Advanced Gauge by xViz. On the left, the target value is set in the Target value *field, and on the right, in the* Maximum value *field.*

If the filter reveals that the plan is exceeded, the chart will disappear altogether (Figure 19-7). This is because the maximum value must be greater than the actual one.

Primary Gauge Maximum value needs to be higher than Primary Gauge Actual value!

Figure 19-7. Outcome when the sales target is exceeded, meaning the sales value surpasses the target

In actual business dashboards, the requirement is often to present 10–15 summary values compactly on the initial dashboard level, all within a single row. This is precisely why, in Chapter 18, we emphasized important features like showcasing additional metrics and icons. If visual elements were utilized, it was typically in a more streamlined form, such as sparklines (trend lines without labels) or simplified bullet charts. Unconventional gauges from the gallery tend to occupy considerable space. While arrows and scales might initially capture attention, they provide limited ongoing utility for continuously monitoring metrics.

Key Performance Indicator (KPI)

In this section we will tell you about a default visual that at first glance looks impressive and seems to meet many of the criteria for a perfect KPI card but has one crucial limitation. The objective of this element is to showcase a value alongside a graphical representation illustrating the fluctuation patterns.

Let's see how the KPI works. For instance, if we input actual sales into the *Value* field and planned sales into the *Target* field, the card stays empty. To fix this, it is crucial to populate the *Trend axis* field. Here, we need to enter the date that signifies when the value will change. If we select the month, the card will then show the value (Figure 19-8).

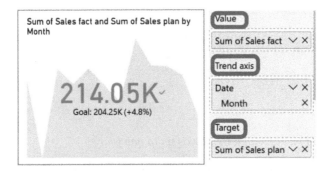

Figure 19-8. Default KPI visual with three filled fields

Now let's compare. In the previous figures (Figures 19-2 to 19-6), we had 2.68 million, and here we have a completely different value.

If we use the same data to create a Multi-Target KPI card, we would get the familiar 2.68 million. However, in Figure 19-8, in the KPI, we see 214,000. Where did this figure come from?

Certainly, the widget exclusively displays the most recent value from the dataset. In our case, this corresponds to the concluding month of the year, December (Figure 19-9). It's perplexing that the card is incapable of showcasing the cumulative total value; instead, it presents the value from only the latest period determined by the selected trend axis.

Try changing the *Trend axis* to a year instead of a month (Figure 19-10). In this case, we get 2.68 million. However, the chart in the background, for which we chose this widget, has disappeared altogether. The sample data shows sales for only one year, so we won't see any dynamics on a yearly basis. If you have data for multiple years, the system will once again display the value for just the last year. Therefore, the meaning of such visualization is completely lost.

Month	Sales fact	Target
September	229.0K	217.7K
October	228.9K	222.5K
November	226.2K	209.2K
December	214.1K	204.3K
Total	2,682.1K	2,577.5K

Figure 19-9. Data for the KPI visual in tabular form. The KPI in Figure 19-8 displays only the Sales fact for December (the latest value).

Figure 19-10. KPI visual with a trend axis set to one year

The concept behind this visual is interesting. It provides flexible formatting options and the possibility of creating a well-designed visualization. However, the value of formatting diminishes when it is unable to showcase the necessary information. In most cases, businesses prefer to see cumulative values rather than just the latest period. If such an option were accessible, we would readily integrate it into our projects. For those who appreciate the idea of a card with a sparkline, we recommend utilizing Card with States by OKViz in such instances (Figure 18-2).

Tips and Notes

When it comes to showcasing KPIs on a dashboard, you have the option to employ unique visual elements available in both the default kit and the AppSource gallery. However, you should exercise caution when incorporating these visuals.

Gauge
> These visuals tend to occupy a considerable amount of space to represent a single value. Regardless of fluctuations in the value, the gauge consistently fills 50% of the arc, lacking meaningful variability.
>
> By introducing a field with the target value, you can include an extra line—a target marker. Nevertheless, this doesn't effectively convey plan exceedance and may even lead to errors, as observed in the example with Advanced Gauge by xViz.

KPI
> The default KPI visual in Power BI elegantly presents actuals, deviations from the plan, and a sparkline. However, it comes with a notable limitation: instead of displaying the cumulative value, you will see the sum for the last period on the time scale.

Download the *.pbix* file with customized visuals (*https://oreil.ly/SNxGv*).

CHAPTER 20

Scatterplots

Scatterplots allow us to analyze data based on multiple variables and determine the presence and nature of relationships among them. For example, you can compare product sales in terms of quantity, cost, and total revenue.

In Figure 20-1, we can observe the distribution of the product portfolio. Among the quantity of units sold, bottle holders lead the way, represented by the far-right point. However, in terms of sales volume, they fall in the middle. The highest dollar sales volume is attributed to helmets, which is the topmost point. The size of the bubble represents the price (the larger the bubble, the higher the price). Mountain bikes have larger bubbles compared to their neighboring road bikes, demonstrating the relationship between revenue and price.

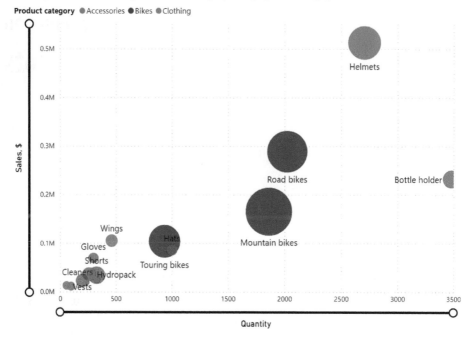

Figure 20-1. Product portfolio on the scatterplot

Pay attention to the fact that on this chart we've included labels for both axes, even in a vertical orientation! We've done this because we have two sets of values to compare. Furthermore, you'll see some handy scale sliders next to these labels. They're quite useful when it's hard to distinguish smaller categories when they're displayed alongside much larger ones. In Figure 20-2, we've zoomed in on the range of values for quantity, focusing on a range from 0 to 700 units, and for revenue, from 0 to 140K. With this zoomed-in view, we can better compare products that might have gone unnoticed when all values were shown together.

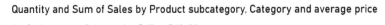

Quantity and Sum of Sales by Product subcategory, Category and average price

Product category ● Accessories ● Bikes ● Clothing

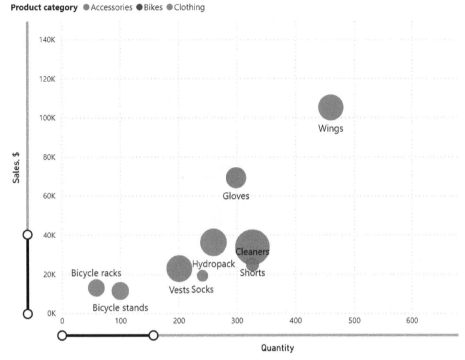

Figure 20-2. Zoomed-in lower left scatterplot area

The scatterplot, although normally considered a basic chart type, is discussed in this part of the book covering risky visuals for a reason. This is because the example with product segmentation, where we can clearly observe relationships between quantity, revenue, and price, is somewhat exceptional. In real-world data, the distribution usually looks more like what you see in Figure 20-3. In this case, we've replaced products with managers while keeping the same scales.

Sum of Quantity, Sum of Sales fact by Manager

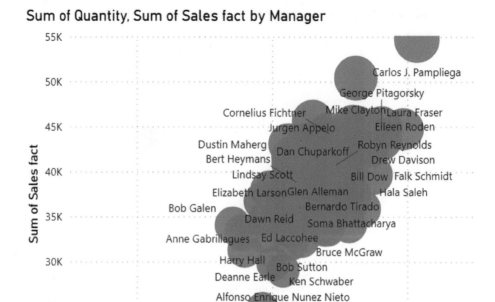

Figure 20-3. Unreadable scatterplot on managers

In general, you can see a clear trend: the higher the quantity of products sold, the greater the revenue. However, two managers are falling behind the main group, but within this group, we can't discern much. The circles and labels overlap, creating a messy spot. Even if we zoom in (in other words, filter out the outliers—Figure 20-4), the overall picture won't change significantly. Yes, it's easier to read the names now, but we can't draw any new conclusions from this visualization.

Sum of Quantity, Sum of Sales fact by Manager

Figure 20-4. Scatterplot on managers with no outliers

For this reason, dashboard scatterplots are rarely informative. With a specific range of data, we can see an interesting relationship, but more often than not, it turns out like the picture in Figure 20-4. In such cases, we have to explain what this combination of dots means and what information a manager can derive from it. That's why we categorize this visual as exotic. It's more useful for personal analytics, data exploration, and checking and filtering hypotheses about relationships between variables. But for regular reporting, it's a rare exception. If you've double-checked that your data clearly shows relationships at a glance, let's discover the key features of this visual.

How to Create and Customize a Scatterplot

As always, we should follow logical steps to make the chart clear and enable useful options.

Step 1: Allocate Data Fields

As we mentioned, this chart is part of the basic set of visualizations. Let's select it and begin with the following fields (Figure 20-5):

Values

> This includes data with product subcategories (bubbles will be created based on these).

X Axis

> Data on the quantity of units sold (the system automatically calculates their sum).

Y Axis

> Data on actual sales (the sum is also automatically calculated).

Figure 20-5. Scatterplot creation

The resulting chart reflects the distribution of product subcategories concerning revenue and the quantity of units sold. It looks quite clear and already provides information for reflection.

Step 2: Add Category and Value for the Bubble Size

To make the data more visually informative, let's add color and size to the bubbles on the chart. In the *Size* field we'll place *Average of price per item*, and in *Legend*, we'll add *Product category* (in our case, it's *Accessories*, *Bikes*, and *Clothing*—Figure 20-6).

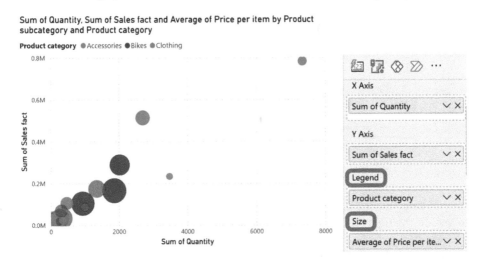

Figure 20-6. Adding average price and product category data to the scatterplot

The conclusions we made earlier are further supported. We can see that the leaders are from *Accessories* (the light blue bubbles) and they have medium price (the size of the bubbles), and the most expensive products belong to the main category *Bikes* (the dark blue bubbles) and they are in the middle of sales.

Step 3: Add Zoom Slider

How do we make sense of the data in the bottom left corner, where bubbles and labels overlap? We engage the *Zoom slider*! Enable the *Format visual → Zoom slider* (Figure 20-7). Scroll bars appear on both axes of the chart. By moving the slider, you can zoom in for a closer look.

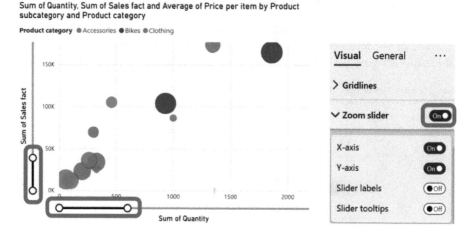

Figure 20-7. Adding a zoom slider to the chart

This will help you see the segment in the bottom left corner, but all the leaders at the top and on the right will go beyond the visible area. In other words, we are displaying an incomplete picture. Keep this limitation in mind!

Step 4: Add Play Axis and Animation

The scatterplot in Power BI has an option to create a "wow effect"—the play axis. We place a parameter in this field, and as it changes, our data will also change. Most often, this is a time scale, although you can use it to view changes by country or by managers. I will choose the *Month* parameter.

Below the chart, a scale with monthly breakdown appears (Figure 20-8). If you turn on the *Play Axis* button to the left of it, the months (in the top right corner) will start to alternate, and the bubbles will dynamically move and change in line with the data changes.

It looks impressive, but you won't obtain any real business information from this animation. Therefore, before using this option, you should ask yourself: why am I using this, and what do I want to convey?

We've examined an educational example and obtained a rather illustrative chart that can provide valuable information. However, be prepared that when presenting it, you might still need to explain what the bubble size and color represent and how to read this chart.

Figure 20-8. Adding an animation effect to the chart—changing the chart by month

Hexbin Scatterplot

What alternatives do we have in the AppSource gallery? Is there really something exotic in Power BI? Meet the Hexbin Scatterplot in Figure 20-9.

Figure 20-9. Hexbin Scatterplot

Like the bubble chart, this visualization shows the position of data points (in our case, managers) relative to actual sales in dollars (x-axis) and units (y-axis). However, these points are placed against a background of hexagonal cells. The color intensity of these cells indicates the density of data points: the darker the cell, the more points it contains. In other words, the shape of the cells doesn't matter; only the intensity of their color matters.

We can see that the brightest cell is located at approximately the intersection of 38,000 and 320 units. This means that most managers achieve this average result. At the same time, two obvious leaders are clearly visible in the upper right corner, and two outliers in the lower left corner.

This is a colorful and impressive visual element. However, it is used very rarely in business reports due to the overwhelming graphical nature, which can make it difficult to discern the essence of the data. Nevertheless, the Hexbin Scatterplot can be suitable for infographics.

How to Create and Customize Hexbin Scatterplot

We won't go into a detailed guide here; we'll just highlight the main features. Let's fill in the three main fields (Figure 20-10):

Details

> Here we place the *Manager* parameter, which is what the points will represent.

X Axis

> We add a numeric parameter that will be placed on the x-axis, which, in our case, is *Sales fact*.

Y Axis

> In this field, we place a numeric parameter that will be located on the y-axis, which, for us, is *Quantity*.

In the settings of this diagram, you have the following options:

- Changing the color and size of the hexagons
- Changing the color and size of the points
- Turning labels and axis titles on or off

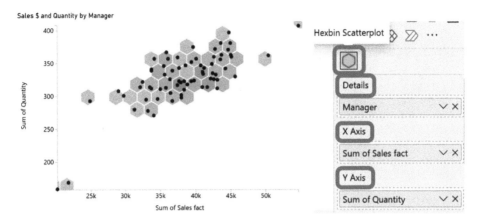

Figure 20-10. Creating a Hexbin Scatterplot

Additionally, in the settings, you can use the option *Disable hexagons* and keep only the points, but doing so may render this diagram less meaningful.

The Hexbin Scatterplot is a direct counterpart to the bubble chart, embellished with colorful hexagons. They can either enhance the overall look or make it less readable and comprehensible. Therefore, all our cautions about the scatterplot apply to this visualization too. Considering the visual load introduced by the hexagons, the risk associated with this visual is even greater.

Tips and Notes

Scatterplots are great for statistics and mathematical data analysis, but their capabilities are limited within the context of business tasks. If you decide to use such a visual element, we recommend selecting one from the default Power BI set. It is well-developed and offers the widest range of customization options while avoiding unnecessary embellishments.

Checklist for a scatterplot:

1. Allocate data fields for x- and y-axis, and category for the plot.
2. Add a category for the legend and a value for the bubble size.
3. Add a zoom slider (if needed).
4. Add play axis and animation. Double check that you really need it!

Download the *.pbix* file with customized visuals (*https://oreil.ly/NevOq*).

CHAPTER 21

Word Cloud

A word cloud is a special visual representation that displays a set of textual values (or categories) using fonts of different sizes and colors. The larger the font, the more frequently that category appears. An example of such visualization can be seen in Figure 21-1. This type of visualization is often used for navigating topics in a blog or on a website: at a glance, it's clear what topics the materials are about and which themes are the most popular.

Figure 21-1. Word cloud sample

Let's see what we can achieve by applying a word cloud for business purposes. To do this, we will attempt to display the best-selling products using the names of product subcategories as tags and the sales volume to determine the weight of the subcategories (see Figure 21-2).

Figure 21-2. Word cloud on sales data

In Figure 21-2, we cannot precisely compare how much mountain bike sales exceed road bike sales or assess the structure of which products contribute to 80% of sales. However, we can qualitatively get an overview of the entire range of products.

Such a diagram is not commonly used in corporate reporting, but there are cases where it effectively presents information in a small screen area. But before we move on to its construction, let's carefully consider when you really need a word cloud and when the data makes sense in a different format.

Alternatives for Word Cloud

First, we'll provide a simpler explanation.

We're sure that you're eager to show your advanced visualization skills. However, some beginners make mistakes by using a word cloud when they should use more common types of charts, for example:

- Bar charts
- Pie charts or treemaps
- Slicers

Let's learn from their errors and understand when it's better to use simpler and more familiar visualizations for data analysis.

Rating: Quantitative Comparison

In Figure 21-2, we showed you an example of displaying sales using a word cloud. But in that case, our goal was to give you a general idea of all the products and get a sense of which ones are selling well.

In this case, it's hard to identify the leaders in the word cloud if the difference between them is small. Also, it's impossible to assess the values, as they are not represented in the visualization, and the font size doesn't reflect the true value proportions. For such a purpose, a bar chart would be more suitable. It allows you to immediately see the ranking of products, the differences between them, and the precise sales figures for each product. You can observe this in Figure 21-3.

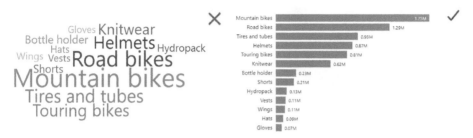

Figure 21-3. Sales rating (word cloud versus bar chart)

Structure: Part of a Whole

It might seem like a word cloud could be a good choice for displaying the structure. Yes, we can easily read the names of all the categories, even those at the end of the list. However, we won't see each one's proportion. In contrast, with a treemap, we can immediately see which products account for about 80% of sales.

So, if you really want to assess the proportion, then use the old good pie chart (if you have no more than 6 categories) or a treemap (if you have around 10 of them; Figure 21-4). And remember, if you have 20–30 categories, they will look messy in any chart.

Figure 21-4. Parts of a whole (word cloud versus treemap)

Cross-Filtration

In some cases, a word cloud can be used as a filter. This might be convenient: we can see all the categories at a glance without a scroll bar. But a word cloud has a significant limitation—this visual allows you to select only one item. In other words, with the Ctrl key held down, you will not be able to select another category, nor will you be able to apply a filter to another visual. So it is better to use a slicer (Figure 21-5).

Figure 21-5. Word cloud doesn't support multiple choice

"Why do we even need a word cloud?" you might ask. The advantages of a word cloud are that, first, it's a compact visual. And second, it displays all categories without the need for a scroll bar. Data can be in such proportion that, compared to the maximum values in the first columns, all other columns are too small. In Figure 21-6, we seem to be using a column chart correctly, displaying the ranking. However, it looks bad; country names are rotated at an angle and very small, so you have to strain to read them. Here's where a word cloud can come to the rescue: we see that most of the responses are from France and Italy. At the same time, we can see the other countries; the text for them is twice as large and arranged horizontally.

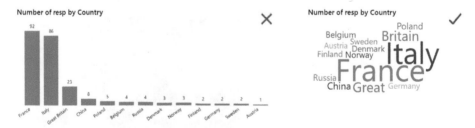

Figure 21-6. The exception: when the word cloud visualizes the ranking more clearly than a bar chart does

So, if you've convinced yourself three times that you need a word cloud for your report, let's move on to configuring it step by step.

How to Create and Customize a Word Cloud

The basic set of Power BI visuals doesn't include a word cloud, but you can download several options from the gallery. Let's create and configure the visualization from Microsoft: in the gallery, you can find it under the name "WordCloud."

In the *Category* field, we enter the data we want to display in the word cloud. In our case, this is *Product subcategory* (it's important that this is text data).

In the *Values* field, we add the parameter by which the font size will be sorted: *Sales fact*. You can see the result in Figure 21-7.

As always, we get a draft where we need to fix critical errors:

- Phrases are broken down into individual words, making it seem like there are more categories than there actually are.

- Words are angled, making it difficult to read.

Figure 21-7. Data fields for word cloud

Step 1: Disable Text Rotation

A mandatory rule is that all labels on the diagram should be strictly horizontal. To fix this issue, we'll uncheck the *Rotate Text* option in the settings panel (Figure 21-8).

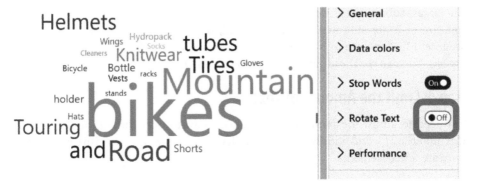

Figure 21-8. How to disable text rotation

Step 2: Combine Split Phrases

By default, phrases are split and scattered. For example, the subcategory *Tires and tubes* displayed with a brown word "tubes," then "Tires" below, and "and" in the bottom left of the chart. To fix this, go to *Visual format → General* and uncheck the *Word-breaking* option (Figure 21-9).

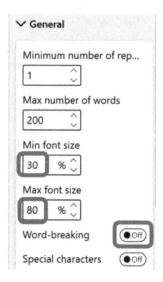

Figure 21-9. General parameters for adjusting text

Step 3: Adjust Text Size

The largest subcategory, *Mountain bikes*, takes about 30% of the chart space. But the font size of lesser subcategories is too small, so it is difficult to read. To solve this issue, set Min font size to 30 (for the smallest words) and *Max font size* to 80 (for the largest). You can see these parameters in Figure 21-9.

Step 4: Limit the Amount of Text

You need to adjust the number of elements, to avoid overloading the diagram. Set *Max number of words* ideally to no more than 20. In my case, this isn't necessary, as there are fewer elements.

Step 5: Customize Chart Colors

The diagram appears too colorful. Unfortunately, you can't select a specific palette or gradient in the settings. All we can do is manually set the color for each category. Let's do this in the *Data colors* section, where you can choose colors within the same spectrum for each product (Figure 21-10).

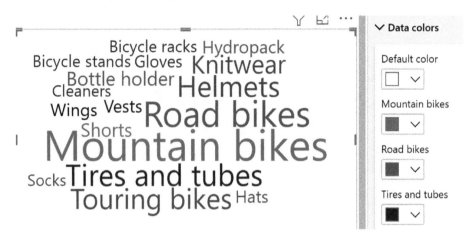

Figure 21-10. Color customization

In the end, we get a visually appealing version (Figure 21-11, right). It can be used to display the structure or as a slicer, albeit with cross-filtering limitations.

Figure 21-11. Word cloud by default (left) and the final view (right)

Another Word Cloud from AppSource

There's also a word cloud by xViz available in the gallery. It's almost identical to the WordCloud widget from Microsoft, but there's a difference: the settings are available only in the paid version. Even rotating the text to a horizontal position is a paid option. The default version is simply unusable, as you can see in Figure 21-12.

Figure 21-12. Default view for word cloud by xViz

The phrases here are divided, so we end up with things like "knitted helmets" and "mountain racks." Plus, half of the words are written vertically at a 90-degree angle, which makes them difficult to read. This version needs some setting up, but the options required for this are found only in the paid version.

Keep in mind that a word cloud isn't meant for precise comparisons of quantities. It's more about providing a visual overview and context. When dealing with specific data, you can use it to showcase rankings, structures, or as a filtering tool, but it often requires some customization for these purposes.

In Figure 21-13, you'll see an example of a dashboard that displays feedback from event attendees. It has a specific layout with two large tables and ample space above them. We've added a word cloud to make the most popular topics stand out in the center. You can select any phrase in the word cloud to read detailed feedback, both positive and negative, about those topics.

So, in specific cases, a word cloud can be a good solution when traditional charts don't quite fit the bill.

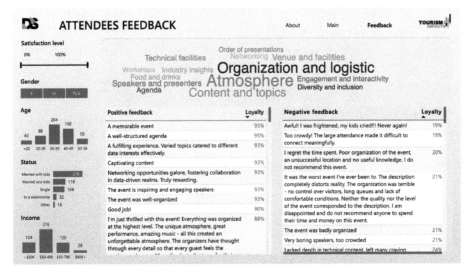

Figure 21-13. Unusual text dashboard with word cloud

Tips and Notes

The key setup rules are as follows: all words are written horizontally, and breaking phrases is not allowed. We recommend using the WordCloud widget from Microsoft—it provides all the necessary options for configuring the result.

Checklist for setting up a word cloud:

1. Disable text rotation.
2. Remove word splitting.
3. Set the minimum (30 pt) and maximum (80 pt) font size.
4. Ideally, limit the maximum number of words to 20.
5. Assign shades within one color palette to category names.

Justified use of a word cloud is in reports related to the analysis of web pages or search queries, as well as when it's important to display the main composition and visually highlight the leaders.

Remember: a word cloud is not a full replacement for slicers. It doesn't work with multiple categories of data. You won't be able to filter data fully with it.

Download the *.pbix* file with customized visuals (*https://oreil.ly/p2Ff2*).

CHAPTER 22

Decomposition Tree

The decomposition tree is an interactive visualization for hierarchical data. The concept is to take a single metric and drill it down into various dimensions. In Figure 22-1, you can see the sales drivers by country. The leader is the USA, and then we expand it by product categories and subcategories.

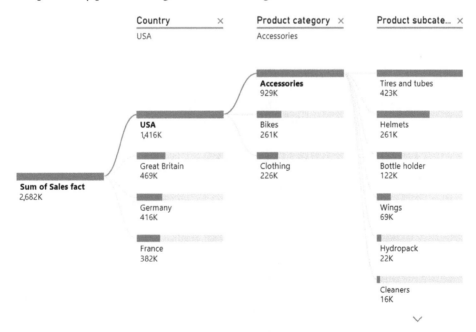

Figure 22-1. Sales decomposition from USA to Accessories

We can continue the analysis in a different direction: let's expand *Great Britain*, and then the *Clothing* category, and see the ranking of products within it (Figure 22-2). In the same way, we can explore the data in different directions.

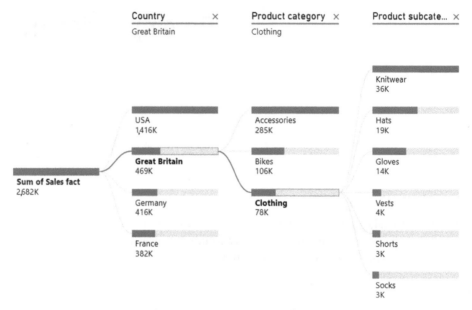

Figure 22-2. Decomposition from Great Britain *to* Clothing

The decomposition tree is part of the standard set of Power BI visuals, so there is no need to download it from the gallery. It is built from a single measure and multiple categories that expand and "branch out" as you move from one to another.

How a Decomposition Tree Works

When building, in the *Analyze* field, you place the parameter you want to analyze and break down into subgroups. In the *Explain by* field, you place the categories by which you will analyze the original parameter—in our example, this is *Country, Product category, Product subcategory,* and *Manager.* The number of such parameters is not limited here.

Initially, you will see only a single bar with the total sales amount and nothing more. This can be confusing at first, but to the right of it, there is a plus sign that allows us to expand the tree in different directions. As you can see in Figure 22-3, we can choose any of the categories, regardless of the order in which we added the fields.

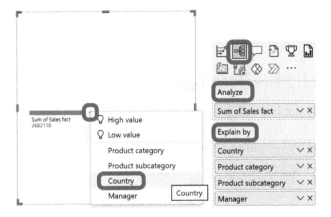

Figure 22-3. Decomposition options from the top level

Furthermore, on the pop-up window in Figure 22-3, there are elements for *High value* and *Low value*. If you choose *High value*, only the items with the highest values will be displayed on the branch. If you choose *Low value*, you will see the underperforming items in that category, which also can be useful for sales analysis. If this filtering is active, a lightbulb is shown to the left of the category name. In Figure 22-4, you can see the sales decomposition path for *Great Britain*, *Helmets*, and *Manager*, with managers having the lowest sales in this category.

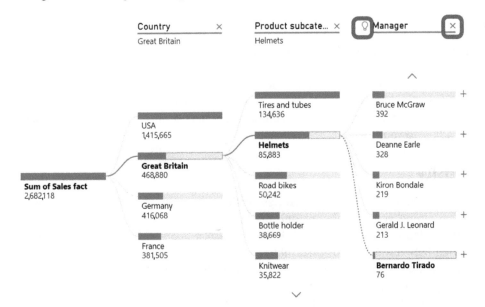

Figure 22-4. Low value decomposition by managers

When you want to view categories in a different order, click on the X to the right of the category name (Figure 22-4) and select a new display order by clicking on the + next to the desired category.

How to Set Up the Decomposition Tree

The examples at the beginning of the chapter are shown in the default chart style. In Figure 22-5, you can see a denser tree in orange. In this style, the data label is emphasized, and the categories are subdued.

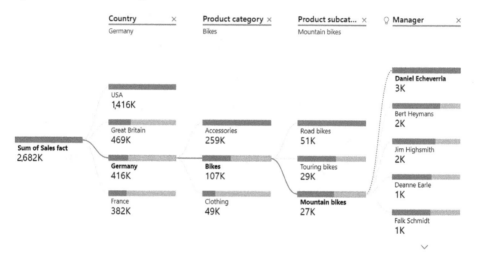

Figure 22-5. Customized decomposition tree

In this case, we won't provide a detailed step-by-step guide because the visualizations don't have traditional elements like x- and y-axes. There are also no common errors, such as missing data labels. Instead, there are special features that you can personalize and adjust to your needs.

Density

In the *Format visual → Tree* settings section, you can adjust the *Density* of the tree, meaning you can choose one of three preset styles. You've seen the default style in Figures 22-1 through 22-4. There's also a *Spare* style, which increases the spacing between bars both vertically and horizontally. You can use this if your tree visualization occupies the entire report page. However, if you want to leave room on the page for other visuals, we recommend the *Dense* option. In this setting, elements will be closer to each other but with enough spacing to avoid merging.

In the same *Tree* settings section (Figure 22-6), you can disable the *Responsive* mode, which automatically adjusts the number of displayed elements when you resize the chart. Then you can specify the *Max bars shown*, which will always be visible on the tree.

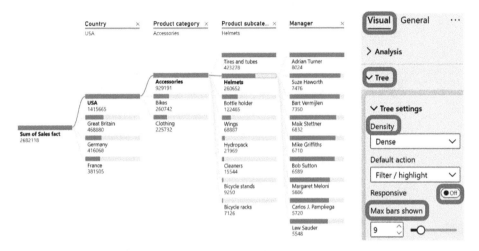

Figure 22-6. Tree settings

Connectors

In the *Format visual → Tree → Connectors* section, you can customize the color and style of the lines (Figure 22-7). There aren't any significant differences between *Default* and *Round*. Next, you can change the color of the *Selected line*, but you won't immediately see the applied changes on the lines—they will remain gray.

However, when you select an element in the line, the left and right sides become orange in our example. Additionally, the color of the bottom borders of the headers will change.

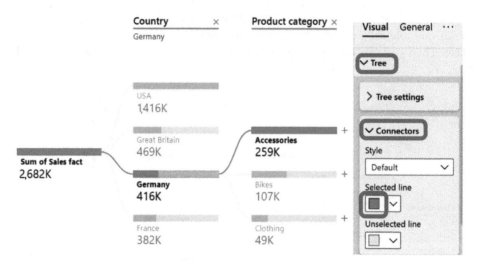

Figure 22-7. Connector color

Bars

In the *Bars* section, you can customize the width and color of the bars, as well as the fill style. The parameter responsible for filling with color is called *Scale to* (Figure 22-8):

- By default, it's set to *Level maximum*, meaning the first item in the list is fully colored.

- When you choose *Parent node* (as shown in Figure 22-8), the color indicates the proportion of a specific element concerning the parent measure (for example, *Accessories* are shown in blue to represent their share of total sales in the USA, and the blue for *Helmets* shows their share of all accessories sold in the USA).

- Selecting *Top node* colors each element to show its proportion concerning the very top level (*Sales fact*). However, in this case, the coloring for levels 3 and beyond won't be clearly visible against the top node.

We recommend sticking with the default *Level maximum*. In this way, each "column" will provide a clear ranking of categories. But there will be some distortion horizontally since the upper bars will all be colored maximally, even though their values differ. There's no perfect solution, and you need to strike a balance depending on your data range.

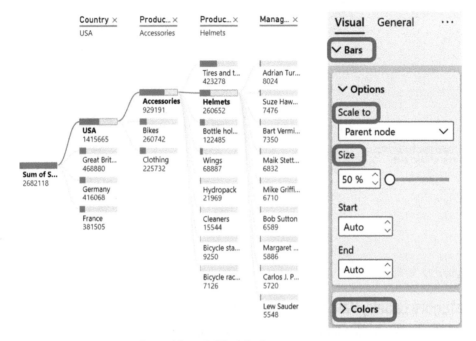

Figure 22-8. Customize the width and fill of the bars

You might be surprised that when you increase the width of the chart area, the bars themselves don't stretch; instead, there's just empty space on the right. You can adjust the width of the bars using the *Size* parameter. In Figure 22-8, we reduced it to 50%, which compressed the tree by half. This option looks too dense, and many category headings don't fit. However, reducing the width to 70%–80% is sometimes appropriate. Just as increasing it beyond 100% is useful if you need to display long category names.

In the same *Bars* menu, you can also change and customize the colors of the bars in the *Colors* section (Figure 22-9). We'll change the main color (*Positive bar*) to orange and select a light background to go with it. Negative values rarely appear in the decomposition tree, but you can also configure a color for them. In our case, all sales are positive, so we'll leave this color as the default.

Figure 22-9. Bar colors

Category Labels, Values, and Headers

These options are configured in the same way as for other charts. Let's describe them briefly:

Category labels
    When choosing the font size, make sure that the labels are fully readable. We've kept the default 9 pt.

Values
    You can increase them to 12, but don't forget to format them in thousands or millions. Although it's set to *Auto*, we were seeing long labels with five to seven digits.

Headers
    These refer to the header of a branch or column. Here you need to ensure that the field names fit (or rename them in the selected fields list).

Subtitles
    Enable this option and you'll immediately see which element is currently selected and expanded.

As a result, you'll get a customized view like the one in Figure 22-10.

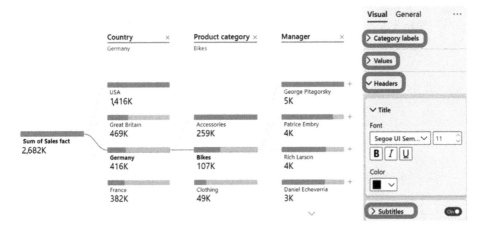

Figure 22-10. Customizing category labels, values, and headers

Simple Alternatives to the Decomposition Tree

It looks dynamic and original, making you want to add this element to your dashboard immediately and let the business team interact with the data. However, in practice, the decomposition tree is rarely used in business reports. And we understand why:

- You need to click the plus signs several times to reach the desired level of detail.
- Working with data labels is inconvenient. By default, they are small, and increasing their size doesn't help much. The chart becomes too wide, and the text volume seems excessive.
- The list is limited in height. For example, you see the top five or nine subcategories, and below them are arrows for scrolling. You don't know how many there are in total.
- You can't see the overall product ranking; it's only built within the selected country. If you expand sales by product field, you'll face the same issue with countries: you'll only see the breakdown within the chosen product.

Bar Charts with Cross-Filtering

Businesses need quick answers to their questions with just one click, and that's the essence of cross-filtering in Power BI. This is how you can simplify information perception and save the user from searching for answers to their questions.

Let's break it down with a simple example, considering we have just two hierarchy levels. In Figure 22-11, you can see a column chart for countries at the top (as there are only 4 of them) and a horizontal bar chart for categories (with more than 10 of them). If we click on *Germany*, we instantly see which categories were sold there and what their share was compared with total sales. And the card will always show us the total prominently.

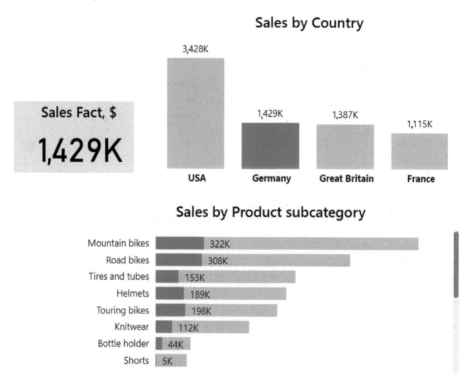

Figure 22-11. Bar charts with cross-filtering for two levels of decomposition

Similarly, we can click on a category and see how its sales are distributed across countries.

Matrix with Conditional Formatting

The previous example was limited to two levels. In Figure 22-12, we can see three levels: countries in the columns, and a hierarchy of category-subcategory in the rows. By clicking on the + sign, we can expand the category and see the breakdown of sales. Conditional formatting highlights the maximum values. The advantage is that we see the overall picture, not just the ranking within a single category.

The decomposition tree visual is more suitable for internal data exploration rather than presenting information to business users. However, in specific cases, the decomposition tree can both be visually appealing and effectively convey the data's meaning.

Product category	France	Germany	Great Britain	USA
⊟ **Accessories**	**185K**	**191K**	**241K**	**826K**
Bicycle racks	1K	1K	3K	5K
Bicycle stands	1K	0K	1K	9K
Bottle holder	27K	44K	39K	122K
Cleaners	3K	3K	3K	16K
Helmets	56K	49K	86K	228K
Hydropack	3K	0K	7K	22K
Tires and tubes	87K	82K	91K	362K
Wings	6K	11K	11K	62K
⊟ **Bikes**	**57K**	**64K**	**105K**	**236K**
Mountain bikes	15K	15K	34K	75K
Road bikes	33K	37K	49K	128K
Touring bikes	9K	13K	22K	33K
⊞ **Clothing**	**41K**	**37K**	**77K**	**200K**
Total	**283K**	**292K**	**424K**	**1,262K**

Figure 22-12. Matrix for three levels of decomposition

Tips and Notes

The decomposition tree is an interactive visualization for hierarchical data. To create it, select the parameter you want to analyze and break down into subgroups in the *Analyze* field. In the *Explain by* field, you specify the categories by which you'll analyze the data.

The default view of the decomposition tree looks good, without any critical issues. However, you can customize the density of the tree, connector colors, bar colors, bar width, and the way bars are filled.

This visual is primarily intended for internal data exploration. Analysts use it to manipulate data and discover interesting relationships. However, on a business dashboard, traditional visualizations are often simpler for users to understand.

Download the *.pbix* file with customized visuals (*https://oreil.ly/ER2aa*).

CHAPTER 23

AI-Based Visuals

Artificial intelligence (AI) is becoming an integral part of digital products, and Power BI is no exception. Each year, Microsoft's ecosystem of analytical products expands, and we often struggle to keep up with all the innovations. Typically, AI features are designed for advanced analysts, leaving business users with a "black box" that can be intimidating to open.

In this chapter, we will explore two elements driven by the AI engine: "key influencers" and "Q&A" (questions and answers). On one hand, it might be challenging to categorize them as exotic, considering they are part of the basic set of Power BI visuals. On the other hand, business users often tend to avoid them initially. This is because, on the first attempt, the outcomes may seem unusual and distant from the "see and understand" principle.

In the AppSource gallery, new visuals with AI features are introduced every year. There's no need for you to implement them right away. At this point, it's simply information to expand your knowledge and familiarity.

Key Influencers

This visual component represents "built-in analytics." AI identifies interconnections and trends within the data, determining which factors impact the chosen metrics.

We will test the visual component using the same dataset on bicycle and accessory sales. Let's attempt to uncover some insights, such as the correlation between sales and product subcategories, as well as the performance of managers in different countries.

On the visualization panel, select *Key influencers* and fill in the fields:

- In the *Analyze* field, add the metric you want to analyze; in our case, it's *Sales fact*.
- In the *Explain by* field, input any parameters that could be influencing factors on sales. In our case, these are *Product subcategory, Country,* and *Manager*.

The conclusion is rather obvious: total sales increase when average sales per category rise (Figure 23-1).

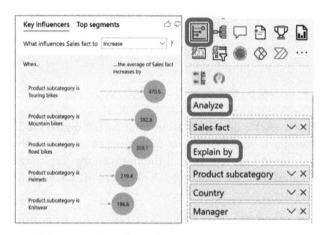

Figure 23-1. Key influencer by default

If we choose one of the categories (in Figure 23-2, it's *Road bikes*), a column chart appears with, again, a quite obvious conclusion: *Sales fact* is more likely to increase when the *Product subcategory* is *Road bikes* than otherwise (on average).

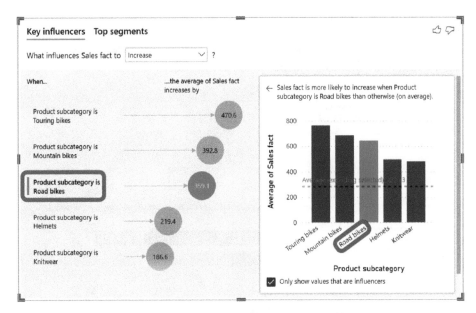

Figure 23-2. Key influencer with the selected subcategory Road bikes

If we navigate to the *Top segments* tab, we'll see that the system has identified five key data segments (Figure 23-3). Some of them relate to sales of specific products, while others pertain to sales in specific countries.

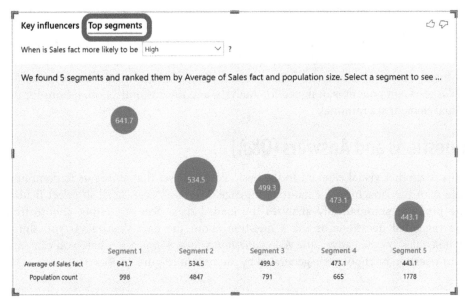

Figure 23-3. View of key influencer in the Top segments *tab*

By clicking on the "bubble" of the first segment, we will navigate to the tab with detailed information about it (Figure 23-4). In our case, the system compares the sales of the leading category, *Road bikes*, with the average sales across the entire category. Additionally, it displays their share in total sales.

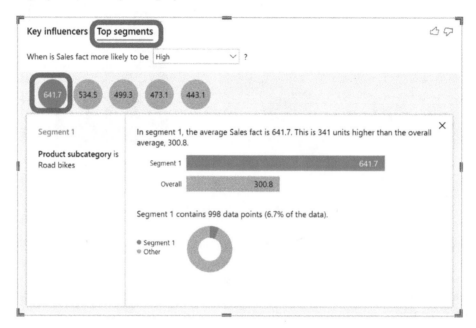

Figure 23-4. Analysis of the first segment, Road bikes

There might be situations where AI discovers interesting insights in your data that you'd like to showcase on the final dashboard. However, in such cases, you'll need to build a separate chart and format it according to the checklist because the *Key influencers* component is designed for analysts, and the customization options for this visual element are minimal.

Questions and Answers (Q&A)

This is another visual element in the basic Power BI set that allows us to communicate with the "machine" in natural language. We don't even need to select fields—the program automatically analyzes the loaded data. You can either choose from the suggested questions or ask a question about the data yourself. If you simply double-click on the canvas, the *Ask a question* window appears, where you can enter your question or choose one generated by the system (Figure 23-5).

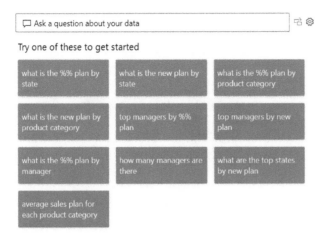

Figure 23-5. Ask a question *window by default*

Suppose we want to find out how many product subcategories we have. We type **How many product subcategories are there?** in the *Ask a question* field (Figure 23-6). If you click the button to the right of the question, "*Turn this Q&A result into a standard visual,* you will get the most suitable chart. In my case, it's a draft version of a card that needs to be customized following the familiar checklist.

Alternatively, compare the sales plan across countries. We type **Compare Sales plan versus Country** and obtain the following result, which, with a single click (the button to the right of the question), can be turned into a ready-made chart—here it will be a bar chart. Remember that any pre-built element in Power BI always requires additional formatting (Figure 23-7).

Figure 23-6. Q&A output

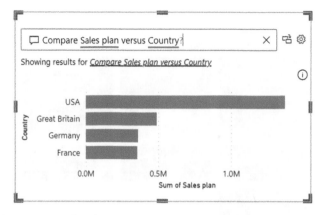

Figure 23-7. Comparing sales plan versus countries using Q&A

Unfortunately, the ability to formulate questions is limited. Suppose we want to find out which managers have achieved the sales plan. Let's try asking, `Who has achieved Sales plan?` In this context, the system doubts what we mean by the word "achieve." Furthermore, in response to "Who," it provides not the managers, but the countries. It generates an extensive table with a breakdown by days (Figure 23-8).

who has achieved sales plan	🔲 ⚙

Showing results for *who has sales plan*

Date	Sales fact % difference from Sales plan ▼
⊟ **Sunday, June 20, 2021**	**88.58%**
⊞ France	1721.28%
⊞ USA	81.38%
⊞ Great Britain	35.07%
⊞ Tuesday, January 12, 2021	88.25%
⊞ Wednesday, May 12, 2021	85.88%
⊞ Sunday, May 09, 2021	80.86%
⊞ Tuesday, December 28, 2021	73.63%
⊞ Sunday, March 14, 2021	66.92%
Total	4.06%

Figure 23-8. Example of an incorrectly formulated question

Certainly, you can find the correct question to get an answer. However, the question must be posed in the language of the machine, understanding the relationships within the raw data, rather than in business language. In our practice, it was easier to select the fields and perform slice and dice of the data in search of relevant insights.

Perhaps, by the time you are reading this chapter, this feature will allow interacting with the machine in a conversational format.

Thus, at the present moment, the Q&A feature can serve as an auxiliary tool for getting acquainted with the data and generating draft charts. It can help discover insights, but then they need to be visualized using separate classic or advanced visuals.

Tips and Notes

In this chapter, we introduced you to two elements driven by the AI. It's not a "ready-made" visuals for the dashboard; it is mostly for data exploration and searching for insights.

Key Influencers
> The algorithm identifies interdependencies and trends within the data, determining which factors influence the selected metrics. It requires two types of data:

> *Analyze field*
>> Add a numerical metric, for example, sales.

> *Explain by field*
>> Add any dimensions that could be influencing factors on sales.

> As a result, you will obtain ready-made visualizations, but the customization options are minimal.

Q&A
> This widget allows us to communicate with the "machine" in natural language. There's no need to even select fields; you can stick with the questions suggested by the system or ask a question about the data yourself.

> However, the question must be posed in the language of the machine, with an understanding of the relationships within the data source, rather than in business language.

> In summary, AI-based elements come in handy for getting acquainted with the data and generating draft charts. With their help, you can discover insights, but then these insights need to be visualized using separate classic or advanced visuals.

Download the *.pbix* file with customized visuals (*https://oreil.ly/m89lu*).

CHAPTER 24

Radar and Aster Plot

For the practice in this chapter, use the practice dataset (*https://oreil.ly/FxwcF*).

The radar chart allows you to compare values across multiple scales. These scales emanate from a central point, visually resembling a radar. A point is placed on each scale, and they are connected to form a polygon. Each category results in its own shape, and when overlaid, they create a pattern resembling a spider web; hence, it is often referred to as a spider chart.

Let's consider an example. We want to compare the preferences of two consumer segments: *Youth* and *Adults*. In Figure 24-1, you can see five smartphone criteria on the radar axes: *Battery*, *Camera*, *Display*, *Memory*, and *Brand*. For the *Youth* segment, all criteria are important except for battery, while *Adults* prioritize battery and memory, with the other factors being less significant. Consequently, we observe distinctive patterns in preference profiles: for adults, it resembles a triangle with an emphasis on two criteria. For the youth, it is more irregular but forms a pentagon.

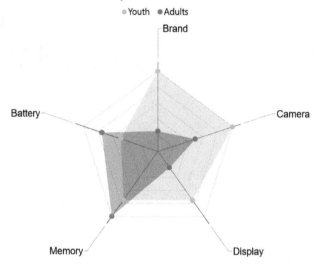

Figure 24-1. Radar chart comparing preferences in smartphone features for different age groups

The next example illustrates a competency profile of managers based on a survey. Eight key competencies were assessed on a 10-point scale. The survey was conducted from three perspectives for each employee: self-assessment, supervisor assessment, and subordinate assessment. In Figure 24-2, we observe that in self-assessment (represented by the dark gray line), the employee (let's call him John Smith) rates himself evenly across competencies, except for stress resistance. However, subordinates (depicted by the blue line) and the boss (depicted by the orange line) rate him much higher. However, there is a discrepancy in the assessment of creativity. The boss considers John's creativity to be high, while his team sees it as low. This might be attributed to John presenting his subordinates' ideas as his own when reporting to the boss.

Radar charts can highlight insights, but they typically require careful examination. This visualization demands an immersion in context and is commonly employed in sociological studies, customer surveys, and employee assessments.

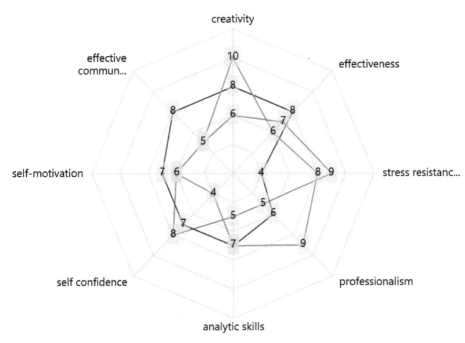

Key Employee Skills

- - Boss - - Self evaluation - - Subordinate

creativity

effective commun...

effectiveness

self-motivation

stress resistanc...

self confidence

professionalism

analytic skills

Figure 24-2. Key employee skills

If you intend to use it on an executive dashboard, exercise caution. It might be challenging for executives who are not deeply immersed in the details to comprehend. This visual is not part of the basic set, and we consider that appropriate. It won't be suitable for financial data, sales, or project management.

We dealt with radar charts when using the Power BI dashboard not for weekly tracking but rather as an alternative to presentation slides. Competency assessment results were showcased on the dashboard, and instead of a slideshow, the analyst narrated an interactive story by clicking on slicers and drilling down into additional data.

But there may come a time when you really need a radar chart, so we'll briefly explain how to build one in Power BI and highlight common mistakes to avoid. Then, we'll introduce you to another unconventional visual: the aster plot. In rare cases, it might come in handy for comparing values across multiple scales.

Radar Chart by xViz

In the AppSource gallery, there are several variants of the radar chart. The simplest one is provided by Microsoft, and you've seen it in Figure 24-1. It has very few customization options. We can only modify colors, add or remove fill, and adjust font size. However, we can't even display values on the chart—neither on the axis nor on the data points.

Therefore, let's move directly to the xViz radar, which provides more options. We'll start with the raw data; to build the chart, we'll need to fill in three fields (*Axis, Legend, Value*), and we'll require a flat table, as shown in Figure 24-3. The nuance here is that we want to display several data series, but they need to be transposed into a single *Value* column. The *Evaluator* field will store the identifier for each row (Self-rating, Boss, Subordinates).

Characteristic	Manager	Evaluator	Value
analytic skills	Andrew Foster	Self rating	9
analytic skills	Joy Perry	Self rating	5
stress resistance	Andrew Foster	Self rating	8
stress resistance	Joy Perry	Self rating	5
professionalism	Andrew Foster	Self rating	9
professionalism	Joy Perry	Self rating	8
self confidence	Andrew Foster	Self rating	6
self confidence	Joy Perry	Self rating	6
analytic skills	Andrew Foster	Boss	7
analytic skills	Joy Perry	Boss	5
stress resistance	Andrew Foster	Boss	6
stress resistance	Joy Perry	Boss	8
professionalism	Andrew Foster	Boss	5
professionalism	Joy Perry	Boss	6
effective communications	Andrew Foster	Boss	9
effective communications	Joy Perry	Boss	6

Figure 24-3. Fragment of a flat table for building the xViz radar chart

Now we can build the chart. Place *Characteristics* in the *Axis* category, and assign *Evaluator* to the *Legend* category for clarity on the meaning of each line. In the *Value* field, input the *Values* using the *Average* format, focusing on the average competency rating rather than their cumulative sum (see Figure 24-4).

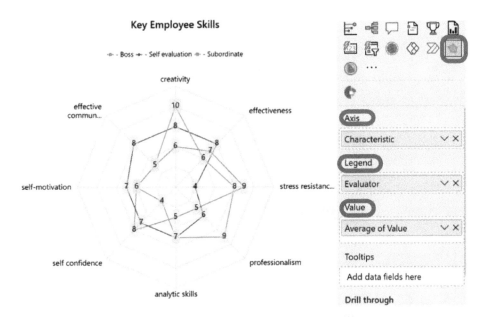

Figure 24-4. Data fields for constructing the xViz radar chart

In this visualization, we have the option to tweak settings, with the most important being the display of data labels. Regrettably, customizing individual series, as commonly seen in line charts, is not feasible here. This implies that each series will feature a black font with a gray background, and it's not possible to, for example, have an orange font corresponding to the line color for the boss's assessment or a blue font for subordinates.

Within the settings, there's a notable feature labeled *Series Type*. This resembles the family of line charts options explored in Chapter 6. By default, we have a basic line, but there's an option to switch it to *Area*. This choice works well with a single series of data or, at most, two. As depicted in Figure 24-5, three overlapping areas create a cluttered pattern. Alternative choices, such as *Area Stacked* or *Column Percentage Stacked*, introduce even more disorder.

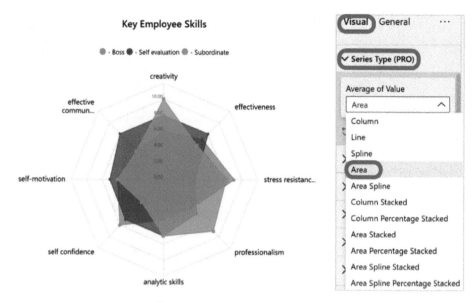

Figure 24-5. Modifying the radar type

Furthermore, you have the option to modify the radar type through the *Chart Options → Chart Type* menu. Besides *Radar*, there are *Polar* and *Radial* types. In the polar variant (Figure 24-6, left), instead of category labels, you observe axis angle values, essentially dividing the circle into 360 degrees. However, this representation doesn't offer additional insights and adds complexity to perception. On the radial side (Figure 24-6, right), we get a composite bar chart curved into an arc, but this curvature complicates understanding. Additionally, it's essential for us to compare values, and their sum lacks significance.

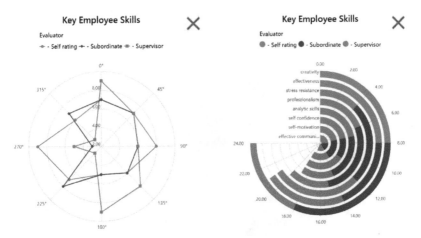

Figure 24-6. Alternative types of radar chart: polar (left) and radial (right)

In rare instances, this could be used for statistical data or creating infographics, but we haven't encountered such visualizations in any real-world dashboards. Exercise caution when considering these features.

Aster Plot by Microsoft

The aster plot is a visualization that, like radar charts, can compare values across multiple categories. It resembles a donut chart, where the value determines the height of the slicer instead of its width. It is similar to a radar chart but with only one data series (multiple series cannot be displayed).

In the AppSource gallery, you'll find the Microsoft Aster Plot. Building it requires just two simple fields: *Category*, where you insert the *Characteristic* field, and *Y Axis*, where you input the *Value*. As shown in Figure 24-7, it displays a colorful shape without any labels.

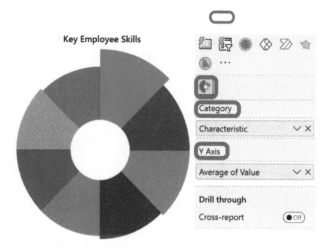

Figure 24-7. Default aster plot

The default appearance seems somewhat odd and incomplete. Let's examine how we can improve it. In the settings, we have the option to activate the grid, central label, data labels, and legend (refer to Figure 24-8).

Figure 24-8. Enhanced aster plot after customization

A significant limitation is that we cannot display category labels, as seen on the radar chart (Figure 24-2). They are only visible in the legend, which can be inconvenient—having to search for a small point and match it with the color of the slicer. Even in the classic pie chart from Chapter 4, there were many more options for customizing data labels (both values and categories, as well as percentages of the total).

This seems to be a situation similar to the nonstandard options in Radar by xViz. It looks eye-catching, but without fine-tuning, it's still impractical for use on a business dashboard. However, there are cases where you can take this unconventional visualization as a foundation and finalize it with additional elements.

In one of our projects, we depicted economic development indicators using a similar aster plot. We created 10 cards, one on each spoke, displaying the indicator's name and its value. In the center, we placed an image of a globe, and above it, another card showing the overall average value (Figure 24-9).

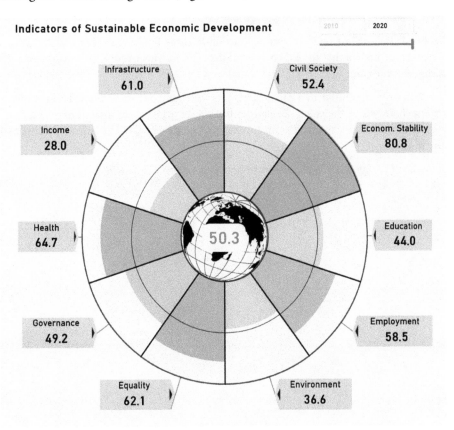

Figure 24-9. Combination of aster plot and 10 cards

This visualization involves more effort than simply adjusting a single element. Experienced analysts may find such visualization unconventional, but it did elicit a wow response from business users.

In summary, using the xViz visual allows us to create a radar chart resembling Microsoft Excel's, while its more advanced features make it somewhat intricate for straightforward understanding. The aster plot presents an original look, but in reality, it remains somewhat unfinished, needing refinement through supplementary elements for a polished look.

Tips and Notes

The radar chart allows you to compare values across multiple scales. If you intend to use it on an executive dashboard, exercise caution. It won't be suitable for financial data, sales, or project management. In rare instances, it could be used for statistical data, customer research, and employee assessment.

To build Radar chart by xViz you need to fill in three fields: *Axis*, *Legend*, and *Value*. The nuance here is that to display several data series, they need to be transposed into a single *Value* column.

The aster plot is similar to a radar chart but with only one data series. It resembles a donut chart, where the value determines the height of the slicer instead of its width. A significant limitation is that we cannot display category labels. They are visible only in the legend.

Download the *.pbix* file with customized visuals (*https://oreil.ly/-97q0*).

CHAPTER 25

Chord Diagram

For the practice in this chapter, use the practice dataset (*https://oreil.ly/jr_H9*).

This diagram is utilized to illustrate relationships between categories, both direct and reverse flows. Chord diagrams are often employed to display population migration between regions and in other forms of infographics. However, there are suitable business applications as well. For instance, it can depict the movement of personnel within company departments, customer flows between market players, or the import and export of goods between countries.

In Figure 25-1, the diagram illustrates product combinations acquired by our customers. It shows how many customers, initially buying bikes, subsequently purchased accessories or clothing. The segments of the circle (arcs) represent product categories that together make up 100% and are interconnected. The length of the arc indicates the total sales value of that category (in the units shown on the figure). The thickness of the connection (chords) represents a quantitative comparison of the relationships between objects, indicating how many customers from one category became customers of another. When we hover over an element, a breakdown is displayed: for example, hovering over the blue chord connecting *Bikes* and *Accessories*, we see that out of all those who initially bought bikes, 6,758 moved on to accessories, and out of those who bought accessories, 877 subsequently purchased bikes.

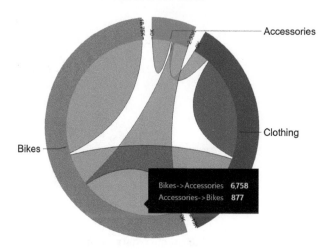

Figure 25-1. Cross-category product sales

Unfortunately, we cannot see the total number of bikes sold. More precisely, we can see it, but it's very small and inconspicuous—if you look closely, at the beginning of the orange arc, there is the number 18.75K. This is the total number of bikes sold, but we cannot increase or change the label's position. In the diagram settings, this is the *Axes* parameter, and it has no settings at all, except for *On/Off*. The only way to see the value is through the tooltip when hovering the cursor over the element.

Figure 25-2 is an example of a chord showing the staff changes between departments. Here's what we see on the diagram:

- The staff structure, how employees are distributed among the four departments, with the accounting department being the most numerous (the longest arc).

- The proportion of employees who stayed in the department and how many moved to another (the chord that "stays within the arc" and does not connect with others shows those who remained).

- The number of employees moving from one department to another. The chord does not indicate the direction (who left the department and who came in). To determine this, you need to hover the cursor, and in the tooltip, you can see that eight moved from accounting to the legal department, and conversely, four moved back.

Staff changes

Accounting

Strategic planning

Project department

Accounting->Legal section   8
Legal section->Accounting   4

Legal section

Figure 25-2. Staff changes between company departments

How to Build a Chord Diagram

This visual is not included in the basic set; you need to download it from the AppSource gallery (search Chord by Microsoft Corporation). Building it is quite simple if your data is prepared in the required format. We need to put them in these fields:

From
> Source categories from which values start their journey.

To
> Destinations where they end up.

Values
> A numerical value that determines the thickness of the chords, representing the magnitude of the flow or quantity associated with each connection.

So, we need three columns, but usually, such raw data is stored in the form of a matrix, as shown in Figure 25-3. In our example, the transition of employees is represented by the values at the intersections of the matrix. For instance, the number 66 indicates that 66 employees stayed in the accounting department, and the number 4 at the intersection of the *Legal* row and the *Accounting* column means that 4 employees moved from the legal department to accounting.

Department	Accounting	Legal section	Project department	Strategic planning
Accounting	66	8	0	5
Legal section	4	34	12	0
Project department	5	2	28	8
Strategic planning	2	7	0	16

Figure 25-3. Initial data matrix for the chord diagram

However, this format of raw data in the form of an adjacency matrix is not suitable for Power BI. Data needs to be transformed into a flat structure, as shown in Figure 25-4. In the *Before* column, all categories are listed as the *Source*, and in the *After* column, they are listed as the *Destination*. Note that if employees do not move anywhere and remain in their department, the name of that department is the same in both *Source* and *Destination* columns.

Before	After	Number
Accounting	Accounting	66
Accounting	Legal section	8
Accounting	Project department	0
Accounting	Strategic planning	5
Legal section	Accounting	4
Legal section	Legal section	34
Legal section	Project department	12
Legal section	Strategic planning	0
Project department	Accounting	5

Figure 25-4. Flat data table for Power BI to build the chord diagram

The table for the chord diagram should include the following columns of data:

Before
> The name of the department from which the employee transition occurs.

After
> The department to which the employee is moving.

Number
> The quantity in numerical format; it is not mandatory to specify the value as zero if there is no transition.

Upload the prepared data into Power BI and add the chord diagram to the report dashboard, as shown in Figure 25-5.

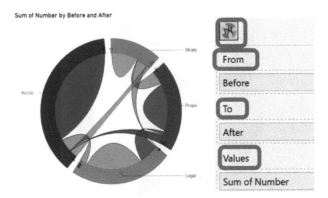

Figure 25-5. Chord diagram construction

As we mentioned at the beginning of the chapter, the chord diagram has very few options for customization. We can change only the colors of the sectors and the font size. To see specific values, you still need to hover the cursor over the sector or chord. Therefore, there is no need to provide a step-by-step guide here; let's move straight to the common mistake.

Common Mistake

Another example is shown in Figure 25-6, illustrating the fund distribution for three different company projects. However, this representation is not entirely correct. The issue lies in the fact that this chord diagram displays two types of data—on the left, funding sources, and on the right, projects receiving these funds. There is no reverse flow from the project back to the sources. Also, the sectors of the circle should add up to 100%. In this case, we cannot combine these two categories (funds and projects) into a single entity.

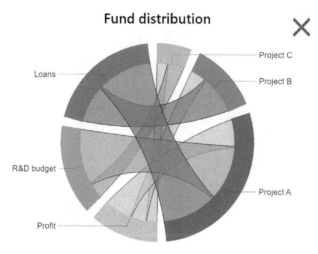

Figure 25-6. Fund distribution for three projects

In infographics, you may encounter similar examples, but we do not recommend this approach for business dashboards. At first glance, the structure is unclear, and you need to hover over each chord to understand the sum. It's easier to build a classic stacked column chart, but you will need to determine what you are emphasizing:

- Projects broken down by fund distribution (Figure 25-7 on the left)
- Fund distribution across projects (Figure 25-7 on the right)

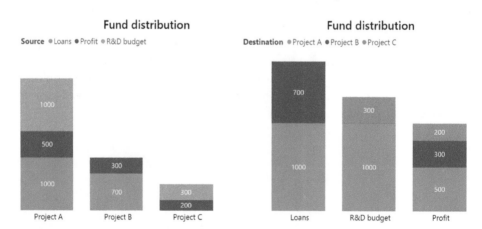

Figure 25-7. Alternative solutions for displaying fund distribution: projects with funding sources (left) and distribution of funds across projects (right)

We understand that the desire is to show "everything at once," but that's where the art of visualization comes in: immersing oneself in the business context and understanding priorities together with the business client.

We have introduced you to one of the most exotic diagrams. If you use it on your dashboard, it will not go unnoticed. The key is to ensure that after the wow effect wears off, the business user doesn't feel disappointed because they can't understand anything.

However, it does provide a chance for you to narrate a compelling story and highlight insights during an interactive dashboard presentation.

Tips and Notes

Chord diagrams are employed to depict relationships, both direct and inverse, between categories.

To create one is quite simple if your data is prepared in the required format. You need to place them in the fields:

From
> Source categories, from which values begin their path

To
> Destinations, where they end up

Values
> A numerical value that determines the thickness of the chords, representing the magnitude of the flow or quantity associated with each connection

The main limitation is that we cannot customize the axis and data labels. To see a specific value, you need to hover the cursor over a sector (category) or chord (changes between categories).

Download the *.pbix* file with customized visuals (*https://oreil.ly/00FzI*).

Conclusion

Congratulations, you have reached the end of the book! You can now be confident in your data visualization abilities, not just at a basic level but at an advanced level, too. Working with clean data sources, you have the skills necessary to choose appropriate charts and create professional dashboards.

Of course, the dashboard is just the tip of the iceberg. To create a good visual, a vast amount of work must go into data preparation behind the scenes. Moreover, a modern dashboard is not simply a static slide but is actually an interactive web application (and is mobile as well). There is much more detail about bookmarks, slicers, and pop-up windows that simply couldn't fit into this book. We encourage you to read more about Power Query and DAX if you're interested in taking the next step.

We are sure that you will continue to enhance your skills and implement analytics in your company. Some companies accomplish these tasks with in-house teams; others outsource analytical services or build hybrid teams.

Here are three examples of how companies can utilize Power BI to improve their services.

A manufacturing company has a clear understanding of its business metrics and requirements for its Power BI dashboards. However, the data is inconsistent and scattered across different sources. The company hired a team to build a data warehouse on Microsoft SQL Server and took on tasks related to data integration and cleansing. At the same time, the company focused on analyzing the efficiency of their processes. Each party concentrated on their core business, and as a result, the company found a way to increase its annual profit by $10 million.

A software company has accurate data, and an in-house team of analysts used it to create more than 100 reports. However, there was a problem—no one but the analysts themselves could make any sense of them. Their stakeholders wanted to see clear and understandable dashboards, so they sent a data team to conduct a review.

They rearranged KPIs into the correct hierarchy and created an executive summary dashboard with drill-through capabilities to operational reports. As a result, business meetings took a positive turn, and stakeholders discussed not "what happened" but "what we will do next." Soon they were able to raise another round of investments.

Another company conducts training sessions similar to what's outlined in this book. They developed guidelines in advance, along with examples showing the "how to" and "how not to" approach for dashboards. These training sessions became a reason to bring remote staff into the office, fostering team-building activities. On the fly, they brainstormed a few more dashboard ideas and created prototypes in Power BI. As a result, the company transitioned to true self-service BI.

These examples highlight the transformative power of choosing the right visuals for data analytics, leading to better business outcomes, improved communication, and enhanced teamwork.

Thank you for reading, and best of luck with your projects as well! Ahead of us lie incredible technological innovations—but remember, dashboards are not just tools for data discovery; they are also for facilitating communication among people. As long as we remain human and are willing to experiment, even using risky visualizations, no machines can replace us.

Take care, everyone!

Index

About the Authors

Alex Kolokolov is an expert in Business Intelligence and dashboards. He is CEO and founder of Data2Speak Incorporated, a company providing data analytics services and consulting.

Alex has taught in MBA programs in the USA as part of the Fulbright Program at Florida Atlantic University and Key West University. With over 15 years of practice, Alex has set up hundreds of management reports in production, banks, and trading companies; he's experienced with software from Microsoft, Qlik, Tableau, and IBM. Based on this experience, he describes universal rules for visualization and working with the requirements of business customers.

Maxim Zelensky, PhD, is a Power BI consultant at Intelligent Business. He is a renowned Microsoft Power BI expert, with a wide range of interests and experience in Microsoft BI and Excel tools. With over 20 years of experience in marketing, sales, and purchasing, Maxim's knowledge of various business aspects and models allows him to offer solutions that best meet the real needs of the business. Maxim started studying Power Query and Power BI in 2015. He spent a lot of time investigating different aspects of these tools and became one of the most recognized Power BI experts, which led to him being nominated for the Microsoft Most Valuable Professional award. He earned this award in 2018-2022, confirming his level of expertise, community influence, and knowledge sharing.

Colophon

The animal on the cover of *Data Visualization with Microsoft Power BI* is an olive baboon (*Papio anubis*), the most wide-ranging baboon species and native to 25 equatorial countries across Africa, from Mali to Tanzania.

On close inspection, their coats are actually a combination of green-grey, black, and yellow, but at a distance, they appear olive. They live in hierarchically structured groups of 15 to 150. Females remain within the same group for their lifespan (with a few exceptions), inheriting their social standing within the group from their mothers. In contrast, males leave their birth group when they have matured and join new groups every few years.

Olive baboons communicate in a variety of ways, including grunts and noises, facial expressions, physical exhibitions, and even fights. They are omnivorous, and within the carnivorous side of their diets, they are both scavengers and hunters. This flexibility in diet contributes to their ability to thrive in a variety of habitats.

The current IUCN conservation status of the olive baboon is Least Concern. Many of the animals on O'Reilly covers are endangered; all of them are important to the world.

The cover illustration is by Jose Marzan, based on an antique line engraving from *Cassell's Natural History*. The series design is by Edie Freedman, Ellie Volckhausen, and Karen Montgomery. The cover fonts are Gilroy Semibold and Guardian Sans. The text font is Adobe Minion Pro; the heading font is Adobe Myriad Condensed; and the code font is Dalton Maag's Ubuntu Mono.

Printed in the USA
CPSIA information can be obtained
at www.ICGtesting.com
JSHW051511171124
73715JS00014B/221

9 781098 152789